CATCH ME A
KILLER

CATCH ME A
KILLER

A PROFILER'S TRUE STORY

MICKI
PISTORIUS

PENGUIN BOOKS

Catch Me a Killer

Published by Penguin Books
an imprint of Penguin Random House South Africa (Pty) Ltd
Reg. No. 1953/000441/07
The Estuaries No. 4, Oxbow Crescent, Century Avenue, Century City, 7441
PO Box 1144, Cape Town, 8000, South Africa
www.penguinrandomhouse.co.za

First published 2000
This edition 2023
Reprinted in 2024

3 5 7 9 10 8 6 4 2

PUBLISHER: Marlene Fryer
MANAGING EDITOR: Robert Plummer
PROOFREADER: Dane Wallace
COVER DESIGNER: Ryan Africa
TYPESETTER: Monique van den Berg

Set in 11 pt on 14.5 pt Minion Pro

Printed by **novus print**, a division of Novus Holdings

MIX
Paper | Supporting
responsible forestry
FSC® C022948

ISBN 978 1 77639 145 5 (print)
ISBN 978 1 77639 146 2 (ePub)

*Dedicated to Calie Pistorius
and all the heroes out there*

Contents

Introduction

Forthwith this frame of mine was wrenched
With woeful agony,
Which forced me to begin my tale;
And then it left me free.

Since then, at an uncertain hour,
That agony returns:
And till my ghastly tale is told,
This heart within me burns.

– Samuel Taylor Coleridge, 'The Rime of the Ancient Mariner', 1798

As a child, it was always my dream to become a writer. I never imagined that I would one day become a psychologist who pursued serial killers.

If I look back, I suppose there were a few subtle indications of the course my life might one day take, but no one could have predicted my future.

There are two words that best describe my childhood: happy and nomadic. My parents divorced before I reached the age of five. Like many children, I reacted by creating my own little imaginary world. There was a certain spot in our garden where my mother had planted rhododendrons. Their leafy branches created a secluded cove, and this became my secret domain. There I ruled supreme. We had a huge garden and my mother used to dress me in red to make it easier for her to spot me, but no one found me in my exclusive hideaway.

Today, I can understand how important the fantasy worlds of serial killers are to them – a place where they have complete control over other human beings and where they have sovereignty over life and death.

My nomadic lifestyle began shortly after my parents' divorce. The first sign was a real estate signboard outside our yard. Since I couldn't read, I asked one of my older friends what it said and she told me that our house was for sale. I removed the board and buried it in my private garden. Unfortunately, fate had other plans. The next day another board appeared. My parents explained the reasons for their divorce to me and I accepted it with childish innocence and trust. All would turn out well in the end. Grown-ups know better.

My mother, my brother and I moved into an apartment complex with a swimming pool. I was petrified of the pool. Although my astrological sign is Pisces, this did not mean that I took naturally to water. I remember that it was my father who took me into the pool for the first time. He held me in his arms and I felt safe. Although my parents were divorced, my father was still a part of my life and he always remained a source of strength to me.

Later, my parents decided to remarry each other, and we all moved into a new house that my father had built for us. This house also had a swimming pool, and my mother taught me how to swim and dive. I went to school and life was fun and free of complications.

That is, until my parents got divorced a second time. This time there was no 'For Sale' sign to warn me. My mother, my brother and I moved into another house. My father remarried and stayed on in our old house with his new wife and her children.

At first it felt odd visiting him at weekends and finding foreign furniture in what used to be 'my' room. But I adopted my new siblings as my own family and regarded them as my brother and sisters. My mother also remarried, which extended my 'new' family even more – with another brother and sister and a stepfather. Suddenly I was no longer the youngest in the family; I was somewhere in the middle. My father's wife's first husband had also remarried and had a daughter. She was the half-sister of my step-siblings on my stepmother's side. I regarded her as my baby sister as well. This may all sound very complicated, but to us children it all made sense. I never regarded my stepmother or stepfather as my own parents, but we got on well as the years went by.

I believe that my childhood experience of complicated family dynamics sensitised me to understanding the subtle intricacies of different relationships and laid the foundations for my becoming a psychologist. I can interpret complex hidden agendas and I am sensitive to nuances. This became a handy skill during interrogations.

———

I left home at the age of seventeen when my mother divorced again. Since then, I have lived in more than thirty different homes, in various cities and even other countries. The effect of this nomadic life was profound. I never developed a sense of belonging, and I could not identify with any particular community. It was difficult to establish roots. Friends came and went, and I learnt to incorporate losses and to move on with my life. I became the captain of my own ship, and my childhood resilience – or obstinance, as some may call it – was infused in my personality's armour. I learnt that I am able to seek the positive in my circumstances. I still find it rather amusing when people advise me to 'move on with your life'!

At the time of first writing this book in 2000, I was a divorced, childless woman in my thirties. At the time of revising it in 2023, I am a single, independent woman in her sixties. I take responsibility for my own mental, financial and physical well-being and I have found a sense of belonging centred within myself, wherever I may be.

Serial killers do not belong, not to anyone. They are never centred and exist aimlessly in the abyss. They belong in prison.

People often ask how my journey of profiling serial killers began. My family was academically orientated. My father was the vice-rector of the University of Pretoria, so it was expected of us to attend university. At the age of seventeen I enrolled in a Bachelor of Arts degree, majoring in languages, since I planned to become a writer. It was a good thing I chose French as a subject, along with psychology and criminology. After completing my degree in 1981, I worked for some years as a journalist. This was solid preparation for my work with the South African Police Service, and, more importantly, it was at this time that I met my future husband, who was also a journalist. We had a fairy-tale wedding and, for most of its duration, a fairy-tale marriage.

After a spell working as journalists in Cape Town, we returned to Pretoria, where I decided to continue my studies in psychology. When I was offered a junior lectureship in the Department of Psychology at the University of Pretoria, I accepted. I lectured during the day and attended my honours course in psychology at night, completing the degree over two years. I continued with my master's and, directly after that, my doctorate, when I had just joined the South African Police Force.

Over the course of my studies, I met three professors who became my mentors. One of them, Professor Kemp, presented a list of assignment topics, inadvertently setting the rudder of my ship on a different course. One of the themes was the psychopathy of serial killers. I can no longer remember if I consciously chose this topic or if none of the other students wanted it, but I ended up with it.

The year was 1992. I didn't know then that what started as a one-off project would become my life's work. I discovered the work of FBI profiler Robert Ressler and read his *Whoever Fights Monsters*. I was particularly struck by his adaptation of a quote from Nietzsche's *Thus Spoke Zarathustra*, which appeared as a warning on the first page of his book: 'Whoever fights monsters should see to it that in the process he does not become a monster. And when you look into an abyss, the abyss also looks into you.'

Although I was writing my master's dissertation on the Oedipus complex, I was already planning my doctoral thesis on the link between Freud's theories and serial killers' developmental phases, expanding on the assignment topic. I had read more than three hundred case studies on serial killers to see if I could find the link. I found it in every one of them. At the end of this book, I elaborate on this theory and illustrate how some South African serial killers fit into the pattern.

During the last months of my internship at the University of Pretoria in 1993, Captain Braam Beetge, a psychologist in the South African Police Force, phoned one of my mentors, Professor Erasmus. Braam was looking for a candidate to join the Force and to become involved in a project on forensic psychology. I had taken forensic psychology as an extra subject with Professor Erasmus and he recommended me. I applied for the post and was appointed in February 1994, the year after I completed my master's degree. It was also the year of my own divorce, although my husband and I remained lifelong friends until he passed away in 2020.

And so the wheels were set in motion as I was appointed to the level of captain in the South African Police Force.

'Whoever fights monsters ...' Serial killers are not monsters; they are human beings with tortured souls. Anyone who derives personal satisfaction from killing another human being has a tortured soul. If we believe them to be monsters, we would expect them to 'foam at the mouth', to behave like

Hollywood master criminals such as Hannibal Lecter, or to be some sort of Antichrist. But they are none of these. They are normal people: your neighbour, your brother, the man walking down the street. So, how will you recognise them? You will not.

I will never condone what they do, but it is also not my job to condemn them – that is the job of a judge. As a psychologist, it is my job to understand them in order to explain their behaviour in a court of law as well as to the general public. How can a teacher teach maths if she does not understand it? My understanding of serial killers does not mean that I have sympathy for them. I have compassion for the abused, neglected children they once were, but a difficult childhood is never an excuse to commit a heinous crime. I do, of course, have sympathy for the victims and their families. Over the years, the deaths of those I loved taught me to value life and sensitised me to the suffering of the families of the victims of serial killers. As a psychologist, I had to control my feelings to avoid overriding my professional judgement, although all psychologists 'tune into' the feelings of their clients to understand their existential dilemmas.

So, to understand them I had to enter their habitat, and this abyss became my mental home for many years. I do not think I consciously chose it: it lured and beckoned to me, and I suppose the crusader blood I inherited from my mother's ancestors answered the call.

At first, I could not control my entering and surfacing from the abyss. Inside the abyss I found a dark and lonely place, closely related to what some may call hell. The abyss is lonely but populated, much I think as the ancient Greeks described Hades. Serial killers exist there, and if one really wants to find them, that is where one has to venture. One cannot begin to under-stand a serial killer's mind if one is unprepared and unwilling to experience their feelings. I did not have to kill to understand why others do, but I did have to go through some harrowing experiences in order to understand. At no stage did I enjoy this.

We are all masters in our own fantasy lives. In our fantasies, we can con-trol what other people think, do, feel, look like and so forth. We can rewind, forward-wind, rewrite the script, play victim, play master, and command the attention and respect we miss out on in reality. It is a pastime and a defence mechanism that all humans employ.

So, after some trigger event challenges their self-esteem, serial killers also retreat to their fantasy lives, but these are vengeful, lustful, aggressive fantasies – originating when they are children – and, when they are old enough, they manifest these fantasies in reality. There is no greater power than the power of life or death over another person. That is the power of omnipotence – it is godlike. It restores the killer's sense of worthlessness, of emptiness. However, reality is never as perfect as fantasy. Therefore, they will kill repetitively – like a drug addict getting their fix. Does this absolve them from being accountable for their crimes? Of course not. Would they kill if a police officer was standing right next to them? No. Do they know it is wrong? Yes. Do they care? No, they do not.

I understand the existentialism of omnipotence and the addictive danger attached to it. Roman emperors, military generals, dictators and despots have fallen prey to it. Perhaps judges having to pass the death sentence also struggle with this existential question, and that might be one reason why the death sentence has been abolished in South Africa and many other countries. Even current presidents, captains of industry, drug lords and some religious leaders fall prey to the addictive danger of omnipotence.

'The abyss looks into you ...' I was acutely aware of my own loneliness, which resounded with the killers', but I also know that I depended heavily on the love and understanding of those people for whom I cared and who cared for me. Yet I did not easily discuss my feelings with others, because I didn't want to draw them into the abyss with me. I didn't want to contaminate them. When I didn't have a serial killer in my mind, I lived a normal life, but when I interrogated a serial killer, I dived into the darkness of the abyss. The abyss is the hell serial killers create for themselves. I became familiar with their feelings of emptiness, loneliness, depression, death, omnipotence and fear. I dived deeply to get a grip on the killer's torment. Metaphorically, in the abyss, I grabbed their hand and then felt like I was swimming back up through the darkness into the light, dragging them with me.

When I broke the surface, there was light. That was the moment when I had to adjust from being the psychologist to being a cop. It was very difficult not to drown and to remain balanced, and the dive often affected me for months after the arrest. I hardly ever had time to work through these experiences because I usually went straight from one case to the next. I am grateful that my mother and father taught me how to dive and swim, both mentally and physically.

I managed to bring most of them to the surface, at least for a little while. I do not claim to have released serial killers from hell, but they opened up and talked to me because they responded to someone who understood them, just as any other human being would. Serial killers do not take responsibility for killing; many told me it was the police's responsibility to stop them. The general belief that serial killers want to be caught is a myth perpetuated by Hollywood and writers of fiction. In real life, if they are caught, they are forced to stop killing. But because they like the omnipotent feeling of killing, they avoid detection as much as possible. Some very arrogant ones may even taunt the police by leaving notes or making anonymous phone calls, but this is rare and it still doesn't mean they want to be caught!

The perception that serial killers target detectives or profilers and have personal relationships with them is another myth perpetuated by Hollywood and authors of bad fiction. It may lend cheap sensationalism to a book, movie or television series, but it is simply not true and makes a mockery of serious detective work.

Fortunately, a detective was always present to take over when I broke the surface after an interrogation. Once the psychological work was done, it was up to the detectives to process the legal side regarding confessions, the pointing out of crime scenes and the trial. The relationship between the detectives and me was one of utter trust. The detectives had to trust me to do my work, and I can understand that it was very difficult for them not to interrupt. In turn, I trusted them to catch me when I surfaced and to take over. The baton had to be passed on firmly, as in a relay race. The first time we perfected this process was in the case of the Phoenix serial killer in 1997. During this interrogation, the serial killer demonstrated to the detectives how he had tied up his victims by practising on one of them.

Although I use the analogy of psychological armour, I never regarded my work as a religious crusade – despite my ancestry. By assisting the detectives in arresting a serial killer, I had a dual goal. As a part of a team, I was preventing the deaths of innocent people, thereby serving the community. Secondly, on a more personal level, I was willing to guide the serial killers out of the abyss – and hopefully into prison. Whether or not they sank back was their own issue and the salvation of their souls is up to God, not me.

I have trained hundreds of detectives in several countries in the investigation of serial killers. I had to prepare them and teach them about the abyss. These were experienced detectives who were quite used to death and horrific crime scenes, yet it takes a special kind of detective to be able to handle this – and to handle me – so they were carefully selected for training. Most of them did not have to venture into the abyss; they only needed to trust me to do it and be there when I surfaced. Some of them did venture into the abyss and survived. Some got scarred, but they survived.

The close bond that developed between the detectives and me had nothing to do with sexuality. Although I am a woman, I was accepted into the brotherhood – a camaraderie and *esprit de corps* that exist between brothers-in-arms – which included women. I departed on a hazardous journey into a very dangerous mental plane with my male and female colleagues, and we had to develop trust and closeness in order to survive and to succeed. We worked long hours, travelled great distances and endured many difficulties. But once a case was solved, they returned to their partners and families. I had sacrificed my own marriage in the interest of my work, but I could see no need for them to sacrifice theirs. And luckily, some of the detectives were women. Looking back, I am proud that we could exemplify the good work men and women can accomplish by fighting injustice together, as a team, and I see no reason why this should be sexualised. Sexualising my part, or that of any woman, in such a brotherhood will only tarnish our honour, loyalty and respect, and shame on those who try to capitalise on cheap sensationalism.

At the end of each of my courses, I knew I had laid the theoretical foundations and that investigating a serial killer would provide the detectives with the experience. I always ended my courses with the words: 'Well, what are you waiting for? Go and catch me a killer.' And they did.

In the six years that I worked as a profiler, I was involved in more than thirty serial killer cases. My level of involvement varied from being completely immersed in the investigation to sometimes just providing a profile. To my knowledge, South Africa had the second-highest rate of serial homicides during that period (the United States of America had the highest). Unconfirmed reports indicate that there had been fifteen serial killers active in Russia during those years. Serial killers can appear anywhere, but there is as yet no official international data bank available to provide accurate statistics.

South Africa still has one of the highest murder rates in the world, illustrating the amount of work that a Murder and Robbery detective has to cope with, and yet South Africa held the record for apprehending serial killers within three to six months of a special investigation team being established, provided the serial killer stayed active. This was the calibre of the men and women I was proud to work with.

I am often asked if there is a particular case that is more special to me than the others. The answer is no. Each detective investigating a case regarded his or her case as special, and their dedication inspired my full attention, in as much as it was humanly possible for me to give. Having said that, the case of the Station Strangler occupied a special place, only because it was my first – every detective will always remember their first case as well. The Station Strangler case also brought me into contact with Mitchells Plain, which is where I encountered the abyss for the first time.

ONE

The Station Strangler

The fair breeze blew, the white foam flew,
The furrow followed free;
We were the first that ever burst
Into that silent sea.
– Samuel Taylor Coleridge, 'The Rime of the Ancient Mariner', 1798

Ten-year-old Elroy van Rooyen and his cousin Ryno were budding entre-preneurs who earned their pocket-money by pushing grocery trolleys for customers to their cars. So, on the afternoon of Friday 11 March 1994, they did not go straight home after school but headed for a large shopping centre instead.

The boys lived with their grandmother on the outskirts of a coastal town, the Strand. Elroy and Ryno grew hungry from the hard work and walked to a café where they ordered French fries. While they were waiting for their food, they fiddled around on one of the game machines in the café. They attracted the attention of a man who had been watching them for a while, who then walked over and offered to pay for a few games. Elroy and Ryno were delighted and invited the stranger to join them in a game.

When their food was ready, the boys left the café and returned to the shopping centre. They sat down on the kerb and ate their hot greasy chips. The stranger followed them and asked them their names, but he did not introduce himself. He asked if they would help him carry boxes to the train station, which was across the way from the shopping centre, and he prom-ised them ten rand each for their efforts. Ten rand was a fortune to a young entrepreneur and both boys jumped at the opportunity.

As they approached the train station, Ryno became uneasy. He realised that the boxes they were carrying were empty and he remembered hearing about the Station Strangler who had killed eleven young boys a few months before in neighbouring Mitchells Plain. He threw down his boxes and begged

Elroy to leave with him, but Elroy refused. He also knew about the Station Strangler, but that was in Mitchells Plain, and besides, he was much too intelligent to be caught by the Strangler. He had often boasted as much to his friends.

The last Ryno saw of Elroy, he was getting into a train with the stranger. His decomposed body was discovered eight days later.

Just a few weeks earlier, I was spending my first day in the South African Police Force. It was 2 February 1994. I had been allocated a large office with standard government furniture at the police headquarters in Pretoria. Over the course of the morning, I had sat in my office reading the policies of the Institute for Behavioural Sciences. It wasn't particularly exciting.

At lunch time I was summoned to the office of the head of the department. We chatted for a while, and he asked me if I knew about the serial killer active in Mitchells Plain in the Cape. I had read about the case in the newspapers. I knew that the Station Strangler had been killing young boys since 1986, but the bodies of eleven boys had been found in the dunes in December 1993 and January 1994, bringing the total to twenty-one. He smiled as I told him what I knew, asked me what I was waiting for and instructed me to take the first available flight to Cape Town to join the investigation team that had just been formed.

My two immediate superiors, Major Jean Nel and Captain Braam Beetge, rushed me through the red tape, and by three o'clock that afternoon I had an appointment certificate in my hand – not a real certificate, but a little card – proudly proclaiming me to be a member of the South African Police Force. My rank was equivalent to that of a captain. I phoned my husband, rushed home and started packing. By six o'clock I was on the plane.

I was nervous and excited and experienced an adrenalin high during the flight. I was also very naïve. I didn't realise then that being called to board a plane with just a few hours' notice was to become a major pattern of my career.

When I arrived at the airport in Cape Town, I looked around expecting to see a uniformed policeman holding a signboard with my name on it. But there was no policeman. I entered the coffee shop and spotted four huge men in civilian clothing. They all sported what I later came to call the 'standard police moustache' and were drinking beer. My instincts directed me.

I asked them whether they were perhaps waiting for me. They all looked up, blinked, frowned and asked if I wanted a beer. I declined. They told me I didn't look anything like they had expected me to. I didn't know what to make of the comment and decided to keep my mouth shut.

One of the policemen was also a psychologist, Captain Sarel Steyn from Port Elizabeth, and another was his assistant, Flippie. The other two men were members of the Peninsula Murder and Robbery Unit. We booked in at the International Police Association House in Cape Town.

Sarel called Flippie and me in for a meeting later that night. He had been in the Force for three years and assumed seniority. He informed us he would work with the detectives, Flippie would work on the victim profile, and it would be my job to compile a profile of the Station Strangler. That settled it.

At 6 a.m. on 3 February 1994, I was ready for my second day in the Force. I had dressed in a black miniskirt, stockings and high heels. Thinking back on what I was wearing that day, I cannot help but be amused. The detectives fetched us and drove us to the Mitchells Plain police station.

Mitchells Plain had a population of about one million people. It was a very poor community and had the reputation of being one of the worst crime spots in the country. Little did I know that I would fall in love with this hornets' nest and that it would change the course of my life.

My first impression of the place was hazy. An early morning mist enveloped the town, casting a grey blanket over the bustling traffic. The streets were tarred and lined with two-storey council houses, which all looked the same. No one seemed to pay any attention to the traffic lights.

The Mitchells Plain police station was situated opposite a shopping centre called The Plain. In those first few weeks, a detective would escort me across the street to the café. I was not allowed to leave the police yard unaccompanied because it was considered dangerous.

Later, I would return to Mitchells Plain whenever I was in Cape Town. I would visit friends there, go shopping and go to the movies on my own. By then I had learnt how to blend in and no one ever challenged me. Fools rush in where angels fear to tread, they say, but I knew that I would always be safe in Mitchells Plain and that I was not being foolhardy.

On that first day, I noticed that there were three caravans parked in the police yard to accommodate the twelve detectives who formed the Station Strangler task team. Lieutenant Johan Kotzé was in charge of the team.

Colonel Leonard Knipe, commander of the Peninsula Murder and Robbery Unit, oversaw the whole investigation. The Peninsula Murder and Robbery Unit is located in Bellville, but the investigation was conducted from Mitchells Plain.

The team was still somewhat disorganised as it had only been assembled the previous week. There was no operations room and no system in place. Sarel took matters in hand and arranged with the Mitchells Plain commander that we could use their conference room as an operations room. We were issued with stationery, furniture, telephones and radios.

I found a corner amid the chaos and read the summary of all the victims that had been found, including those discovered prior to December 1993.

The bodies had been found in varying stages of decomposition. The youngest was eight, the oldest fifteen. All the boys were of fragile stature. Many were found with their hands tied behind their backs. In cases where the bodies were discovered before decomposition set in, it was possible to establish that they had been sodomised before being strangled with their own clothing.

On 27 January 1994 an angry and hysterical mob had gathered at the police station demanding to be involved in the search. They descended in their hordes on the surrounding dunes, under police guidance. Among others, they found the body of eight-year-old Fabian Willowmore, the youngest victim. He was lying next to his best friend, eleven-year-old Owen Hoffmeester. He had been strangled with his best friend's vest. Owen had been strangled with Fabian's underpants. A note was found in the trouser pocket of another badly decomposed body.

The report I read had no photographs, which allowed me to distance myself from the actual horror that was being recorded.

That afternoon the detectives brought in a suspect they had picked up, and Lieutenant Kotzé requested that I interrogate him. I had never interrogated anyone before, and had to rely on my enthusiasm and therapeutic skills as a psychologist. I was not trained as a police officer, nor yet as an interrogator, but as a psychologist I could recognise a psychopath when I met one.

To protect the identity of the person, I will call him Willie. Willie lived with his girlfriend in Mitchells Plain and he was regarded as a suspect because he had volunteered to assist the investigation team and because he ran martial arts classes for young boys. I think it must have been his child-hood dream to become a policeman and this was his chance to be involved in an investigation. There was no way that Willie was going to let the oppor-tunity pass. Some serial killers have tried to insinuate themselves into the investigation of their own cases, to obtain inside information. At that stage we thought Willie was a good suspect, but he was totally unlike the man that the detectives eventually arrested.

I had met psychopaths before, but Willie seemed like the archetype. He was manipulative, he lied and obviously had only his own interests at heart. He had run away from home as a child and often played truant. He had no idea where his family was and he had travelled extensively around the country, but like a good criminal, he recognised Mitchells Plain as the ideal hideout. He had also had several previous encounters with the law.

He was also very charming. Psychologists have fancy words to describe the characteristics of a psychopath, but there is a common layman's term that often describes them best: bullshitters! I interviewed Willie for an hour or two and then I let him go. The detectives would keep tabs on his move-ments, but for the moment Willie had no idea that he was regarded as a suspect.

I left the operations room after 4 p.m. and found the detectives in one of the caravans. I was still astounded by the magnitude of Willie's psycho-pathy, and as I climbed into the caravan I swore aloud. The detectives looked up, and for the first time they smiled at me. They seemed to focus on me as a person. They asked hesitantly if I wanted a beer. This time I did not decline. Since they had no glasses, I took the dumpy and drank straight from the bottle. They relaxed and started talking. Lieutenant Johan Kotzé asked me what I thought of Willie and whether I would like to see the 'graveyard' – meaning the crime scenes. I said I would. He jokingly recommended that I dress in jeans the following day. In other words, no more minis, stockings or high heels!

I didn't know what to expect the following day, but I certainly did not expect the scrambler motorbike. I put the helmet on, swung my leg over the seat and settled behind Johan's back. We rode through Mitchells Plain, and for the first time I got an idea of the labyrinth of its streets. I expected Johan to ride fast, but he stuck to the speed limit in the residential areas. The houses were mostly double storeys with tiny little yards. Later, when I considered buying one, I discovered that each house had a small lounge, dining room and kitchen downstairs with two bedrooms and a bathroom upstairs. One could hardly turn around in the bathroom. Large families occupied such a dwelling. The Station Strangler lived in one too.

Johan turned the bike onto the open road and opened the throttle for the first time. We approached the dunes and he parked the bike. The dunes were steep and we climbed them in silence. The heat simmered on the white sand as Johan led me to the different spots where the bodies had been found. I knew the Strangler had picked those spots because they were so remote that no one would hear the muffled cries of the young boys. The children must have trusted the man completely to have followed him there.

As the February sun burnt down on us, I imagined how it must have felt to discover decomposed bodies in those dunes during the midsummer heat. Johan and I didn't talk much; he merely described what had happened at each of the scenes. I had studied the crime scene photographs the night before and could match them to the spots in the dunes.

There was a strange wind blowing as we sat quietly at one of the crime scenes. It rustled the leaves of the vegetation and blew small waves along the sand. Both of us were in a pensive mood. I became aware of a very peaceful atmosphere, which was not what I expected. I expected to pick up a nuance of violence there. But there was nothing – just the wind rustling the leaves, and a sense of desolation and peace. All the action was long past and I could not recover any of it.

I prayed for each of the victims at every scene, although I knew their suffering was over. I prayed for the Station Strangler too, because his anger and pain will remain with him until he dies, and I prayed for the detectives.

At one of the scenes we discovered the dismembered hand of a child. The body had been removed but somehow the small, fragile hand had been left behind in the sand. Johan put it in a plastic bag he found on the scene. I had to hold the bag when we drove back. It was my first direct experience with violent death and it upset me greatly.

I did not see much of Sarel for the rest of the week. He worked mostly with the detectives while Flippie and I tackled the paperwork in the operations room. I collected as much background as I could on the case to draw up the profile.

Back home in Pretoria, as I analysed the information, I could feel the Strangler entering my mind. It was a strange experience. I couldn't concentrate on anything else and thought only about him.

When I returned to Mitchells Plain a week later, it felt like coming home. The hooting cars, shouting brokers, laughing schoolchildren, barking dogs and blaring sirens created a cacophony unique to that place. It struck a resounding chord in my heart.

The Station Strangler investigation commenced shortly before the country's first democratic elections in April 1994. In the meantime the South African Police Force had asked Interpol to refer them to an international expert on serial killers. The name of Robert Ressler, ex-FBI agent, came up. The Force corresponded with Ressler, but it was decided that his visit should be postponed until after the election, since it was considered too dangerous to bring him out to Mitchells Plain at that stage. I had been overjoyed at the prospect of meeting Ressler, as I had read his book, and was very disappointed when his visit was put on hold.

One Saturday night I experienced my very first police 'braai', which was an institution in the Force. Any detective worth his salt would have a grill in the boot of his car and a glass in the glove compartment. I was told we were going to a beach house at Monwabisi Strand, so I was expecting some sort of holiday home.

We arrived at Monwabisi Strand and left the cars in the parking lot at the beach. Then we climbed into a 4 × 4 and drove down the beach for a kilometre or two. We eventually arrived at a little ruin of a building about half the size of a single garage. No doors or windows, just four walls and a roof. This was the beach house.

It was still daylight and I went for a swim in the sea. One of the detectives warned me not to lie on the beach. When I asked why not, he replied that my skin was so white that they would not see me and might accidentally step on me. I put my jeans back on again after that comment.

The braai was typical Police Force style. Meat, drink and bread rolls. No middle-class salads or fancy trimmings, no cutlery or plates. When dusk settled and the fire was crackling, Johan and Boeta brought out their fishing rods. I joined them at the edge of the surf as they cast their lines.

Boeta was standing a short distance from where Johan and I were sitting.

At first we were silent, but when we started talking we continued for most of the night. Johan taught me a lot about the Force and the detectives, what to expect and what not to do. I told him about serial killers and how their minds worked. We drank brandy and Coke.

It was a beautiful night, cool after the sweltering heat of the day. The waves chased each other up the beach, the stars shone bright and I could spot the Southern Cross clearly. Boeta's silhouette projected a sense of security. Behind me I could see the fire burning and the detectives standing around it. A few of them had brought their wives and children along.

And I knew that behind those dunes lay Mitchells Plain. I also knew that the Strangler lived there. He was never out of my mind.

I found Johan very complex. He was moody, adventurous, unemotional and determined. He listened intently to what I had to say. We discussed a dream we both had of training detectives to investigate serial killer cases exclusively. Later, this dream was realised for me, but that was the night the dream was born, and it was also the night when I realised what I could offer the South African Police Force. It was only later, when the Force became the Service, that I realised the contribution that I could make to the community as well.

It was a happy night and I felt very far removed from Pretoria, my childhood, my past and, unfortunately, my marriage. Johan's fishing rod suddenly jerked and he jumped up. He laughed when he saw what he had reeled in, but wouldn't show me what it was until we reached the fire. It was a shark, and he had caught it at the very spot where I had swum a few hours earlier. He released it back into the sea, where it belonged.

When we all drove back through Mitchells Plain at two the next morning, I felt secure and confident, and slightly tipsy too.

Back at my office in Pretoria, I continued working on the profile. I followed the FBI's recipe. To draw up a profile, one first has to gather all the ingredients. Firstly this includes all the information available on the crime scenes – the position of the body, clothing, weapons used, description of ligatures and any physical evidence left behind by the offender. Next is a summary of the victims, called a victimology report. The victimology report contains information on each victim's background, habits, family structure, age and occupation. Forensic science has advanced so much that the identity of a victim can be established by reconstructing a skull, lifting fingerprints, tracing dental records, analysing bone structure and, of course, with DNA.

Many serial killers try to conceal the identity of their victims by removing their clothing or identity documents, some by cutting off fingers or hands to remove their fingerprints, and some defile a victim's face, but even serial killers cannot defy nature. The process of rigor mortis takes a certain number of hours after death and some serial killers may try to delay this process by, for example, freezing or burying a body, but this can be detected by forensic experts. Criminals always make the mistake of thinking themselves cleverer than the police, but they forget that any police force has experts who work as a team and the collective intelligence of the team far surpasses that of one criminal.

After the victimology report, information is gained from the post-mortem examinations, laboratory reports and ballistic reports. This includes the cause of death, description of wounds, contents of the victim's stomach, DNA results, calibre of gun used, and so on. The preliminary police report includes all information in the dockets – for example, who found the body, a description of the crime scene, the time the crime was committed, the neighbourhood and the socioeconomic status of the community. A summary of the local crime statistics is also included.

The last and most important ingredient is the photographs. Photos of each crime scene, where possible of the victims when they were alive, and of the post-mortem examination, as well as an aerial photograph and maps of the area, all complete the picture.

Analysing all the information, one makes a decision about the homicide type and style – for example, whether he is an organised serial killer, and whether he is lust-motivated. Decisions are also taken regarding the level of risk the victims were exposed to, as well as the risk the offender took when committing the crime. A sex worker would be regarded as a high-risk victim, while a housewife living on a well-guarded property is a low-risk victim. A killer who operates in the dark of night and takes precautions to hide his identity has a low risk, while one who blatantly commits the murder without regard for being detected takes a greater risk. Serial killers' arrogance and growing confidence sometimes cause them to take greater risks.

Once it is established exactly what kind of criminal one is dealing with, a reassessment of the crime is made. The profiler tries to reconstruct the sequence of events at each crime scene. Was the victim conscious when he or she accompanied the offender to the crime scene? Were sexual deeds committed before or after death? Did the offender try to conceal the body or remove the evidence?

The last step is to write the profile. This includes a description of the offender's sex, race, age, level of education, occupation, and place and type of residence. I also include the possibility of military training, whether he uses a vehicle, and extensive assumptions about his childhood. The offender's social status as well as his social interactions with both sexes are deduced. I also try to predict whether he would suffer from a mental illness or personality disorder and elaborate on what it might be.

I have found that most serial killers suffer from personality disorders rather than mental diseases. People with personality disorders have rigid personality structures and often have difficulties with interpersonal relationships, but they are not mad. On the other hand, people suffering from mental diseases may lose contact with reality, hallucinate and deteriorate in their general functioning.

Serial killers generally present themselves as normal people to the rest of the community. They go to church, visit restaurants and buy groceries just like everyone else. They are someone's son, someone's brother, someone's neighbour. I sometimes think of them as nice people who have this nasty habit of killing others.

Roy Hazelwood, a retired FBI agent, taught me that serial killers are mostly men for the following reasons. A man's sexual sense is sight and a woman's is touch. Men are aroused by what they see. They buy pornography and buy sexy underwear for their lovers. Most voyeurs are men. Sexual crimes are very visual. Sadists want to see the pain they are inflicting upon their victim.

Another reason is that when a man has been sexually abused as a child, he will take it out on others, while a woman will tend to take it out on herself. If a man wants to dominate a woman, he will demand sex, and if a woman wants to dominate a man, she will refuse him sex. Also, women's sexual problems relate to pain while men's relate to performance. Women mostly equate love with sex, while men do not necessarily equate sex with love.

To draw up a profile, one needs extensive knowledge of the social sciences, including psychology, criminology and ethnology, as well as experience and a gut feeling. A profile is an educated guess based on a network of facts and not a description of a ghost, as some of my critics have described it. My profiles matched the suspects we arrested in 95 to 99 per cent of cases. That is no ghost story.

I spent all my energy on the profile of the Station Strangler and had none to spare for my private life. He totally occupied my mind and I thought I knew him completely. He was no longer a stranger to me.

My profile was completed by the end of February. I described him as a local man who lived and worked in Mitchells Plain. He had to be a local, as a stranger's presence would almost certainly have been monitored by the community and brought to the attention of the police. FBI research has found that serial killers usually commence killing in their early twenties. As this man had been operative for eight years, I predicted that he would be in his late twenties to early thirties. I surmised he would be of the same race as the victims, as a man of any other race in the company of a boy would have been immediately noticed by the public, who were very suspicious of such activities. The man was clearly familiar with the area. He also knew the dunes very well and must have spent much time there, perhaps playing there as a child.

I said he would either be a teacher, a policeman, a social worker or a minister of some sort. Someone who preferred the company of children, someone children felt they could trust. I predicted that he would have been sodomised as a boy when he was the same age as the victims.

Serial killers do unto others what was done to them either directly or in a symbolic manner. When something horrible happens to a child, he will later try to master it by repeating it, but he will be inclined to reverse the roles. An abused child is the passive victim and the abuser is the active aggressor. In his fantasies the child identifies with the aggressor and takes on the active role, while some other person or object becomes the passive victim. We are all heroes in our own fantasies, where we can control every event and even manipulate other role-players' emotions, appearance and dialogue. The difference is that serial killers act out their fantasies. They have no conscience to inhibit them.

The note that had been found in a victim's pocket read: 'Station Wrangler. Number 14, many more to score.' When this little boy was killed, the case had not yet broken in the media and the Station Strangler could not have been aware that the police were investigating the case as a series. He therefore had no reason to communicate with the detectives by leaving a note on the victim. When the first names were printed in the newspapers, another boy's name appeared next to number fourteen, indicating that he was the fourteenth victim to be found.

It seemed that this must have irritated the Strangler. I realised that he must have returned to the fourteenth victim and placed the note in his pocket, indicating the correct chronological order. This proved two things. Firstly, the Strangler must know exactly where each of his victims lay, and, secondly, he was a perfectionist. It was therefore likely that he would dress very neatly. I included this in the profile and many people wondered how I came to this conclusion.

Early in March I returned to Mitchells Plain. The profile had been released to the public. This was an unusual move, but we needed the community's cooperation, and the response was enormous. As so often happens, countless grudges were brought out in the open. People were reported to us who did not even remotely fit the profile. Having the detectives pull the offending party in as a suspect in the Station Strangler case provided sweet revenge for many people.

One individual wrote letters to a newspaper in which he mentioned the blood of the victims saturating the cracks on the pavements. I recognised some of the lines in the letters as extracts from letters that David Berkowitz, alias 'Son of Sam', had written. Berkowitz was a serial killer who had operated in 1977 in New York. A book had been published about this case and the letters were reproduced in the book. I alerted the detectives to this, and they went to all the libraries in the surrounding Cape Town suburbs and checked who had borrowed the book. The man who had written the letters to the newspaper was traced. I think he was unpleasantly surprised by the excellent detective work that led the team to him. He explained that he had just wanted to play a hoax. We decided not to prosecute him.

I met up again with Willie, who was still regarded as a suspect. One Friday he arrived at the caravans claiming that the Station Strangler was using the subterranean sewerage system in Mitchells Plain. He proposed forming his own task team to inspect the sewerage canals in order to relieve the detectives of this duty. We told him it sounded like a good plan, but put him on hold. If he was the serial killer, he could clear the drains of evidence before we could get to them.

The following Sunday morning he arrived at the caravans accompanied by a 'squad' of teenagers all fully equipped and dressed in brand-new army kit. Willie had been a very busy man that weekend. He had gone to the army and told them that he was assisting the Station Strangler task team, explaining his suspicions about the sewerage system. They had good-naturedly fitted him and his squad out with army uniforms, webbing belts, boots and all. The Sea Rescue Unit had supplied him with metres and metres of rope. A chain store was persuaded to donate enough tinned food to last a month. All of this was done without the official consent of the Force. Willie was a psychopath *par excellence* and could manipulate any unsuspecting person.

We stared at Willie and his squad, dressed and armed to the teeth, ready to descend into the sewers. For a while we were at a loss as to how to deal with him, but luckily Willie had overlooked one small detail. He had forgotten to get batteries for the torches. We stalled him by saying that we would buy batteries early on the Monday morning and he could hit the sewerage system then.

That Sunday night some of the detectives went to Willie's house, searched it thoroughly and then brought him in for intensive interrogation. Some of us played good cop, pretending not to understand why the others were investigating him, but we were all in it together. Early on Monday morning we cleared Willie as a suspect, issued him his batteries and sent him off into the sewers. At least he didn't bother us for a while, emerging only now and again to show us pieces of old clothing that he had found. Whenever we drove around Mitchells Plain, we joked about Willie being somewhere beneath us.

Understandably, the community of Mitchells Plain was caught up in hysteria. Under different circumstances, it would not have been unusual for a child to live with his parents for a while, then move in with relatives or grandparents without informing his parents. The parents would just assume that he was living with relatives and would show up sooner or later.

This was the reason that most of the victims were not immediately reported missing. There were so many people living in one mother's house that it was only when she noticed that one of the supper plates had not been touched that she missed the boy. Gardens were small, and the children spent most of their time on the streets. They played soccer, visited game shops and walked long distances to the beach unaccompanied.

But since it had become known that a serial killer was active, things had changed. Parents accompanied their children to and from school. Any unknown man seen walking with a boy was regarded as a suspect and chased. One woman claimed the Strangler was a woman who harvested semen from men and planted it on the boys. Another woman told us her husband had sex with chickens. We picked him up and he told us that he thought it would be an interesting pastime. We interviewed child molesters to learn how they approached children. The team of twelve detectives worked through two thousand suspects from February until April, when we finally arrested the right man.

But before that, the community went mad. They burnt the crime scenes, destroying valuable traces of evidence; they stormed a police station and wrecked the fence because they thought a suspect was being held there. They mobbed a private house and detectives had to be lowered by helicopter onto the roof to remove people from the premises. We could not search a suspect's house during the day for fear that retaliation by the community and vigilante squads might result in innocent people being harmed.

Although the Station Strangler had killed the first child in 1986, the murders did not follow a set pattern. Months, even years, passed before another body was discovered. Also, the bodies of the children were scattered among the vast and often impenetrable dunes surrounding Mitchells Plain and neighbouring Belhar, Modderdam and Kuilsrivier. It was mostly when a passer-by was lured from a footpath by the smell of a decomposing body that it would be discovered.

Murder was a common occurrence in Mitchells Plain because of gang violence. Initially, only one detective from the Peninsula Murder and Robbery Unit, Warrant Officer Reggie Schilders, investigated these killings. Reggie was up against tremendous odds, first of all to find the bodies, then to link them, and lastly to identify a suspect. The suspect he was up against was a cunning man who made use of the vast uninhabitable land and who relied on the bodies not being discovered in time for any evidence to be secured from the scenes.

During the time Reggie was investigating the case, no one in the South African Police Force had done any research on serial killers. The idea of involving an investigative psychologist was foreign to Reggie and to all the other detectives. By the time the community and the police had discovered the bodies during January 1994, Reggie had retired.

The fact that such a large number of children were killed and discovered over a period of just a few weeks prompted the Force to assemble the investigation team. Detectives were seconded to the team on the basis of their ability and availability. Since the detectives had so many murder dockets to investigate at any given time, a single murder would not have warranted assembling a whole team. There just wasn't enough manpower for that.

By setting up a task team and by involving the community in the search, the Force was sending a message that the case was receiving serious attention. Most of the community leaders understood this, but when the lives of children are at stake, no one can predict the reaction of any community. They vented their anger by burning the vegetation, not realising that they were destroying evidence. The vigilante action of storming a house was not unique to Mitchells Plain – vigilantes have acted similarly in other South African serial killer cases. It is the duty of the investigating officer in charge to involve the community without jeopardising the investigation and to manage vigilantes. When emotions run high, this can be a daunting task.

As public interest grew, it was inevitable that we would also be harassed by the press. They followed us everywhere.

We worked twenty-four-hour days. I learnt to sleep and eat whenever I could. Although there was a barracks in the police yard, they could only provide us with coffee early in the morning, and over weekends the detectives who were off duty would bring those on duty food that their wives had prepared. I felt sorry for the wives, knowing how little they saw of their husbands during those three months. Some of them had problems at home, but luckily there were no divorces. I was not so lucky. I didn't see my husband often, and sometimes I didn't even have the time to say goodbye before I boarded a plane.

We were allocated an assistant to manage the administrative duties in the caravans. One day she commandeered two of the detectives and they set off to the shopping centre across the road. When they came back, they had secured a promise from a chain store that she could fetch ingredients free of charge every day to prepare lunch for us. It was their contribution to the investigation. By lunch time that day, all the detectives had clocked in and we were treated to snoek sandwiches.

I returned to Pretoria and found myself totally disorientated. My environment seemed alien. It was difficult to adjust to normal hours and a daily routine. I felt like a junkie going cold turkey. One night my husband found me sitting in our lounge, smoking. I could not sleep. He asked me what was wrong and I replied that there was a madman in my head. Wisely, he just put his arms around me.

I knew the killer was active that night. The next morning I phoned Johan and asked him what he had been doing the night before. He said that he had gone fishing but that he had had a strange premonition. I told him I'd felt the same. A few days later I was back in Mitchells Plain again.

The investigation was still running at full steam, but the detectives were tired and despondent. The work was never-ending. Their mood had suddenly changed. Morale was low, they bickered among themselves and I felt unwelcome. A sinister cloud had descended on the whole investigation.

Saturday 19 March was my thirty-third birthday. Willie was out of the sewerage system and hanging about the caravans irritating us. I sent him to buy some beer so that we could celebrate my birthday before retiring that night. He came back with a dozen beers and a bunch of yellow roses, bought with my money. I appreciated the thought. My husband had also sent me a bouquet from Pretoria.

At about lunch time that day, the call that we all dreaded came through. A body had been found near Faure, a few kilometres from Mitchells Plain.

We rushed to the scene. The body was lying in a hollow between the dunes. I approached it hesitantly. This was the first murder victim I had ever encountered. I looked at the child lying on his stomach before me. He was wearing underpants. His hands were tied behind his back and he had been strangled with his tracksuit pants. His small red sneakers and a toy were lying next to him. His skin had blistered and revealed the flesh. He was covered with maggots.

I crouched down on my haunches and prayed for the child. I did not feel sick, nor was I put off by the stench. A strange thought crossed my mind. When that little boy had dressed in his tracksuit pants one morning, he had no idea that he would be strangled with them that afternoon. I had never come so close to the Strangler before. Now I was being physically confronted by his handiwork. There was no doubt in my mind that this was one of his victims, although it was not possible at that stage to ascertain whether the victim was a boy or a girl, because the body was covered by maggots. I could hear them eat. The child was later identified as Elroy van Rooyen.

The restless crowd had multiplied and some of the detectives tried to keep them away from the scene. A short while later the press arrived. We avoided them, denying that it was the Strangler until we could confirm our facts. The Mitchells Plain community was already hysterical, and it would have been irresponsible to whip up emotion in the Faure community as well. We sat on the dunes waiting for Johan and the Forensic Unit. The detectives were edgy, irritated by the public and the journalists. I was aware only of the strange wind again. The fact that it was my birthday did not cross my mind until much later when we returned to the operations room and I noticed the beers. We did not drink them that day.

We went to neighbouring police stations to check on reports of missing children but could not establish the identity of the victim. By Monday afternoon we had the results of the autopsy. The boy had been killed on the night Johan and I had had the premonition. I felt strange, and the foul mood of the detectives did nothing to relieve my trepidation. I left the police yard and wandered about the shopping centre alone. I was no longer afraid of being accosted. At times I would climb onto the roof of one of the caravans and just stare at Mitchells Plain. Although things had changed within the investigation, Mitchells Plain still held its hypnotic spell over me.

I remember one morning spotting a young woman walking across the open veld. The sun had just broken through the mist and the wind was playing with her dress and her long black hair. She was barefoot and had a moody expression on her face. She was beautiful. I have never wished to be anybody else, but at that moment I identified with that girl. I wished I had grown up in Mitchells Plain. I wished I had lived in one of those tiny council houses and played on those dusty streets as a child. Never in my life had I felt that I belonged to any community. But this place, one of the worst crime spots in the country, was where I felt at home.

Mitchells Plain offered me the chance to be myself, something I had not expected, and although I was confused by it at first, I grew strong from it. I was depressed because my marriage was breaking up despite the fact that I still loved my husband, and yet I was also exhilarated by my transformation.

A week after we found the body, we had a breakthrough. A woman, Mrs Fouzia Hercules, was waiting for her daughter outside a shopping centre in the Strand one Friday afternoon when she noticed a stranger approach two little boys who were sitting on the kerb eating French fries. She noticed him because she knew most of the locals and he was a stranger. She saw him walk towards the station with the two boys. The boys were carrying boxes. She recognised the boys as the grandchildren of a friend.

At a school meeting a week later, she heard that one of these boys, Elroy, had been missing for a week. Everyone knew that the Strangler had struck again. She went to her friend, Ouma van Rooyen, and met little Ryno, the surviving boy. They came to us in Mitchells Plain to tell us what they knew and Ryno and Mrs Hercules compiled an identikit of the man.

The focus of the investigation moved to the Strand, a town about twenty kilometres from Mitchells Plain. The night before I returned to Pretoria, we got information that the Strangler might be living at a certain address in a squatter camp in the Strand. At four o'clock the next morning we moved into the squatter camp. The detectives were heavily armed with automatic machine guns. I was excited because, although it was a dangerous mission, they had decided to take me along.

The squatter huts were built of corrugated iron and cardboard. There were no formal streets – only little alleys no wider than a metre that criss-crossed through the shacks. Numbers were painted on the shacks, but not in any chronological order.

Silently and stealthily, we moved like shadows, trying not to draw attention to ourselves or wake the dogs. Some barked at us, but no one seemed to be awake. The detectives were trying to find the right shack. We stopped at one of them and I crouched down to pat a dog who seemed friendly. One of the detectives came up behind me and firmly dragged me away. He was not antagonistic but he was concerned. He quietly explained to me that I was in a possible line of fire and that anyone could shoot at me through the corrugated iron. I sincerely appreciated being shown the ropes and after that I stayed behind Barry Chamberlain, who was huge.

We found the right shack. Johan knocked on the door. A man opened up and urinated on the ground next to Johan while he spoke to him. The man was agitated but allowed us in. I was surprised at how comfortably the shack was fitted out. There were carpets and furniture. We started searching the house and a woman woke up. She began swearing at us, which seemed to wake the rest of the community. We did not find the person we were looking for and Johan decided it was time we retreated.

Barry grabbed my hand and we ran through the squatter camp. I don't think I would have made it on my own, but he led me safely out. We drove to the house of a detective who lived in the Strand. He woke his wife, who made us coffee. Then Boeta drove me to the pier on the beach. I walked to the end and sat down. The waves were washing in beneath me and the sky was painted pink with the first rays of dawn. It was breathtakingly beautiful.

I caught a flight back to Pretoria at ten o'clock that morning. For the first time, my husband and I seriously discussed separation. Although I loved him, I could not stay married.

I carried on with my work, trying desperately to fit into the routine of office hours. My superiors supported me, but I was very unhappy. I no longer had daily contact with the detectives and most of them seemed strangely hostile towards me. Two weeks of uncertainty passed.

Then, on the morning of Friday 13 April, Detective AJ Oliver called me. AJ and I had formed a close bond by then. He informed me they had arrested the Strangler the previous night. His name was Norman Afzal Simons.

A nurse working in a private clinic had reported to the investigation team that she suspected one of her patients might be the Station Strangler. He fitted the profile and resembled the identikit. The team had kept observation on the man and found that he often left the premises of the clinic at night. The nurse reported that the man had been admitted to the clinic at his own request. He claimed to suffer from depression, but he did not participate in the therapy sessions and refused to take his medication.

One night the team followed the man through Mitchells Plain as he drove back to the clinic. They pulled him over and Johan asked him to follow the detectives to the operations room, which he did voluntarily. There Johan began interrogating him, but he told Johan he would prefer to write down the story of his life. Johan gave him a pen and paper and waited.

Eventually he finished and Johan read his story. The man wrote that he had been sodomised by his brother. He intimated that he was the Strangler, but did not confess. It was midnight by the time he had finished. The man said it was too late for him to return to the clinic. Johan offered to let him sleep in the caravan and he accepted. A few detectives kept watch over him and when the others returned the following morning, the man was still asleep.

The detectives sprang into action and did some background searches on the man. The more they found out about him, the more it seemed likely that he was the right suspect.

When he awoke, he accompanied them to the house that he shared with his mother, stepfather and sister. It was a council house a few blocks from the police station. The detectives conducted a thorough search. In a cupboard in his room they found clothes belonging to his deceased elder brother.

AJ told me that Sarel had been called in from Port Elizabeth and had accompanied them on the house search. I was hurt that I hadn't been included, but I was also excited. I booked a flight. Two of the detectives fetched me at the airport and took me to a hotel.

The next morning I heard that the detectives had held a braai the previous evening to celebrate the arrest. They did not invite me. I did not ask them why. On the Saturday morning they came to fetch me from the hotel. I accompanied Colonel Knipe, Johan and Sarel and one or two other detectives to Valkenberg Psychiatric Hospital where Simons was going to be interviewed by a highly qualified psychiatrist, Dr Tuviah Zabow. He informed us that Simons suffered from a personality disorder.

I observed Simons during Dr Zabow's interview. He was a twenty-seven-year-old teacher who worked at a primary school in Mitchells Plain. He seemed effeminate, and was soft spoken and well dressed. So far he fitted my profile, but I didn't have a chance to talk to him during the interview.

I still have difficulty describing the rejection and anger that I felt. I had been so involved in the case, but I was left out at the end. I was aloof and unapproachable that morning. A light drizzle had started falling when we left the hospital and I got into one of the cars. But Providence had not forgotten me, although it seemed the detectives had. They were talking to Dr Zabow on the porch.

As I sat in the car staring at the rain and waiting for the detectives, the back door opened suddenly and someone got in. I didn't turn around at first, because I thought it was one of the detectives. I stared ahead, but the silence was screaming at my back. The abyss was right there, gaping behind me and I could not ignore it.

I turned around and stared into the dark eyes of the man who had been haunting my thoughts and mind for four months. We were alone in the car, and in the abyss. I introduced myself to him and he shook my hand. He had strong hands. We started talking. He wanted to know what would happen to him and I told him that I honestly didn't know. I saw him as a frightened individual and felt empathy well up in me.

I dived into the abyss without a second thought. At that stage, no memory of his murders crossed my mind. Only he was there. I asked him questions about his life and found out that he was fluent in French. We started speaking in French. A detective got into the car to escape the rain, but couldn't understand what we were talking about. Simons told me that he loved classical music, that he enjoyed being a teacher, and that it was his dream to visit Denmark. In those twenty minutes, I got to know him as a person and not just as a phantom. I knew him so well already. I tried my best to reach him, but circumstances did not offer me the time.

We returned to the Peninsula Murder and Robbery Unit and Simons was taken away to be booked into an undisclosed venue for his own protection. The rest of us went to Mitchells Plain.

At that stage I was hurting badly. I was leaving my husband, I felt rejected by my friends the detectives and felt betrayed by Sarel. I had also looked into those dark eyes and into the abyss. Yet the sun was shining in Mitchells Plain. It was bright and sparkling after the rain. I broke the surface of the dark waters and my soul lifted and seemed to catch one of the high winds. I felt myself soaring like a seagull above that beloved place. By the time we reached the caravans, a smile had broken through. The others responded to the smile and I realised not all of them had turned on me. It felt good to be back. Not just good, but exhilarating.

There was a lot of work to be done. Johan was not there because he had accompanied Simons. The rest of us split up and decided to do some more background searches. I teamed up with Barry and AJ and some of the other detectives who weren't antagonistic towards me.

We went to Alpine Primary School, where Simons was a teacher. We were shown his classroom. While the detectives interviewed the headmaster, I chatted to one of the teachers. He was still in a state of shock. He told me that it was the duty of the male teachers to patrol the school grounds during the lunch breaks to ensure the safety of the pupils, but that Simons had refused to do so. Of course, he didn't realise then that Simons saw no need to patrol the periphery of the school grounds, when he knew the Strangler was already inside. He also told me that the Standard 3 (Grade 5) teachers had decided that their pupils should do a project on the Station Strangler to make them aware of the danger. Simons refused to let his class do so. Lastly, he said that the teachers locked their classrooms during school hours with the children safely inside. Simons used to knock on the doors and jokingly cry out: 'Open up, it's the Strangler.' No one took him seriously.

We worked till late that night. I walked over to the shopping centre to buy some cigarettes and was pleased when the café owner addressed me by name and discussed Simons's arrest with me. No one could believe that the beloved community leader, a well-known primary school teacher who presented isiXhosa lessons to ex-convicts, was the feared Station Strangler. Serial killers are usually such normal people that their communities often react with disbelief.

I reached my hotel room late that night. On the Sunday no one came to pick me up. I spent the day lying beside the pool feeling miserable again. I knew they were talking to Simons and they were excluding me again.

In the early evening the detectives came to pick me up. Simons was ready to make a confession. We went to the Murder and Robbery Unit. Some of the detectives were avoiding me, feeling guilty it seemed, but the others included me. During the afternoon's interrogation session, Simons had even demonstrated to Johan how he had managed to kill two boys at the same time. At about 10 p.m. we drove to the magistrate's office in Bellville where Simons was to make his confession to a magistrate. We sat outside on a wall and waited for two hours. The mood had lifted slightly and we managed to joke a bit. Finally, Simons emerged. He gave me a friendly greeting.

Johan told us that Simons said he would prefer to point out the crime scenes that night, because he feared doing so during the daylight hours. It was a wise decision. Johan organised an independent detective to conduct the pointing out. It is advisable that an officer who has no intimate knowledge of a case officiates the pointing out of crime scenes. Then there can be no allegation that a suspect was deliberately taken to a scene of which a detective had first-hand knowledge.

It was decided that the rest of us would follow their vehicle at a distance, far enough not to interfere with the process, which would have been illegal, but close enough to be on standby should trouble erupt in the community.

It was about two o'clock on Monday morning when we reached Mitchells Plain. The car in front of us stopped at certain places, and we waited while Simons and the independent detective got out and Simons pointed out scene after scene. The whole process was recorded and photographs were taken at every scene. Then they returned to the car and the procession started off again. Simons pointed out several scenes in the Mitchells Plain area that were all correct to my knowledge. All of us knew where those bodies had lain.

It was strange to be driving through Mitchells Plain in this manner. This time we were not looking for the Strangler. This time he was in the car in front of us and the community of Mitchells Plain was completely unaware of the stealthy convoy creeping through their streets. Only the dogs were awake. If the people had known we were there, they would have lynched Simons.

Suddenly Johan's car pulled over near the dunes closest to the beach. We all got out. Over the police radio, we were informed that Simons had pointed out a spot in the dunes where he had recently left a body that we had not found. Johan radioed for the fire brigade to bring spotlights to the area. We waited. The detectives tried to squeeze themselves into a single car since it was bitterly cold. I sat on the kerb of the road with my back to them, looking at Mitchells Plain, dreaming, oblivious to the cold. I composed a poem in Afrikaans, in the dialect of the local people.

The fire brigade arrived and drove out to the dune. Johan found the spot the detective had described to him and we started searching, but the lights couldn't reach it. We searched that dune with cigarette lighters. Damp sea sand filled our shoes and the wind bit through our windbreakers. We found some child's clothing, but no body. Wild dogs inhabited those dunes and the body could have been devoured.

We returned to the caravans after the unsuccessful search and sipped steaming black sugarless coffee. I reached the hotel at 6 a.m. At 9 a.m. Sarel and another detective hammered on my door. They told me that Colonel Knipe didn't see any purpose in my remaining in Cape Town, because no one was allowed to talk to Simons. He was due in court at 10 a.m. to be charged. Sarel told me there was a flight leaving for Pretoria at 10 a.m. and that I had to be on it. I grabbed my bags and caught the plane. Years later I wished that I had talked to Colonel Knipe and asked for an explanation.

———

During the rest of April and the month of May, I ignored the investigation team. Their rejection still hurt, but I decided that I would stay in the Force. I buried myself in writing, falling back on my experience as a journalist. I remembered my dream that I had that night at Monwabisi – to train detectives to investigate serial killer cases exclusively. I did research and wrote the curriculum for the first course in Basic Investigative Psychology, which focused on serial killers, serial rapists, sadistic lust murderers and auto-erotic death. The principles of my thesis were included in my lectures as well.

Ressler never got the chance to consult on the Station Strangler case and so I faxed him my profile of the suspect with some of the details about Simons's life. This was the first time that he had had any insight into the profile I had compiled. He responded that my profile was 98 per cent accurate. I was too hurt to be proud of my achievement, but very determined to prove myself.

My husband and I finalised our divorce in June and he held my hand in court. Afterwards we went for coffee. He remained one of my closest and best friends and I will always be able to say that for seven years I was happily married.

Sometime in June I got a call in my office in Pretoria that AJ was waiting downstairs at reception. AJ had always backed me up and I was excited about seeing him. I had met his wife, Abby, and his little boy, Kurt, and often had dinner in their home in Mitchells Plain. I rushed downstairs but stopped in my tracks when I saw that Johan was with him. We went up to my office and AJ went to the office next door to call his wife. I felt uncomfortable with Johan but somehow his moodiness had lifted and he seemed like his old self. He invited me to have coffee with him after work. When AJ came back, they filled me in on the details of the case that I had missed out on since I had last had contact with them.

After work we went to a coffee shop. There was a fire burning in the hearth. The atmosphere was cosy and I felt my antagonism melting. Johan told me that he had accompanied Simons to court on that Monday morning and that afterwards he had gone to my hotel to apologise for the detectives' behaviour. He found that I had left and thought that I was upset with them. I told him about Colonel Knipe's order and he was surprised – he had not known about it. He explained that policemen who were not involved in the case were jealous about the investigation and objected to the manner in which I had been so closely involved.

The idea that a psychologist should participate actively in an investigation was foreign to them, and the fact that I was, for the most part, the only woman on the team made it worse. They did not understand the *esprit de corps* – the camaraderie – that existed between us. Some of the detectives' wives had objected to me joining the party the day after the arrest, so I was not invited. The detectives had avoided me because they thought it was the safest way to cope with the situation.

Colonel Knipe thought the best way to deal with matters was to get me out of the way. I could understand that with the pressure of catching a serial killer and having the international press all over him, he did not need personal complications. I finally understood and appreciated the fact that Johan had told me the truth. I just wished that they had told me at the time. I began to understand the Police Force better and had learnt a hard lesson. Jealousy may sometimes cause people to wilfully misinterpret innocent situations, just to further their own agendas. Such people do not consider the effect the rumours they spread may have on other people's lives. Years later, many of them apologised to me, but the damage had registered. It left a scar.

Johan told me more about Simons's life. He was born on 12 January 1967 in Cape Town. His biological father was Xhosa and his mother was coloured. He never had any contact with his biological father. His stepfather was also Xhosa. He had been sent away from his nuclear family as a toddler and stayed with relations in Johannesburg, East London and Durban. At the age of five he was living with an aunt in Queenstown and attended school there. During this period of his life, he mainly observed Xhosa customs and traditions. During his confession he spoke about an '*umfufunyana*', which is a name given to an older woman who has magical powers. He said this woman had a bad influence on him.

During his teenage years he returned to live with his mother in Mitchells Plain. He later worked as an intern in a children's home, and as an office clerk, and finally qualified as a teacher in 1992. He could speak seven languages, including French. The murders began in 1986, when he was completing his matric. Apparently he killed no one while he was studying to be a teacher, and I can only presume that this was because he was happy as a student. He is a very intelligent man and needed mental stimulation. From 1991, Simons had begun booking himself into various psychiatric hospitals and clinics. He was diagnosed with depression and various personality disorders. It seemed as if he was trying to get help, but he never revealed to the psychiatrists that he might have killed people.

Simons suffered from several identity crises. First of all, being of mixed race, he had a cultural identity crisis; secondly, he had a religious identity problem, switching from Christianity to the Muslim faith and then back to Christianity, changing his name from Norman to Afzal in the process; and, thirdly, as a gay man, in those years, he was ostracised.

He revealed to the detectives that his elder brother had sodomised him between the ages of eight and fourteen – the same ages as his victims. My profile had been accurate.

In his confession, Simons said that the spirit of his deceased brother had entered him and that this spirit had forced him to kill. His brother had died mysteriously in 1991. This illustrated how he identified with the aggressor and took on the active role while the boys represented himself and became the passive victims. In my opinion, Simons committed suicide on a psychological level every time he killed one of those boys.

Simons wrote the following in his confession: 'I am nothing. I am dirty. I am filthy and not worthy. I am sorry for letting you down. Don't get caught in the same thing. I really regret everything. It's hard, it is very hard to be possessed by unknown forces. These forces cannot be explained by medication. I salute you with love for a better and understanding and peaceful South Africa.'

With these words, Simons was trying to express what it felt like to be inside the abyss.

TWO

Cleveland, Pinetown and Witbank

And I had done a hellish thing,
And it would work 'em woe:
For all averred, I had killed the bird
That made the breeze to blow.
– Samuel Taylor Coleridge, 'The Rime of the Ancient Mariner', 1798

On 1 July 1994 I walked the block and a half from my office to the head office of the newly renamed South African Police Service (SAPS). I was looking for Colonel Kobus Jonker, the Service's expert on the occult. Occultism is not a crime, but many crimes are committed in the name of the occult. I needed some background information since satanic murders and serial homicide share an element of ritualism and I wanted to teach the detectives to differentiate between the crime scenes. The main difference between serial killers and Satanists is that serial killers have a deep psychological motive for killing, while Satanists who kill profess that it is 'because the devil made them do it'. Also, most serial killers work alone, while Satanists form cults and are showmen who need an audience.

Colonel Jonker's office was on the fifth floor. I was searching for the office when a man emerged from another door and asked me who I was looking for. When I asked for Colonel Jonker, he told me that Jonker was out of town but offered to show me his office.

Colonel Jonker's office was a chamber of horrors. Bibles locked in chains and other satanic paraphernalia were on view in display cabinets, and a coffin stood upright in a corner. He kept these exhibits as mementoes of his work and often used them to illustrate his lectures. The man explained to me what the objects were used for. When we left the office, he invited me to have a cup of coffee with him. Since it was winter and I wasn't looking forward to the walk back to my office, I agreed.

As we entered his office in the corner of the corridor, I noticed the name on the door: Brigadier Suiker Britz. I realised I was in the company of one of the South African Police Service's legends. Suiker Britz would become my boss, my mentor and my guardian angel.

He invited me to sit down. Since I had spent about fifteen minutes with him in Jonker's office and had listened to his jokes about ghostbusting, I felt at ease. He asked me what role I had in the Police Service. I explained my work to him, mentioning my dream to train detectives in the investigation of serial killers. He said that he had heard about my profile on Simons. He was wonderfully easy to talk to and I could not imagine why he had such a fierce reputation.

Brigadier Suiker Britz was in command of all Murder and Robbery Units in the country, including the Peninsula Murder and Robbery Unit where Colonel Knipe was commander. He had previously been in charge of the Pretoria Murder and Robbery Unit, but when he was promoted to brigadier he was transferred to head office and put in charge of the toughest bunch of detectives in the Service. Murder and Robbery is regarded as the elite among the specialised units and these detectives are a breed of their own.

The brigadier was a short man, overweight, with a big moustache and bright blue eyes. His face showed signs of hard living, but there were laughter lines etched around his eyes and his smile was genuine, lacking the cynicism of some of the other senior staff members. I sat there for more than an hour listening to his stories. He asked me to bring him the lectures I had written on serial killers.

I took the set of lectures to him the following week. My experience as a psychology lecturer had come in handy in compiling this curriculum. He paged through them, adjusted his spectacles, looked at me and said he was of the opinion that it would be better if I could be transferred to his department. I was elated and discussed it with Captain Braam Beetge, my immediate supervisor at the Institute for Behavioural Sciences. Although Braam was my boss, we were friends as well. He accommodated my eccentricities and covered for me when I followed my head instead of the rules. Maybe I danced to a different drum, but I got the job done well. I needed to be accommodated, not managed, and Braam knew that. As Captain Frans van Niekerk later told me, in the SAPS it was better to apologise than ask for permission.

At the Institute for Behavioural Sciences, it was mainly my duty to develop a forensic psychology project, but I also had to undertake therapeutic duties for members of the Service who had psychological problems. I didn't mind this too much, since I was a qualified psychologist, but I hated attending meetings and often avoided these on some pretext or other. Braam and I decided to keep Brigadier Britz's suggestion to ourselves until there was more certainty about it. A transfer might not be welcomed since it would create a precedent for other psychologists to break away from the Institute for Behavioural Sciences.

During July and August I carried on with my research. I spent more time in the University of Pretoria library than at the office. It gave me an excuse to avoid those meetings.

I was contacted by a Sergeant Piet Viljoen of the Cape Town Detective Branch to compile a profile on a serial rapist in Cape Town. I didn't want to go to Cape Town since the hurt of the Station Strangler investigation was still close to the surface. Piet flew to Pretoria instead and discussed the details of the case with me in my office. It took me about a day to compile the profile and when I handed it over to him, he said that it fitted his main suspect like a glove. I didn't know that he already had a suspect in mind.

The suspect was a policeman who kept surveillance on the apartments of his victims before he eventually broke in and raped the young women who lived there. He was a compensatory rapist. A compensatory rapist is a man who compensates for his inferiority complex by raping women. The rapes confirm his masculinity to him, but after the rape he feels extremely guilty and tries to compromise by apologising to the victim.

I predicted that the suspect would have some kind of police or army training, since he could climb up drainpipes, jump from two storeys, and he left no evidence. Piet went back to Cape Town feeling more secure about arresting his suspect. I didn't realise then that I had won an important ally. Two years later Piet would be the investigating officer in a serial killer case in Cape Town, and I was lucky to have already won his trust.

I went to visit Brigadier Suiker often and spent many hours sitting in his office listening to him. A camaraderie developed between us. He suggested that I present a lecture on serial killers at a Murder and Robbery course to test the material. He asked me if I would like to attend the course as an observer. When my commanders consented, I was over the moon.

At that stage I had moved in with my sister. She was a horticulturist and was working at the University of Pretoria. She had also separated from her husband and was going through a bitter divorce. She lived in a house on the university's experimental farm. The farm was situated in a residential area, but once you drove through the gates the bustle of the city was left behind. There were cattle and other farm animals and it was very peaceful. A third woman shared the house with us. Between us we had six cats, four dogs and a few goats on the property. The house was an old farmhouse with wooden floors, a fireplace and exquisite pressed-steel ceilings.

When I moved in, I was still recovering emotionally from my divorce. I knew I wasn't very good company and would sit brooding in front of the fireplace every night, or else I would lock myself in my room and lose myself in my music. By day I worked myself to a standstill and by night I withdrew into myself.

My sister had her own problems, but our friend was a practical woman. She was always the one who ushered me to bed at night and fed me headache tablets the next morning. One night she came into my room, took the glass of wine from my hand and switched the music off. She told me it was time to get a hold of myself, and, besides, they needed me to do my share of the household chores. I listened to her advice.

I completed the Murder and Robbery course and then attended a course at Tell Academy in Johannesburg, where I was trained in interrogation and interview methods used by the FBI.

At about this time, the newspapers were carrying disquieting reports that a serial killer was on the loose in the Cleveland area in Johannesburg. He was preying on unemployed adult women. The tally was already ten victims.

Brigadier Suiker called me in to discuss the matter. The cases were transferred from the different detective branches to the Brixton Murder and Robbery Unit in Johannesburg. On 28 September I accompanied the brigadier to Brixton. I hadn't known we were going to be visiting crime scenes and I was wearing high-heeled shoes again. The crime scenes had all been processed, and although the bodies had been removed I still wanted to visit them in order to tune into the serial killer's mind before I drew up the profile.

The commander of the Brixton Murder and Robbery Unit and the investigating officer, Sergeant Timothy Nkomozulu, escorted us. The crime scenes were near the Cleveland mine dump areas. They were located in the open veld close to the highways, mine dumps and an industrial area. The Brixton commander was nearing retirement and not inclined to accept my new ideas. But he had the sense not to be openly hostile in the presence of the brigadier.

At the first crime scene, they told me the killer had written a message on the legs of the victim, nineteen-year-old Maria Monamu. The message read, 'I am not cross with you, we will stay here until you understand', and 'She is a beach'. Maria had been a scholar in Pretoria. Her body was found on 16 July 1994.

We walked to the second crime scene, that of the fifth victim, an unidentified adult woman who was discovered on 7 September. I noticed that a menstrual pad was lying on the scene. I asked why they had not collected it. The commander seemed irritated by my question, but the brigadier said if I wanted it collected, they should bag it. I handed Sergeant Nkomozulu a pair of plastic gloves and an envelope I carried in my handbag for such purposes and he bagged it. The commander became even more irritated. I was a psychologist and should not play detective by carrying gloves in my handbag. Later it was found that the body of the woman had been buried without anyone taking DNA samples from her. The menstrual pad saved the day as it made it possible for her blood group to be determined, enabling the differentiation of her DNA from the killer's. It hadn't been such a stupid idea after all.

We moved on to the next crime scene, which wasn't easy in high heels. This was the crime scene of the seventh victim, Daphne Papo, who was murdered on 9 September and discovered on 21 September. The commander told me that I wouldn't find anything on that scene, since he had personally supervised its processing. He seemed smug.

I asked him if he would mind if I spent some time there. He had no objections. I knelt down and silently prayed for the victim, as I had done at all the previous crime scenes. I scratched around with a stick, trying to capture the feeling of the place. I gradually became aware of the same peaceful wind rustling through the trees that I had experienced in Mitchells Plain. I didn't try to analyse the coincidence, just allowing the experience to wash through my mind. As I scratched, I came upon a condom wrapper. Sergeant Nkomozulu was watching me. We saw the wrapper at the same time. He clicked his tongue and shook his head and called his commander and the brigadier, who were standing a short distance away. The commander was red-faced. He said he couldn't believe that he could have missed the wrapper. Brigadier Suiker just asked the sergeant to bag it and made no further comment. The wrapper could have had the killer's fingerprints on it.

At that moment I knew I wasn't going to be very popular in Brixton.

The crime scene of the third victim, twenty-six-year-old Amanda Thethe, was close by. She was murdered on 6 August and discovered the following day.

The eighth victim, an unidentified woman, was found a little further from this spot in a gully. She died on 16 September and, like Daphne Papo, was discovered on 21 September.

The crime scenes of the second, fourth and sixth victims were a little further away, behind a building, but within walking distance. The second victim was twenty-five-year-old Hermina Papenfus, who died on 29 July and was discovered two days later. The fourth victim, Betty Phalahadi, died on 2 September, and her body was found the following day. She was also twenty-five, as was the sixth victim, Dorah Moleka Mokoena, who was killed on 9 September and her body discovered on 19 September.

The body of twenty-four-year-old Amanda Molake, a student from Pretoria, was discovered on 7 September, as was the body of twenty-four-year-old Margaret Ntombeni Ledwaba, another student from Pretoria. These bodies lay on the other side of the highway, a short distance from the other scenes.

Brigadier Suiker requested the commander to cooperate and provide me with all the information I needed for a profile. Since Pretoria is half an hour's drive from Johannesburg, I compiled the profile at my office. I had a lot of information, but not nearly as much as I needed. The women had all been strangled with their clothing and it seemed as if all of them had been raped. Some were completely naked, while others were half naked. In one case the killer had placed the victim's jewellery on top of her naked body. Some of the victims came from Pretoria, which indicated that the killer used a vehicle to drive from Pretoria to Johannesburg.

I realised that this man was very arrogant. He had dropped a body at a certain site at the end of July 1994. The detectives found it and removed it. Two months later, on 2 September, he left another body at the same spot. Again, it was found and removed. Then, scarcely two weeks later, a third body was found at the same spot. This pattern emerged only after I started analysing the data. Had I been involved earlier, I could have told them that serial killers are very possessive about their 'graveyards' and they could have kept the scenes under observation. By the time I recommended this procedure, it was already too late. The killer had read in the newspaper that a task team had been assembled and he had fled.

I was mostly isolated from this task team. I recommended that they set up an operations room, which apparently they did, but I never saw it. I felt very uncomfortable and unwelcome at Brixton and would go there only when Brigadier Suiker invited me to accompany him. I discussed my unease with him and he explained to me how fortunate I had been with the Station Strangler squad when the detectives had at first readily accepted me.

He tried to explain the dynamics of a Murder and Robbery detective to me. They were a closed unit who distrusted outsiders, they would not easily be convinced of new methods, and they detested interference. I realised that the only way I would be able to break into their ranks was with his help and by excelling at my job. If he backed me up and believed in me, they would slowly follow his example. If I showed them that my work could assist them in their investigations, they would be more inclined to trust me.

I drew up the profile, describing the killer as a man between the ages of twenty-three and thirty, since these were the ages of the victims. He would drive an expensive car, for the victims would not be enticed to get into an old vehicle. I said he would have a speech defect because he had written on the body of a dead woman, which indicated that he had experienced difficulty in communicating with her while she was alive.

I never felt happy with this profile. First of all, the image of a ladies' man did not correlate with a speech defect. I thought that maybe he could communicate well on a superficial level, but that he was unable to communicate deeper feelings to a woman. This implied a rejection by the mother figure. He had called one of his victims a bitch, which indicated his anger towards women, and I surmised that there must have been a recent rejection by a female that had triggered the murders. I predicted that he worked with his hands and was a member of the middle class. I always had a nagging feeling that I was missing something, but I couldn't figure out what it was.

In August 1994 the body of thirty-two-year-old Joyce Mashebela was discovered near Atteridgeville in Pretoria, and on 7 October the body of thirty-year-old Peggy Bodile was found in the same stretch of veld. The victims were partly dressed or naked and had been strangled with their own clothing. They had also been raped. It was decided to include them in the Cleveland series because of the similarities of the crimes. Since the bodies were discovered in the Pretoria Murder and Robbery Unit's precinct, their commander, Colonel Henk Heslinga, who was a friend of mine, involved me in the investigation.

I had established that the killer preferred Friday evenings for murder. On the afternoon of Friday 27 October, Colonel Henk informed me that he had arranged for a police helicopter with infrared night sight to fly over the area that evening. Since it was still early, he invited me to have supper with him before the flight. We went to a Portuguese restaurant and I ate garlic calamari, which was very oily – something I will never do again in my life.

When we arrived at the air base, it had started raining. I did not mention that I had never flown in a chopper before. The pilot didn't mind the rain – there was a killer on the loose. We lifted off and flew over the crime scenes. I had a helmet on my head and could see the infrared screen. By that time it was raining heavily. I was feeling extremely sick and when the lightning started to flash around us, I had to concentrate exceptionally hard not to throw up over Henk. I really could not have cared less whether we spotted the killer or not.

By the time we landed I was a wreck. Scarcely had the chopper touched Mother Earth than I leapt out and ran to the nearest bush, where I vomited until I had nothing left inside me. Henk thought it was a big joke. I drove home with my pride injured and slept late the following morning.

By that evening I felt much better. But at one o'clock on Sunday morning I awoke to the sound of a white police car screeching to a halt on our lawn, its siren wailing wildly and our dogs in hysterics. Before Henk could reach the back door – there were two big Labradors he had to get past – I already had my jeans on. When I opened the door, he told me that Mr Sydney Mufamadi, the minister of safety and security, had summoned us to his house. While I got ready, Henk phoned the Brixton commander in Johannesburg and told him to get over to the minister's house as well. Within ten minutes I was good to go and we drove to Minister Mufamadi's house. He lived on the presidential residential property in Church Street, Pretoria.

The minister welcomed us at the front door. He was dressed but walking around in his socks. He told us that two women had phoned a radio talk show and said that they could have been picked up by the Strangler. The radio station had contacted the minister directly and he had driven to two towns in his private car to pick up the witnesses. This was highly irregular. He asked Henk and me to interview one of them, while an expert compiled an identikit with the assistance of the other witness.

While we were interviewing the woman in the minister's lounge, he came in and asked us if we wanted coffee. A few minutes later he reappeared, carrying a tray. I don't know whether he made the coffee himself, and I also don't know of many policemen who have been served coffee at three o'clock in the morning by the minister of safety and security without his shoes.

By the time the Brixton commander arrived, most of the work was done. Henk took me home, where we had more coffee, and I told my sister and our friend about being served coffee by the minister. We would later establish that the witnesses had not encountered the killer and the identikits they had helped compile did not fit the suspect. I got into bed at four o'clock that morning and by eight o'clock Henk was back again, asking me if I wanted to go on another chopper ride. I did, and I think I won back the respect I had lost on the Friday night. My stomach behaved. As we flew over Atteridgeville, I was surprised to see a jackal running on the hill. I didn't think there was any wildlife so close to the city, but this is Africa, after all. We did not spot any new victims or the killer.

In November 1994, Henk involved me in the investigation of the murder of a prominent professor who was found in his bath with multiple stab wounds. Although there had been similar cases elsewhere in the country, it was not the work of a serial killer, since the main motive was robbery.

Serial killers are differentiated from other murderers by motive. They have a deep psychological motive, whereas passion, greed, revenge or some other identifiable motive can be present in other killers. I spent many days and nights working on this case.

In the meantime my proposal for a course for detectives had been approved. I was told that this was a miracle, since it had been known to take up to two years to get a course set up.

Brigadier Suiker was impressed with my work. He told me that he was not a man to be impressed by just a pretty face and needed someone who would keep the scoreboard rolling. Apparently my scoreboard already had a few points on it. By 18 November 1994, my transfer had been finalised and I moved into my new office at the Detective Services at head office. Brigadier Suiker had a huge office vacated for me, furnished with an equally huge desk and a conference table. He also managed by some means to secure a private telephone line for me. I didn't ask any questions.

On 24 November 1994 I embarked on a tour of the country to select the first group of detectives for my course. They would be Murder and Robbery detectives who would be psychometrically evaluated and I would interview them as well. I had more than eighty applications. I needed men and women who were open to innovative ideas, had an understanding of psychology, and the experience to manage a serial homicide investigation. I could select two per unit and there were nineteen units dispersed across the country.

One of those I selected was Captain Vinol Viljoen of the Pretoria Murder and Robbery Unit. He later investigated the Atteridgeville serial killer and became one of my closest friends and confidants. I also selected Captain Frans van Niekerk and Sergeant George Mothlamme from the East Rand Murder and Robbery Unit. I had worked with Frans on a case involving a sadist who had killed a young girl. Frans had worked on the Norwood serial killer case before I joined the Service, and was also to become involved in the Atteridgeville case, as well as some gay serial murders at a later stage. Brixton withdrew their nominees. The detectives were continuing with the Cleveland serial killer investigation, and I decided to concentrate on my trip to select more detectives for my course rather than worry about them excluding me. I had learnt from the Station Strangler investigation not to take it that personally.

On Saturday morning, 5 December 1994, Brigadier Suiker and a captain from the Narcotics Squad came to collect me at my home. I was teased about the amount of luggage I had. Luckily I am a small woman, for I had to fit into the back of the brigadier's Mazda MX-6. I made myself comfortable by curling up on the back seat, drew the brigadier's jacket over myself and slept like a kitten.

Our first stop at about 6 p.m. was Beaufort West, where we checked into a cheap motel. We had bought meat on the way, and Brigadier Suiker and his friend Jakkals were already building a fire outside for the braai when I emerged from my room with a bottle of brandy. They both laughed, commenting that I had already picked up the bad habits of a detective. But by the end of that trip, my bottle was still half-full and my boss often teased me about this. The bond with my new boss was strengthening, and was based more on camaraderie and respect than on seniority.

The next day we completed the rest of the journey to Cape Town. They booked me into a hotel and left for the Strand, where they would be staying. I had a swim in the pool, cooling off after the hot drive through the Karoo.

Early the next morning Johan Kotzé and Reynold Talmakkies fetched me and took me to the Peninsula Murder and Robbery Unit. I hadn't been there since we arrested Simons and I hadn't seen or spoken to any of the detectives, including Johan, for months.

Johan and Talmakkies were the only two volunteers from the unit, which made my task easier as I already knew them and both had also participated in the Station Strangler investigation. We finished the psychometric evaluation during the morning, and Johan said he had a chopper ride organised for that afternoon. I declined, not being much in favour of choppers, telling him that Talmakkies and I would find something else to do and that we would pick him up later that afternoon.

Wasting no time, Talmakkies and I took the car and drove to Mitchells Plain.

Talmakkies knew me well by then and did not interrupt my thoughts. He just kept on driving through the streets. I relaxed and drifted lazily into the ambience of the place. It was all there, of course: the children playing in the streets, the dogs dodging the cars, the drug dealers on the corners, the gangsters swaggering on the sidewalks, the housewives hanging up laundry, the brokers selling vegetables, the snoek sellers and the women in their bright saris.

We stopped at the police station. Our caravans had been removed and the operations room had been converted back into the parade room. I greeted my friends and we had coffee with Barry Chamberlain. I felt good about being back. Talmakkies drove to the beach, parking at a place where I could stare at the dunes where the children had been slain and where I could watch the sea. I was in a peaceful mood, thinking how much I had learnt about myself and the Police Force in the time since I had last said goodbye to Mitchells Plain.

———

The next day I climbed into the back of the MX-6 and we set off on the rest of our trip. I selected a very young sergeant named Derrick Norsworthy as well as Sergeant Ivan Mpambani in Port Elizabeth. Three years later Derrick would arrest a serial killer using a brilliantly devised interrogation strategy. Most of the detectives I selected had attended the Murder and Robbery course with me in September. This would be the first course in Investigative Psychology and I needed men and women who knew me and who would support my ideas. I interviewed them all and assessed them with psychometrics. Brigadier Suiker was very patient with me throughout this process. He often had work in the towns we visited, but sometimes he had to wait for hours while I finished my assessment of the detectives.

Back in Pretoria, I spent a few days at home before leaving for KwaZulu-Natal to select more detectives. This time I was accompanied by another psychologist and Brigadier Suiker stayed at home. I think he realised that I was capable and would behave myself.

We returned to Pretoria on 15 December, the day the Brixton Murder and Robbery detectives arrested David Selepe, the Cleveland serial killer, in Mozambique. Brigadier Suiker informed me of the arrest over the telephone. I was excited and wanted to meet the killer. He told me he would arrange an interview after the detectives had interrogated him and taken his confession and seen to the pointing out of the crime scenes. I felt slightly disappointed, but I trusted him and knew he would keep his word.

He asked Warrant Officer Polla Ferreira to accompany me to Newcastle in KwaZulu-Natal to complete my selection of detectives. Polla is a beautiful petite blonde whom no one would believe to be a detective. One should not be deceived by appearances, though. One of her hobbies is driving. It rained heavily on the night we returned to Pretoria, but I knew Polla could handle the car on the wet road, so I sank back into my seat, listening to the radio. Suddenly the thunderstorm vented all its fury on the earth. Lightning flashed across the sky, thunder rolled and the rain came down in sheets. It was a terrible night.

We listened to the news on the radio, and it was in those circumstances that I heard that David Selepe had been fatally wounded by the Brixton detectives. He had attacked them while pointing out a crime scene. I was supposed to have interviewed him the next day.

The storm raging outside was nothing compared to the one inside me.

For the second time that year I had been denied the opportunity of talking to a serial killer. I wondered how long it would be before another opportunity arose. Little did I know that one of South Africa's most notorious serial killers was already active very close to my home.

David Selepe had fled to Mozambique to escape arrest. I do not know how the detectives identified him or how they traced him to Mozambique. I was not involved in Brixton's investigation to the extent that such information would have been shared with me. In all fairness to Brixton Murder and Robbery, I have to say that their attitude changed over the years, especially when they had more serial killer cases to investigate.

After his arrest, Selepe was kept in custody in the cells at the Brixton Murder and Robbery Unit. He confessed to killing fifteen women in Johannesburg, Boksburg and Pretoria. He said he could point out the crime scenes in Cleveland and three near Atteridgeville in Pretoria.

My profile of Selepe was not that far off the mark, but I was still unhappy with it. He was in his late twenties. He had many girlfriends as well as a wife. He was described as very charming. He was driving a Mercedes-Benz when he was arrested and he had newspaper clippings of the Cleveland serial killer case in the boot of his car. I had predicted in the profile that he would be interested in the media coverage of the case.

Selepe projected the image of a businessman. He was involved in the Vision Girls' School in Pretoria, a private college where women were trained as secretaries. This was, of course, an excellent source of potential targets, and some of his victims were students there.

Although the man was dead, something was bothering me. I should have heeded my gut feeling, but I was weary of the detectives' scepticism and didn't want to cause trouble by asking them questions about the suspect. Selepe's DNA grouping was 1212, a number that later returned to haunt us.

I took a few days' leave and spent a quiet Christmas with my family. And then from 9 to 27 January 1995 I presented my first course in Investigative Psychology in Pretoria.

Brigadier Suiker sent Polla on the course – 'to check up on you', he later told me with a wink. Sadly, Johan couldn't make it, because he had to prepare for the Station Strangler's trial. It was disappointing because we had both dreamed of this course, but he visited us during the last few days and presented a lecture on Simons's investigation.

The Wednesday before the course ended, we all went to Vlakplaas for a braai.

Vlakplaas was the notorious farm from which Captain Dirk Coetzee and Colonel Eugene de Kock and the C10 unit operated. This was the so-called Third Force, which was allegedly involved in doing the previous government's dirty work. Later, after the establishment of the Truth and Reconciliation Commission, headed by Archbishop Desmond Tutu, the men were invited to apply for amnesty. Amnesty would be granted for gross human rights violations if they were found to be politically motivated and if the violator had not personally benefited from the acts he had committed.

I met several of the members of C10. Most of them were ordinary middle-class Afrikaans men. They had served their country during the Angolan War and had then joined the Police Force. They were brainwashed into an ideology and believed they were acting on the government's orders. When the proverbial papaw hit the fan, the general feeling was that they were hung out to dry. Colonel de Kock was put on trial and sentenced to two life sentences and two hundred and twelve years in prison, but Captain Dirk Coetzee got a post with the new government's National Intelligence Agency. Most of the men waited years for amnesty.

The Truth and Reconciliation Commission allowed the families of victims the opportunity to hear for the first time the truth about what had happened to their missing loved ones. Family members and surviving victims could apply for compensation. In some cases, the men who had committed the deeds and the families of the victims hugged each other after the hearings and some degree of reconciliation was achieved. The history of the country was left with an ugly wound, though. (Eugene de Kock was granted parole in 2015 and was released in 2022. Dirk Coetzee died of cancer in 2013.)

By the time we visited Vlakplaas, the members of the C10 covert unit had been disbanded and the farm had been taken over by the Endangered Species Unit, but some of Vlakplaas's traditions remained. Any newcomer to the farm had to drink a glass of what was called 'Spookpis' or 'Leeutande' (Ghost Urine or Lion's Teeth). The drink consisted of several white spirits – vodka, cane, etc. – that had fermented in the sun for a few days. To this concoction was added raw garlic – the so-called lion's teeth. *Macbeth*'s witches' brew would taste like Kool-Aid compared to this stuff. Captain Vinol Viljoen handed me a full glass. I drank it. I didn't pass out, but I couldn't remain standing on my feet. I spent the rest of the party sitting in the car, too scared to move. I wasn't sure how I got home. Apparently, someone dropped me off and my sister put me to bed.

But the course was a success, and the detectives requested an advanced course.

A week later, I set off for Cape Town to attend the Station Strangler's trial, which commenced on 27 February 1995. The Attorney General of the Western Cape had decided to charge Simons only with the murder and kidnapping of Elroy van Rooyen, the last victim, since there was insufficient evidence in the other cases. We expected the Strangler's trial to last a few weeks – we never anticipated that it would take six months. Those were the worst six months of my life. I attended court every day and documented every word of the trial.

For the first month I booked into a holiday apartment close to the High Court in the centre of Cape Town. The trial began well. The press attended and the public gallery was filled to capacity each day. Many of Mitchells Plain's gangsters were there, as well as the mothers of some of the victims.

During the first month of the Station Strangler trial, Inspector Andy Budke from the Pinetown Murder and Robbery Unit in KwaZulu-Natal phoned me. Two girls had been raped and murdered, while two had escaped their assailant. I flew to Durban for a week, while the Cape Town High Court was in recess. Inspector Budke and Detective Bushy Rambhadursingh met me at the airport. Both of them had attended my course.

The offender was what is known as a blitz attacker – someone who does not have the confidence to charm a victim into accompanying him. He prefers to attack an unsuspecting victim from behind. The detectives had named their suspect the River Strangler. He had overpowered a teenage girl as she sat reading next to a river, not far from her home. Her body was found floating in the water by her father. Stray dogs had eaten at her face, a horrendous discovery for a parent. Because the body had been submerged in water, there was very little evidence.

The other victim was also a young teenager who had been walking along a road in the neighbourhood. A woman driving past saw the girl being attacked from behind and thrown down an embankment, but by the time she returned to the spot, the girl was dead. Her head had been bashed in with a blunt object and she had been raped. The offender escaped. Two other young females came forward and recounted similar stories of a man attacking them from behind. One of them had fought bravely and managed to escape, and the other attracted help by screaming. I interviewed both girls and we got a good enough description to draw up an identikit.

Over the course of that week, we set up an operations room and a task team. We called in all the detectives in KwaZulu-Natal who had attended my course. The fact that we did this caused a rift between Pinetown Murder and Robbery detectives and the task team, but the commander of the Durban Murder and Robbery Unit, of which Pinetown was a satellite, Colonel Vlaggies Roux, eased their tempers.

I worked endlessly on the profile. The surviving victims mentioned that they had smelt marijuana. I described the suspect as a disorganised serial killer who was lust-motivated. A disorganised serial killer would more likely be mentally ill than be suffering from a personality disorder. The fact that the man used a blitz attack meant he lacked the self-confidence to approach a victim. The murders were spontaneous and unplanned. Organised serial killers plan their murders, while disorganised ones act on the spur of the moment. This killer took a great risk by attacking a woman in broad daylight with traffic passing by. That he was motivated by lust was clear, for he raped the women brutally. I thought the man might have been affected by excessive smoking of marijuana. He had long dreadlocks and it was possible that he was a Rastafarian, who tend to smoke marijuana every day as it is part of their culture.

I finally completed the profile by the end of the week – it usually took me three weeks. I flew back to Cape Town on the Sunday evening. The River task team was disbanded soon after I left because there were no more attacks, but Andy promised me he would catch the man before he retired from the Police Force.

During this time the South African Police Force became the South African Police Service and Brigadier Suiker was promoted to the rank of general, which later changed to commissioner when the powers that be decided we should demilitarise. Generals became commissioners, brigadiers became directors, full colonels became senior superintendents, half colonels and majors became superintendents, captains remained captains, warrant officers became inspectors, and sergeants and constables retained their ranks. It was all very confusing to us, especially since some of those not directly involved in line-functioning police work were given civilian ranks. Although I was a member of the Detective Service, I was a psychologist, so I was promoted to become a senior supervisor. Who I was supposed to supervise I still do not know, because at that stage I was the only member of my unit, which I called Investigative Psychology. My rank was equivalent to colonel.

Upon returning to Cape Town from Durban, I decided the holiday apartment was too expensive. If I cost the Service too much, they would recall me back to Pretoria and I wanted to attend the whole trial. Talmakkies arranged for me to move to a covert police camp about fifty kilometres from Cape Town where I could rent a house for five rand a day. There was a police base at one end of the camp and a few houses on the other side. The houses were usually used for witness protection purposes, but when they weren't in use they were available for other members of the Service.

My little house had three bedrooms, a lounge, kitchen and bathroom. There were no carpets on the floor, no TV, radio or telephone. I tried to make it look homely, but failed. The camp was close to Mitchells Plain, but rather isolated in the veld. It was a very dangerous area and I had to get through the security gates before nightfall or risk being hijacked or attacked.

For five months I lived in this place that seemed like a prison camp to me. Sergeant AJ Oliver, who had the responsibility of preparing the Station Strangler docket for the trial, looked after me. During this period we established a lifelong friendship. By now I was so at home in Mitchells Plain that I would do my grocery shopping there and sometimes visit friends, like AJ and his family, on my own. No one bothered me – I was regarded as a local. I had become quite proficient at speaking their dialect as well.

In the mornings I would get up at five o'clock and drive to the Strand. The camp was situated halfway between Cape Town and the small seaside town. I would pick up Elroy's grandmother and Mrs Hercules, our main witness, in the Strand and then we would drive to a squatter camp and pick up Elroy's mother. As a psychologist I was not expected to transport witnesses, but AJ couldn't manage all of the driving, and the rest of the Station Strangler task team were too busy to assist him. It was dangerous for a woman to enter squatter camps alone, but as soon as it became known that I was working on the Station Strangler case, no one bothered me. It took me two hours to get everyone to court on time. I took them home again in the afternoon and then sped off to get through the camp gates before nightfall. Then I confronted the loneliness. There was nothing in that house. Sometimes I would go to bed at five o'clock in the afternoon just to escape being awake.

One weekend I noticed a stray cat in the dunes behind my house. It was the ugliest cat I had ever seen. She was scrawny, and her coat was all the colours of the rainbow. Within three weeks she was sleeping on my bed. At least I had company – I was missing my own pets.

During the Cape Town High Court recess in April 1995, I returned to Pretoria for two weeks. I arranged with the camp gardener to feed the cat, threatening him with death if she wasn't there when I returned. It was a pleasure to sleep in my own bed again, with my own Siamese cat, who had gone grey because she missed me and probably thought I had died. It was good to see my sister too.

Shortly after my arrival in Pretoria, I got a call from Captain Rudi Neethling of the Middelburg Murder and Robbery Unit in the province of Mpumalanga. They had arrested a young male who was suspected of killing three women in Witbank, but the suspect, Nolan Edwards, claimed that he was suffering from amnesia.

Polla and I set off for Middelburg, about two hours' drive from Pretoria. We interrogated Nolan for a day. He agreed to meet us the following week at a dam near Witbank, where the murders had supposedly taken place. He claimed that members of the right-wing Afrikaner Weerstandsbeweging (AWB) were involved.

The investigating officer, Sergeant Elmarie Lambourn, Polla and I sat on the lawn on the banks of the dam and talked to Nolan. I was playing good cop, listening empathetically to his lies. We had already established that he'd had a traumatic childhood.

Nolan kept repeating that he could not remember what had happened during the murders, but we were convinced he was not telling us the whole truth. Yet, as he had been a boxer, I was concerned that the blows he had taken could have caused brain damage and that he might conceivably be suffering from amnesia.

Polla was quiet while I was talking to him, but at the right moment she lost her cool and confronted him, saying that it was obvious he was lying to us. She can sound quite angry for such a small blonde. We had not planned beforehand when she would take over, but her intuition guided her. I was grateful for her intervention because I was also losing my patience, but I was supposed to be playing good cop.

Nolan then started crying and told us he was scared of telling the truth because he was afraid that the AWB would victimise his wife. He admitted to killing the women. As the investigating officer in the case, Elmarie stopped him, warned him of his rights and called for an independent officer to take his confession. Nolan also agreed to point out the crime scenes.

Nolan said that he had killed the first woman, Joanna Mnisi, in his apartment. He claimed she came to the door and made sexual advances towards him. This apparently reminded him of his childhood when the mother of a friend and her charwoman had indecently assaulted him. Nolan had an aversion towards sex as a result of this incident. He told us that he had lost his temper and stabbed Mnisi to death. Afterwards he phoned a friend. They wrapped the body in a carpet and dumped it at the side of the road.

The other two victims, Sithuphugi Sibiya and Beauty Maleka, were sex workers who worked at a certain hotel. Nolan told us that he had picked them up and driven them to a quarry. They were raped, shot, and their genitals were mutilated. Nolan admitted to the murders but denied the rapes. He had grown up in a conservative Afrikaner home and had right-wing connections. Apparently, killing the women was acceptable to him, but having sex with them was taboo, as they were of a different race. He could not explain the fact that the DNA samples of the semen found in those women matched his.

I testified at Nolan's trial. During the trial he claimed that he suffered from Multiple Personality Disorder (MPD), or Dissociative Personality Disorder as it is now called. In my opinion, a serial killer cannot suffer from MPD because the cause of MPD differs from that of serial homicide.

When children are abused at a young age, as Nolan was, they have several options of mental defence mechanisms. The person with MPD develops split personalities as a defence mechanism, thereby repressing the abuse to the subconscious, but he does not develop revenge fantasies. The serial killer does develop revenge fantasies, thereby acknowledging the abuse, and he acts out these fantasies. The two defence mechanisms are totally different and do not overlap. A serial killer cannot, therefore, suffer from MPD because his defence mechanism is vastly different from that of the MPD sufferer.

It also seemed very suspicious for someone on trial for murder to suddenly claim that he was suffering from MPD. Very convenient, I would say. Mr Justice David Curlewis was of the same opinion and sentenced Nolan to ninety years for the murders.

Nolan was very anxious about going to prison and being exposed to other men. Abuse at the hands of an adult male when he was a child was something he still recalled strongly. This was not a person suffering from amnesia or MPD.

I undertook to report his fears to the psychologists at the Department of Correctional Services, with whom I had a good working relationship.

In 1999 three judges of the Appeal Court acquitted Nolan of the murders of Sibiya and Maleka. He was acquitted of the murder of Mnisi on a technical irregularity, which means he could still be charged with the murder. Speaking at his parents' home after his release, Nolan said he took the blame for the murders because he feared for the lives of his wife and son. His wife has since divorced him. Today Nolan is a free man.

In May 1995 I returned to my little house in the Cape 'concentration camp'. The stray cat was still there.

The trial continued. There were amusing times in court and there were tough times too. The confidence of the two state prosecutors, Advocate Mike Stowe and Advocate Annette de Lange, ebbed and flowed like the tide. But we thought they were doing a great job and trusted them completely. On one occasion, all the detectives were called in for a consultation. This was the first time that all of us would be together again. I was apprehensive about seeing them, but by this time I was better equipped emotionally to handle them. In the event, I had nothing to worry about. They accepted me and a glimmer of the *esprit de corps* returned.

The reason the trial was taking such a long time was because the State had decided to prosecute Simons only on Elroy's kidnapping and murder. There was not sufficient evidence to charge him with the other murders. Simons's confession to the other murders and his pointing out of the crime scenes could therefore not be presented during the trial. It would have been illegal. Since the State based most of its case on circumstantial evidence, namely on the eyewitness reports of Mrs Hercules and Ryno, the defence put in a major effort to discredit everything the State presented. Because of this, Simons was advised to plead not guilty. Simons often claimed that he was ill, and then the trial had to be postponed to the following day.

Eventually, on 14 June 1995, Norman Afzal Simons was sentenced to ten years' imprisonment for kidnapping and twenty-five years for the murder of Elroy van Rooyen. After his sentence had been passed down, I went to the holding cells below the court and spoke to him. He was in a dazed state, as if he couldn't quite believe what was happening to him.

By then he completely denied the homicides and seemed to have convinced himself that he was innocent. He told me that he loved children and showed me the cards and letters of support he had received from his pupils. I would never deny that he loved children, or that he was a good teacher, but he was found guilty of murder by a High Court and I think that anyone with a little investigative experience would realise that the crime scene of Elroy van Rooyen was a carbon copy of all the other crime scenes of those Mitchells Plain boys. Simons decided to appeal.

On the afternoon of his sentencing, a few of us met the prosecutors in a tavern. We celebrated and it felt great, but not the same as it feels when one arrests a suspect. The case was closed and the detectives would move on to new cases. Simons would go to jail and we could all carry on with our lives. I went to see him the following day at Pollsmoor Prison. At first he refused to see me, but eventually he came out. He did not want to talk to me about the murders or his feelings and I felt him slipping away from me, but then he turned around and walked up to me and hugged me with tears in his eyes. The moment lasted a few seconds, but it felt endless. In those few seconds several thoughts flashed through my mind. I was back inside the abyss. I could feel all his pain, but I could also sense the fear of the child who had died in those arms. I could hear Simons's cries mingled with the child's. It was a hollow sound, ringing with raw pain. I had tears in my eyes as Simons walked away. It was the last time I saw him.

Simons wrote me several letters from prison. They were friendly and quite witty too. He had converted back to Christianity and was preaching to his fellow inmates. He was kept in the psychiatric ward of the prison for his own safety for a long time. The gangsters of Mitchells Plain apparently still had a contract on him.

Simons's appeal was eventually heard by five judges in the Appeal Court. On 27 March 1998 his sentence was converted to life. The five judges agreed that Norman Afzal Simons was responsible for the death of Elroy van Rooyen. I doubt that he will ever be charged with the murders of the other children.

Simons was released on parole in July 2023. The community was up in arms, as they should be. It is my conviction that a serial killer should never be released.

But is it fair to call Simons the Station Strangler and a serial killer, if he was only convicted of one murder? Several rumours have circulated that the detectives arrested the wrong man, that the DNA on some of the victims did not match Simons's, and that more boys were killed after his arrest. In my view, these rumours are unsubstantiated. Simons made certain admissions and demonstrations to the detectives during the interrogation, and he pointed out the crime scenes, but this was inadmissible in court, because he was only charged with one murder, which according to the state prosecutor, Mike Stowe, had the strongest supporting testimony.

Simons was arrested by the investigation team of the SAPS as the suspect in the Station Strangler serial killer investigation, and he was convicted, albeit of only one murder, in a trial resulting from that investigation. It is plainly absurd to postulate that if a serial killer is arrested in an area, no future murders of similar victims in that area will ever occur. Would no more women be murdered in Atteridgeville after David Selepe was arrested? That notion would be disproved by another serial killer.

THREE

Atteridgeville

Are those her ribs through which the Sun
Did peer, as through the grate?
And is that Woman all her crew?
Is that a DEATH? And are there two?
Is DEATH that Woman's mate?

– Samuel Taylor Coleridge, 'The Rime of the Ancient Mariner', 1798

When I returned to Pretoria the week after Simons's sentencing, the newspapers were again reporting rumours of a serial killer operating in Atteridgeville, a township just outside Pretoria.

No one was allowed to confirm to the press whether a serial killer was operative or not, unless it was me or one of the detectives who had completed the Investigative Psychology course. But leaked information and speculation are almost inevitable. Rumours such as these could have a devastating impact on our chances of an early arrest. The killer might move on and kill other people elsewhere, and it is never a good idea to scare a community unnecessarily.

The press tend to run with a story, often causing more harm than good. One line the press was taking bothered me particularly. They were questioning whether David Selepe, the Cleveland serial killer who had also confessed to killing the Atteridgeville victims, was the wrong man, and they were asking whether the police had shot an innocent person. I was convinced that David Selepe was involved in the Cleveland murders. The press did not take into consideration that Atteridgeville has had many serial killers in the past, and it would not be the first time that two serial killers had struck at the same time in the area.

The most notorious of these Atteridgeville serial killers was the Panga man, Elias Xitavhudzi, who murdered sixteen women during the sixties and dumped their bodies near Atteridgeville. In 1956 an unknown man murdered and mutilated six boys over a period of five months. During the seventies, a man dubbed the Ironman clubbed seven people to death with an iron bar. He was never arrested. At the same time, Joe 'Axeman' Kgabi hacked eight people to death. General Britz was one of the investigating officers who arrested Kgabi. Johannes Mashiane, also called the Beast of Atteridgeville, strangled and sodomised twelve boys during the eighties, but jumped in front of a bus during a police chase in October 1989. Atteridgeville seemed to have fallen out of favour with the gods a long time ago. This history of multiple serial killers operating in one area should put an end to the myth that no more murders will be committed after a serial killer is arrested, and that if new bodies are discovered later, then the 'wrong man' has been arrested.

Captain Vinol Viljoen of the Pretoria Murder and Robbery Unit, who had completed my Basic Investigative Psychology course, had pulled in the dockets pertaining to the latest cases. We studied them carefully, noting that the bodies had been bound in some instances but not in others. We decided to monitor the situation, and remained hesitant to comment on whether or not a serial killer was operative.

I made a big mistake when I initially evaluated the case. I concentrated on the differences in the crime scenes, not noticing that there were more similarities than differences. I didn't have time to dwell on the case because on 22 June 1995 the South African Police Service sent me to Scotland to be trained by Robert Ressler and Roy Hazelwood, two retired FBI agents who were regarded as the world experts on serial killers and serial rapists respectively.

It was great to meet Robert Ressler in person after I had made contact with him during the Station Strangler case. He had a distinguished manner and was very kind and rather introverted. He asked me to present the Station Strangler case on the course. I had only a day to prepare for this, but my experience as a lecturer in psychology at the University of Pretoria stood me in good stead and the presentation went well. Ressler often spent his evenings with me discussing serial killers in some Scottish pub. At first I was so in awe of him that I just wanted to listen, but later I relaxed, and as we walked the streets of Dundee, I explained the Atteridgeville problem to him. It was then that he pointed out the similarities to me. He said he would love to come and help us, if it was possible.

Ressler congratulated me again on my profile of the Station Strangler and explained the FBI's work methods to me. Apparently, profilers in the USA occupy offices at Quantico and seldom visit a crime scene to draw up the profile. I think it is vital to be at the crime scene and to tune into the killer's thoughts and fantasies. According to Ressler, profilers in the USA did not work on an investigation alongside the detectives, as I did in South Africa. After I had read John Douglas's book *Mind Hunter*, I realised that Ressler was one of the FBI agents who was more actively involved in profiling, but that his workload was such that he could only manage crisis control and often issued profiles over the phone.

Roy Hazelwood read my profile on the Station Strangler as well. I still remember how he took off his spectacles, glanced at me and said: 'Boy, but you're really good.'

Ressler and Hazelwood taught me so much and I will always appreciate that they often shared their vast knowledge with me on an informal basis. Together, they had thirty years of experience and research, in addition to that of John Douglas and Dr Ann Burgess, an expert on rape, to back them up. They supplied me with volumes of literature that was unavailable in South Africa. I considered this more valuable than gold.

During the course, the concept of an international data bank on serial killers was first discussed. We were all enthusiastic. I knew I had to set up a South African data bank on serial killers and that it would be a mammoth task since there was no data on them as a specified category of criminal. A year later I teamed up with Dr Mark Wellman of Rhodes University in Grahamstown and Professor Dap Louw of the University of the Free State to coordinate this research.

Vinol assembled an Atteridgeville task team at the Pretoria Murder and Robbery Unit on 17 July 1995, shortly after I returned to South Africa. It consisted of Polla, Inspector Thinus Rossouw and Sergeant John Engelbrecht from the Nelspruit Murder and Robbery Unit, as well as a handful of untrained detectives. Vinol briefed us on the dockets that he had collected.

The first docket concerned the badly decomposed body of a woman discovered in Atteridgeville on 4 January 1995. The skin of the woman's torso had already burst open due to decomposition, exposing her intestines. Her dress was drawn up over her breasts. The second victim was Beauty Soko, whose decomposed body was found in Atteridgeville on 9 February. The skin of her torso had also decomposed and the intestines bulged out. She was naked, but her clothing had been placed on top of her body and kept in place with stones.

Twenty-four-year-old Sarah Mokono, the next victim, was found naked in a construction ditch in Atteridgeville on 6 March. Her body had been covered with soil, but her breasts had protruded from the shallow grave. Next was Letta Ndlangamandla, whose body was fully clothed, but she had been strangled with a bra and her hands were tied with a bra as well. She was found on 12 April. Eight days later the body of her toddler son was discovered not far from his mother's body. He had a bloody bruise on his head, but he could have died of exposure. Both were found in the veld near Atteridgeville. Twenty-nine-year-old Ester Mainetja was found on 13 May. She was lying on her back and the lower part of her body was naked. She had been strangled with clothing.

Victim number seven was Elizabeth Mathetsa, who was discovered on 25 May in Rosslyn, a few kilometres north of Atteridgeville. She was completely naked. Twenty-five-year-old Francina Sthebe was found on the hill in Atteridgeville on 13 June. She was sitting next to a tree. She had a dress on, but her panties and the strap of her handbag were tied around her neck and then around the tree. The badly decomposed body of Nikuwe Biko was discovered on 26 June in the veld. Her head and arms had already been torn from her torso by wild animals. Her hands had been tied behind her back and her feet were tied together. I recalled the jackal I had spotted from the helicopter.

The very day after the team was established, we found our first body in a forest near Westford Hospital in the Atteridgeville area. Granny Ramelo was found lying on her stomach. She was clothed, but had been strangled with a piece of clothing. The forensic experts accompanied us to the crime scene. When they turned her over, maggots could be seen feasting on the rotten flesh of her face. The stench was overpowering, and again, as in Mitchells Plain, I could hear them eat.

We found the decomposing body of a woman every week after that. Mildred Lephule's badly decomposed body was found in a ditch next to a railway line at Bon Accord dam, which is north of Atteridgeville. The charred remains of an unidentified woman were found just above this ditch beneath a tree. Twenty-five-year-old Elsie Masangu's body was also discovered near the charred remains of the previous victim. The body of Margaret Radebe was found lying with legs spread-eagled on the other side of the dam. Someone had unleashed the powers of hell in the Atteridgeville and Bon Accord dam areas.

Our stress levels rose with the number of bodies found. Vinol and I would have disagreements that sometimes erupted into screaming matches. We always made up, though. Vinol was a huge detective, who could also be described as cuddly. He could raise his voice and presented quite an intimidating figure, but he also had a soft heart, once one managed to break through to him. We were about the same age, but I regarded him as an older brother and he spoke of me as his 'sister'. The fights were part of the process of getting to know each other better. I prefer direct confrontation to backstabbing. We sorted out our differences and became friends for life.

The Pretoria Murder and Robbery Unit was located in a beautiful but dilapidated old building on Church Street, next to the historical home of Paul Kruger, who was president of the South African Republic (or Transvaal) from 1883 to 1900. The double-storey building had a backyard and some outbuildings. It was in four small, dingy back rooms that we set up our operations room, and Vinol managed the investigation from there. It created a distance between us and the rest of the members of the Pretoria Murder and Robbery Unit.

In between attending crime scenes, Vinol spent the first two weeks of the investigation trying to secure resources for the operations room. He managed to get hold of some cardboard noticeboards, which we put up on the walls. I arranged the photographs of the victims on the boards in the order in which they were killed. The moment I did this, I spotted the mistake I had originally made.

At first we had looked at the bodies in the order in which they had been found and we were confused by the differences in the methods of bondage. Since this aspect did not correlate, we did not want to announce that they had all been killed by the same man. But when I placed them in order of death, we could clearly see how he had progressed in his method. At first the hands were left untied, then they were tied in front, and then at the back, making it easier for him to control his victims.

As I compiled the profile, I realised that it had much in common with the profile of Selepe, the Cleveland killer, that it could have described the same man, but there were subtle differences. However, a profile describes a personality and not a person, and two people can have similar personalities. I predicted that the killer would be in his late twenties. I said he would be a flashy dresser and a sophisticated ladies' man. The murdered women were not prostitutes. They were career women who would not have accompanied a derelict, but would be more inclined to engage with someone who resembled a businessman. He needed charm to lure them.

While I was working on this new profile, the nagging feeling that I'd had when I compiled the Cleveland profile returned. I remembered Selepe had talked about women he had killed in the Atteridgeville area, and I remembered the bodies Henk and I had investigated the previous year. Now Selepe was dead and his 'ghost' had returned to haunt us.

This knowledge did nothing to reduce our stress. Sometimes Vinol would just sit and stare at the photographs of the victims in silence. He smoked more than I did, and I began to buy an extra pack of cigarettes in the mornings. Late at night when he had run out of smokes, he became agitated, and that was when I offered him the pack I had bought. I considered it part of my responsibility to monitor the stress levels of the investigating officers in a case. The abyss can be a horrible and confusing place to someone who is unfamiliar with the territory. These were experienced detectives who had seen and processed horrendous crime scenes before, but it was quite a different journey to enter the mind of a serial killer.

I had a vision of a certain killer in my mind as I worked on the profile, but I could not detect him in the abyss as clearly as I did the Station Strangler. The feeling was vague and left me confused. I did not wake up at night, nor did he interfere with my own personality. He remained aloof. I did not go to look for him inside the abyss. It is not a place one can walk in and out of freely. It has to beckon one, and the call that I heard was too distant to trace.

One day, we got a call from the Atteridgeville police station. They had arrested a man who claimed to be the Atteridgeville Strangler. Vinol sent the detectives to fetch the suspect. He had attacked the daughter of a friend in her home at Atteridgeville and tried to rape her, but she screamed for help. When help arrived, the man was found trying to strangle the woman. He was restrained and then he claimed to be the Strangler. I told Vinol that there was no way that this man could be the Atteridgeville Strangler. Although the picture I had formed in my mind was vague, I knew instinctively that he was not our suspect. Vinol still had to interrogate him, for the man had clearly attempted to rape and murder the woman.

We interrogated him at intervals for two days. He claimed to have Multiple Personality Disorder and tried to entertain us with his interpretation of personality changes. It was the biggest load of bullshit that I had ever encountered. He said he was a German soldier. The moment Vinol spoke a German word, he jumped to attention and pretended to be a soldier. Then he pretended to be an Arab, and even a woman. I confronted him, telling him it was one of the poorest attempts at faking Multiple that I had ever seen. But he insisted that he had the disorder and asked us to hypnotise him.

I contacted Braam Beetge, my former supervisor at the Institute for Behavioural Sciences, who had since resigned and was in private practice. He arrived that night and agreed to hypnotise the suspect. While he worked with him, it became clear to both Braam and me that the man was play-acting. We told Vinol. He persisted with the interrogation and the suspect came up with certain information that might have linked him to the murders. Vinol decided to send the man for a pointing out with an independent officer and a confession to a magistrate.

By the time the suspect was sent for a confession, it was already after midnight. Unfortunately, one of the Service's liaison officers had visited us and alerted the press that the Atteridgeville Strangler had been caught. Of course, all the news editors altered the front pages of their newspapers to carry the headlines that the Strangler had been arrested.

Later that night, when they returned from the pointing out, it was established that the suspect had pointed out the wrong crime scenes. He didn't have a clue about the murders and had confessed only to what he had read in the newspapers. He was employed at the court and was in financial trouble. He thought that if he confessed to being the Atteridgeville Strangler, it would divert attention from his financial difficulties. Vinol was furious and sent everyone home.

Later, in the early hours of the morning, as Vinol was trying to catch some sleep, his telephone rang. There was a man on the other end asking for details about the arrest. Vinol, who had just been woken up and was feeling irritable as a result, demanded to know which newspaper the man was working for. The man answered patiently that he was not a journalist; he was

Minister Mufamadi, the minister of safety and security. Vinol apologised profusely and explained the situation to the minister, who was quite accommodating, given the circumstances. This episode made Vinol more agitated than ever.

During this time I had also started to convert Ressler and Hazelwood's lectures into material for an advanced course on investigative psychology, which I had promised the detectives I would develop for them. I had to do this in my own time, though, and I sat many a night typing away at my computer at home. Ressler had given me permission to use his material, with due acknowledgement.

I withdrew a little from the Atteridgeville investigation. My profile had been completed and an ill wind had settled on the case, as it had after a while in the Station Strangler investigation. Since my childhood I have been very sensitive to nuances. I knew we could sort out any hostility once the case was over. It was still the same story of Murder and Robbery detectives closing ranks, especially when they were under pressure. We were friends, but they still weren't prepared to trust me completely, although we were making progress slowly. Perhaps my problems with the detectives were clouding my judgement, which could have been another reason why I couldn't find the killer as I had found the Station Strangler in the abyss. After the Atteridgeville case, I learnt to clear my mind of other problems when I was working, because I couldn't afford to allow anything to divert my attention. My mind became the tool that I had to use, like a ballistics expert would use a machine, or like computers would be used to assist the detectives. This, of course, did not bode well for my personal relationships.

On the evening of Sunday 18 September 1995, I answered a call from Superintendent Rudi van Olst, commander of the East Rand Murder and Robbery Unit. They had found the bodies of eight women in the veld near the Boksburg prison.

Boksburg is situated to the east of Johannesburg, about an hour's drive from Pretoria. By six o'clock the next morning, I was at one of the most horrific crime scenes I had ever seen. Decomposed bodies were strewn over the veld, some only metres away from others. Maggots were feasting and the stench penetrated our nostrils and clung to our clothing.

One of the bodies was fresh. Another of the women was lying on her stomach and was dressed in jeans. There was a patch on her jeans where she had wet herself in fear. Some of the other bodies were badly decomposed. The flesh on one body had mostly rotted away and the bones were protruding. Her legs were spread-eagled. A mass of maggots the size of a rugby ball were crawling where her genitals had once been. One could have literally lifted them away with a spade. The woman had a pair of panties drawn over her face. At another spot, only skeletal remains were left on the scene. Everywhere one turned, there seemed to be a body. It resembled a massacre.

Captain Frans van Niekerk, who had completed my course, was appointed investigating officer and took control of the scene. Frans was a few years younger than me. He was a handsome man with dark hair and bright blue eyes that reflected his intelligence. He usually had a very laid-back demeanour, but I saw his mind in action that day and he reminded me of a panther. Watching the animal lying lazily on the branch of a tree, one would never expect it to be both agile and dangerous, but when it leapt into action, one would quickly have to revise one's opinion.

It took us two days to process the crime scenes, sending the dogs in and collecting forensic samples. Two more bodies were discovered by the police dogs. At one stage I felt so tired and disgusted that I walked to the place where our vehicles were parked. The dog handler and his dog walked up to their truck. The dog handler took a spade from the back of the truck and poured water from his water bottle onto the spade for the thirsty dog. As I watched the animal lap up the water, the sight of the innocent dog who had done such a splendid job warmed my heart. If the dog needed only a little water to be able to carry on, then so did I. I drank some water and returned to the crime scenes to take notes.

An odd thing about the scene was its proximity to the Boksburg prison. There was also a mine dump and a railway line close by, the trademarks of the Atteridgeville Strangler. And the modus operandi was the same. What caught my attention, though, was that the veld adjoining the killing field was littered with ant heaps. At each ant heap, and there were about a hundred and forty of them, we found black and red candles tied together with black and red wool, an empty plastic Coke bottle, knives tied with red and black wool, little mirrors, feathers, and women's underwear. This appeared to be traditional healer paraphernalia.

I made the mistake of picking up a piece of underwear at one of these ant heaps. Frans explained calmly to me that I could have disturbed evidence. I appreciated the fact that he taught me something about processing a crime scene rather than berating me. Other detectives would quite rightly have been furious. I have never again disturbed evidence on a crime scene and I made sure to read up on the procedures.

Unfortunately, the news about the crime scene was leaked to the press. The following day, the national police commissioner, George Fivaz, circled the scene in a helicopter and the world's press made a nuisance of themselves. President Nelson Mandela visited the scene personally and met all of us. He was aghast at the magnitude of horror on that patch of land.

I recognised the Atteridgeville Strangler's work. There were many resemblances to the victims we had found in Atteridgeville. They were not dressed in the apparel of prostitutes, and all seemed to fall into a certain age group – between twenty and thirty years old. The Atteridgeville Strangler had progressed from tying the victims' hands behind their backs to tying them to their necks. This gave him even more control over the victim. He also had a preference for using underwear to tie them up. At Bon Accord dam he had left bodies in close proximity to one another. I presumed he would walk a living victim up to the corpse of a previous one, to intimidate her. All these signs were present at the Boksburg crime scene.

I felt that someone had shone a spotlight into the abyss, and this scene of carnage was the one that the light had fallen on. Do not shine a light into the abyss, for the sight will forever be imprinted on your memory. I was struck with horror, and my senses were numbed. But I did my job automatically, concentrating more on taking notes and trying to help than on picking up any vibes of the killer. I was not aware of any wind, only of the dirt on my hands, the dust and the stench that clung to my clothing, and thirst.

I was glad when Vinol was called in. He teamed up with Frans. Two teams from the East Rand and Pretoria Murder and Robbery Units were simultaneously working on this case. Information was shared and there was no hostility or 'jam stealing', a term we used to describe glory hunters.

Fortunately, the detectives had found a handbag and its contents far away in the field, and they were able to identify one of the victims. When they traced her place of employment, they met her colleagues, who were able to describe the man she was last seen with. This information brought the detectives onto the direct trail of the killer, but I was unaware of these developments.

———

In the meantime, Commissioner Fivaz had asked me to invite Ressler to South Africa to assist with the investigation. He arrived on 23 September 1995 and stayed a week. Ressler studied my profile and told me that there was nothing he could add to it. After visiting the Boksburg scene, I had added a new element to the profile: two killers might be involved.

The victims would have had to walk kilometres over the open veld to reach the crime scenes. They would not have been able to walk that distance if they were tied up. Once they were there, they would definitely have seen the other bodies and tried to run. How would he have been able to restrain them and tie them up when they knew they were going to be killed? Ressler gave the investigation team some tips, which worked. We also took him to visit all the crime scenes in Atteridgeville and Bon Accord.

Since I was hosting Ressler, I didn't have much contact with the detectives working the case on the ground. I still felt that they would regard my interest as interference and preferred to stay out of their way. My personal feelings were not as important as their catching the killer.

Commissioner Fivaz asked Ressler to review Selepe's case because of allegations in the press that he might have been innocent when he was shot. At last I was able to get an insight into the Cleveland dockets, which Brixton Murder and Robbery had denied me.

There were several disturbing facts. Selepe had mentioned two accomplices, namely a certain Tito and a certain Mandla. Mandla was found to be in jail and therefore discarded as an accomplice. Sergeant Nkomozulu of the Brixton Murder and Robbery Unit, who had accompanied the general and me to the Cleveland crime scenes, had also interviewed Mandla in prison, after which he was eliminated as a suspect.

Ressler confirmed that Selepe had to have been involved in the serial murders since he had confessed and pointed out some crime scenes correctly. He had been caught on camera using a victim's credit card and his DNA grouping of 1212 matched the semen found on the crime scenes. The detective who had shot him was acquitted during the inquest held into Selepe's death.

What concerned me terribly was that the Atteridgeville Strangler also had a DNA grouping of 1212 – however, many people can have the same grouping.

On the Friday before Ressler returned to the US, Commissioner Fivaz held a press conference. Ressler was very complimentary and told the commissioner he regarded me as the second-best profiler in the world – he being the best, of course. The press were like vultures, bombarding the poor man with questions. They didn't know that by then the investigation teams had already identified their suspect as Moses Sithole. I didn't know either.

Co-workers of the woman whose handbag had been found had told the detectives that Sithole had offered her a job. They traced Sithole's address in Atteridgeville, but he had left his home a few weeks before. Sithole later admitted that he had watched Ressler on television and thought that he talked 'shit'.

During the press conference, I got a call on my cellphone from Inspector Theo Goldstone in KwaZulu-Natal. Theo had also completed my course. He had arrested a serial killer in Donnybrook, who was thought to be responsible for killing eighteen people. My heart soared and sank within seconds. I was proud of Theo for applying the knowledge he had learnt on my course, but I was distressed because so many people had died. At least the killer, Mhlengwa Zikode, was in custody.

From 18 to 27 October 1995 I presented the first Advanced Investigative Psychology course to the detectives who had attended the basic course, at a police training academy in Silverton, Pretoria. Frans and Vinol couldn't be there because they were busy with the Atteridgeville investigation, but Johan Kotzé, Andy, Bushy and Theo attended. Theo filled us in on the Donnybrook case. He had done a good job at compiling a profile himself.

Organised serial killers sometimes have an active interest in the progress of the investigation into their crimes. This does not mean they want to get caught – on the contrary, they use the information to avoid detection. Moses Sithole was no different. He read the newspapers daily. He also phoned a reporter at *The Star* newspaper and, using a pseudonym, offered to hand himself over to her. I don't think he had a special reason for speaking to that particular reporter – she just happened to be the one who answered the phone when he called. At one of the press conferences, I had warned reporters that the killer might contact one of them. This reporter kept her wits about her and reported the call to us. Frans and Vinol asked her to persuade Sithole to meet them at a train station, if he called her again.

Sithole did phone again, using an alias, and described some of the crime scenes over the phone. But he denied having anything to do with the murder of Letta Ndlangamandla and her two-year-old son, whose body was found close to hers. Sithole claimed that he loved children and would never hurt them.

The reporter phoned me and told me that she felt sorry for the man who had phoned her and that she had a certain empathy for him. I understood her plight. I think she had had a little taste of what I was confronted with on a daily basis. Serial killers are not born evil; they develop into killers as a consequence of what happens to them during their childhood years, but this is still no excuse for murder – or any other crime. The tragedy of serial killers lies in the dichotomy that they feel compelled to kill innocent strangers in order to express their own pain and anger, causing more pain and anger. Like the ouroboros symbol– the serpent perpetually biting its own tail – it is an existential crisis manifestation. I warned the reporter not to look into the abyss.

The meeting at the train station was bungled by overeager cops who had nothing to do with the investigation but decided to interfere. Sithole fled and the team weren't able to trace him. After that, Commissioner Fivaz agreed that Vinol and Frans could publish his photograph in order to elicit the public's help in tracing him.

While my course with the detectives was still in progress, I got a call from a journalist at one o'clock one morning. He wanted me to comment on the fact that Sithole had just been shot. I declined to comment and immediately phoned General Britz. He confirmed that Sithole had indeed been shot, but that he had only been wounded, and he promised me that I would have an opportunity to talk to him once the detectives had finished their interrogations. The memory of Selepe being shot without an opportunity to talk to him and learn from him was fresh in my mind.

What had transpired was that Sithole had contacted a relative and asked him to bring him a firearm. The relative informed the police. Frans and Vinol set a trap for Sithole at the mine compound where he was supposed to meet his relative. They had arranged with the authorities that Inspector Francis Mulovhedzi would pose as a security guard and wait at the gate for Sithole to arrive. The other security guards were not told of Francis's real purpose.

When Sithole arrived, he asked the guards to call his relative. Because he was the new man, Francis was ordered to go and fetch the relative. He argued because he did not want to let Sithole out of his sight. Sithole became suspicious and ran. Francis gave chase. Sithole disappeared down a dark alley and lay in wait for the detective. Francis called out that he was a member of the Service and asked him to surrender. But Sithole rushed at Francis and attacked him with an axe, injuring his hand. Francis drew his firearm and shot him in the hip and the leg. Sithole was taken to hospital and was interrogated there as soon as he was declared fit by the doctors.

Again, I felt I had been cheated and left out at the last minute – for the third time now. I had not been alerted to the arrest and I was not to be present during the interrogations. I felt like a little girl who wasn't allowed to play with her bigger brothers simply because she was a girl. No matter how many degrees I had, how hard I worked, or how much I shared my knowledge with the detectives, when it came to the crunch, I was still an outsider.

At that point I wanted to resign. When the course was completed, I made an appointment with General Britz and told him that I had had enough of being treated as though I was an ignorant outsider. He talked me out of resigning. He told me he believed in me and once again explained the mind of a Murder and Robbery detective to me – by nature they were a very suspicious bunch. It seemed to me that I could figure out the mind of a serial killer, but not the mind of a Murder and Robbery detective. I was deeply disappointed.

Vinol and Frans interrogated Sithole in hospital. At first he did not want to talk, but as soon as a female detective, Sergeant Cecile Prinsloo, was brought in, he opened up. He seemed to want to brag in front of her. He masturbated while lying in his hospital bed relating his crimes. He described how he would bind the women and masturbate while he watched them dying. He said he raped only the pretty ones. Cecile was unmoved. In time he recovered enough to be able to point out the crime scenes. He even pointed out bodies we had not found before.

Moses Sithole did not have a happy childhood. After the death of his father, Simon Tangawira Sithole, the family lost their home in Vosloorus, a township on the East Rand. Their mother, Sophie, could not care for her six children, so they were placed in an orphanage in Benoni, also on the East Rand. From there the sons, including Moses, were moved to another home in KwaZulu-Natal. Moses ran away from the home. He returned to Vosloorus, where he stayed with his older brother Patrick. But when Patrick left for Venda, which was then a nominally independent state, Moses sold his brother's house without his permission. He did odd jobs, often finding work on farms. He said he had learnt to drive tractors on one of those farms. He also worked on the gold mines on the Witwatersrand and as a cleaner in a shop. When he could afford to, he visited nightclubs. He had many girlfriends, but there were no long-lasting relationships. He travelled to Botswana and Swaziland, but mostly he lived in the Johannesburg and East Rand areas, including a hostel in Rosherville, which is adjacent to Cleveland.

In 1989 he was arrested for rape. He claimed that he was innocent and had been wrongly pointed out at an identity parade. By then he had already been arrested for fraud and theft. Sithole was sentenced to seven years for the rape. He was fond of classical music and reading, and became a member of the prison choir. He did not serve the full sentence but was released in 1993 for good behaviour.

The first body was discovered in Atteridgeville a month after his release. Around that time, he formed the 'Youth Against Human Abuse Organisation', which had the alleged purpose of reuniting orphans with their families. He presented himself as a businessman and designed employment application forms, using his sister's telephone number in Atteridgeville as a contact number. Sithole phoned his sister regularly to collect his messages. This was one way in which he recruited victims.

For a while he moved in with a woman called Martha in Atteridgeville and fathered a little girl. He helped Martha's brother Funyana to fix cars. He deserted his family about a month before his arrest, relying on his wits to stay alive and avoid detection. He slept mostly at train stations.

In the profile, I described the suspect as someone who would dress well and flash money to impress the women. After his capture Sithole denied that he had money, but the co-workers of one of his victims affirmed that he flashed money and had invited the victim for lunch the day before her death. His own sister, Nokwazi Makabeni, also later confirmed to a daily newspaper that Moses was usually smartly dressed and that he loved good shoes. The profile also predicted that a car played a role in the crimes. Sithole claimed he had no driver's licence and used taxis to transport his potential victims, but later there were many unconfirmed reports by women that Sithole had approached them in a vehicle and offered them lifts. The profile also predicted he would have had previous convictions for fraud, theft and rape, which he had.

While awaiting trial in prison, Sithole was heard to have made the following comment: '*Hurt has been my daily bread, hurt has been my prayer, hurt has been my feelings all the time, hurt has been there every hour, every minute, every second, every day, every week, every month and every year ...*' To me, these words reflect the abyss.

On 21 October 1996, Moses Sithole was charged in the Pretoria Supreme Court with thirty-eight murders, forty rapes and six robberies. He pleaded not guilty. Captain Leon Nel of the East Rand Murder and Robbery Unit had been appointed the investigating officer responsible for preparing the dockets for court. Mr Justice Curlewis presided, and the state prosecutors were Advocate Retha Meintjies and Mr George Baloyi. The defence was handled by Advocate Eben Jordaan and Ms Lena van Wyk. As in the Station Strangler's case, the trial was attended by community members who often demonstrated in front of the court buildings. Sithole cried only once during the trial, and that was when his girlfriend Martha refused to allow him to hold his infant daughter in his arms.

Moses Sithole was sentenced to 2 410 years and will spend the rest of his life in the C Maximum Facility of Pretoria Central Prison. Here prisoners are kept in solitary cells and are allowed only an hour's exercise each day in a small, paved courtyard.

After Sithole was caught, the nagging unease I had felt during Selepe's case became clearer. First of all, it was not Selepe who had written the message on one of the victim's legs, but Sithole. Selepe did, however, point out this crime scene. Now I knew why the profiles were so much alike. I am of the opinion that they must have worked together, at least on the crime scenes in Cleveland and Atteridgeville. I had drawn up a profile based on what I thought was Selepe's victim, when it was actually Sithole's. No wonder the profiles were not as accurate as I wanted them to be and no wonder they overlapped.

Sithole denied working with anyone and some of the detectives were unwilling to believe me. There was still a further problem to be resolved. Sithole had been sent to prison for seven years for rape and started killing when he was released. That was why he had killed those women within sight of a prison. But Selepe had also confessed to murdering people in the Boksburg area, as well as in Cleveland and Atteridgeville.

I was also puzzled by the paraphernalia we had found at the ant heaps. Then Frans traced a religious group who claimed the paraphernalia belonged to them but that they had nothing to do with the murders. The leader of the group was cleared of any involvement.

I figured that there must have been someone else who inspired the Cleveland and Atteridgeville killers. I could never pick Sithole or Selepe up in my mind as I had been able to with the Station Strangler. I had no doubt that they were actively involved in raping and murdering the women, but I was sure that they had been inspired by someone else. Although serial killers usually work alone, there have been rare cases where they form alliances.

But Sithole had denied that he had worked with anyone else. Selepe had named Tito and Mandla, but he died before he could elaborate on their roles. Selepe did not mention Sithole. The only reason they wouldn't mention the name of the mastermind behind the killings would be because they were either scared of him or because they revered him, or one of them was the mastermind. These men could have met in prison and formed a pact to kill women, since they believed women had wronged them.

I was certain that the arrest of Sithole was not the end of the saga. I knew we were still looking for someone else, but I realised I had no proof and that my feelings remained hypothetical. I had never met Sithole or Selepe, so I could never explore this line of thinking.

Later, in 1996, when the Nasrec serial killer emerged in the Johannesburg area, not far from Cleveland, I knew that my gut instinct had been right. This man also strangled women and raped them.

FOUR

Donnybrook

Ah! well a-day! What evil looks
Had I from old and young!
Instead of the cross, the Albatross
About my neck was hung.
– Samuel Taylor Coleridge, 'The Rime of the Ancient Mariner', 1798

Donnybrook is a rural settlement nestled in the hills of the KwaZulu-Natal Midlands. To someone who has never visited Africa but who can imagine rural African life, Donnybrook would fit the postcard picture perfectly. Round Zulu huts constructed from mud and wattle, with thatched roofs, adorn the hills. A few huts clustered together, known as a kraal, house an extended family. Footpaths snake up and down the hills, linking the kraals with one another. Women balancing clay pots filled with water on their heads walk these paths every day. There are cattle and chickens and small-scale agriculture to sustain each family. Driving past on the main road, one might marvel at what appears to be a peaceful, typical rural African scene, but this has not always been the case.

In the 1990s, KwaZulu-Natal was rife with political warfare. Supporters of two political parties, the African National Congress (ANC) and the Inkatha Freedom Party, regularly attacked one another. Thousands of semi-automatic rifles were hidden in those picturesque huts, and arms caches lay buried in the surrounding forests.

Faction fighting has been part of Africa's heritage for centuries, especially in this area, and in the nineteenth and early twentieth centuries the Boers and the British added their blood to that which already saturated the soil of KwaZulu-Natal. There is even a river called Blood River in this province. The sound of automatic gunfire has since replaced the ancient war cries, and sophisticated modern weaponry has replaced the 'knopkieries', spears and shields of the past.

It was against this background that the Donnybrook serial killer wreaked his own havoc during 1994 and 1995.

I was attending the press conference held by Commissioner Fivaz in honour of Robert Ressler on 29 September 1995 when my cellphone rang. I was surrounded by reporters and although I recognised the voice of Inspector Theo Goldstone of the Port Shepstone Murder and Robbery Unit, I couldn't make out what he was saying. I slipped out one of the side doors and sat down on the steps outside.

Theo's news shocked me. He told me they had caught a serial killer who had murdered several men and women in Donnybrook. He asked me to come to KwaZulu-Natal as soon as possible. At that stage my work schedule made it impossible for me to leave Pretoria, and besides, the suspect was already in custody. I asked Theo to discuss the case with me during the Advanced Investigative Psychology course that I would be presenting in Pretoria the following month.

Theo filled us in on the case during the course but there were many loose ends remaining, so I promised to return to KwaZulu-Natal with him.

On the evening of 6 November, I flew to Durban. Theo picked me up at the airport. It took us almost four hours to drive to the Midlands. It shouldn't have taken so long, but it was raining heavily that night. Theo told me that Donnybrook had a small hotel with a few rooms, but that the detectives preferred to stay at the Himeville Arms, which was more comfortable although it was further away. We had to drive into the Drakensberg mountains. It was a treacherous road, especially during a thunderstorm, and cattle often appeared on the road without warning. The road was lined with forest on both sides, and in the torrential rain it reminded me of the old Dracula movies. I wouldn't have been surprised if huge bats had attacked us from the enveloping mist.

But we reached Himeville safely. After that frightful trip I just wanted to retire to a warm and comfortable bed, since I had to interview a serial killer the following day.

The Himeville Arms reminded me of an old English country lodge. We went straight to the pub, where I met Sergeant Dionne van Huyssteen from the Port Shepstone Murder and Robbery Unit. He was the investigating officer whom Theo was assisting in this case. Dionne was a handsome young detective who would have fitted into the role of the dashing hero and ladies' man, had this story been set a century earlier.

Mike, the proprietor of the hotel, asked me what I would like to drink. I asked for a cup of hot Milo and instead was handed a wine glass filled with ice-cold chocolate liqueur. By midnight, when I retired to my room, the liqueur, the fire, the friendly locals and the German shepherd that had fallen asleep on my lap had warmed my heart and lifted my spirits.

The following morning we were up and ready to leave at seven o'clock. Theo looked none the worse for the previous night's partying, and Dionne, having youth on his side, looked bright-eyed and bushy-tailed. We drove through the countryside, which was breathtakingly beautiful after the rain. KwaZulu-Natal is always green. The Midlands are surrounded by the majestic Drakensberg mountains, but the vegetation sloping towards the ocean is tropical. Port Shepstone is situated on the coast, and the detectives fondly referred to their unit as Jurassic Park – they even had a dinosaur as their emblem. When they were not in the office catching up on admin, or out investigating, they were in the ocean, surfing.

We spotted some cattle in a field and, to my surprise, the detectives pulled the car over and Dionne started mooing over the public address system. The cows lifted their heads, answered the call and came rushing towards the fence. I found this hysterical, and it pleased the detectives to amuse me. A little frivolity helped lighten the mood, but certainly did not detract from the seriousness of our work.

Donnybrook was too small to be called a village. There was a hotel, a general store, two or three other shops and a police station, all on the main road, which was also the only tarred road. A little above the police station was an empty house, which used to be occupied by the station commander, and we used this as our office.

Theo and Dionne had filled me in on the case while we were driving. From April 1994 to September 1995, the suspect had allegedly been involved in thirty-eight crimes. These included murder, attempted murder, rape, attempted rape and housebreaking. His usual modus operandi was to kick open the door of a hut in the middle of the night, immediately shoot any male present, drag the female outside, rape her and then shoot her. He also waylaid unsuspecting females along the road. He would overpower them, rape them and then shoot them. He left the bodies exactly where he had killed them. He was not a sophisticated criminal, for he left evidence at the scenes and some of his victims escaped. They weren't able to describe him, however, because he always wore a balaclava.

Although the community had been terrified during this period, the local police did not link the cases. If the prevailing circumstances of political warfare, faction fighting and the generally high rate of rape are taken into consideration, one can perhaps understand why they weren't linked. The community, however, *did* link the cases. They had also unfortunately taken the law into their own hands on two occasions and had lynched two men who they thought were responsible. Violent mobs and vigilantism are rife in South Africa.

It seemed that the first four murders and one attempted murder were politically motivated. The victims were all men. After that, a pattern emerged from which the obvious deduction was that the intention was rape. The ages of the females ranged from nine to fifty-four. All lived within walking distance of one another.

On the evening of Thursday 13 April 1995, Thandi Priscilla Gwala and her friend Makhosi Lushaba got out of a taxi at the Bulwer Trading Store in the Donnybrook area. They were waiting for Thandi's boyfriend, who was also Makhosi's brother. An unknown man approached the two women and boldly told Thandi that he wanted to have sex with her. The women were shocked and Thandi told him off, whereupon the man lunged out and grabbed her. Makhosi rushed to her friend's aid and the man released her, but he produced a firearm and fired several shots at the two women. He wounded Thandi in the shoulder. As she tried to run away, he grabbed hold of her and instructed her to remove her underwear and to bend forward and touch her toes. He then raped the petrified and bleeding woman and disappeared into the night.

Six days later, on the evening of 19 April, Sibongile Mkhize and her lover Hendrick Ngcobo had retired to bed in their hut. Later that night they awoke to the sound of the door being kicked open. Before Hendrick could react, a man burst in and opened fire, killing them both.

Then, on the evening of 9 June, Mzozayo Pius Phoswa was visiting his sister-in-law Ntombi Florentine Phoswa at her kraal in St Charles Location in the Donnybrook area. Mzozayo was chatting to Ntombi at the kitchen table and her children were playing in the room when the door suddenly burst open. A man wearing a balaclava and wielding a pistol threatened them. Mzozayo leapt up and tried to disarm the man. The man fired a shot, wounding Mzozayo in the chest, whereupon Mzozayo fled. The man then turned the gun on Ntombi and killed her. None of the children were wounded.

In the early hours of Saturday 24 June, a woman and her nine-year-old daughter were asleep in their hut in Seaford Location in the Donnybrook area. The woman woke up to find a man wearing a balaclava shining a torch in her face. She tried to raise the alarm, but when he fired a shot she decided it would be best to keep quiet in order to protect her child. The man then took her into the other room and raped her over a chair. He returned her to her bed, where he noticed the little girl cowering. He turned on her and raped her as well. Because the man had a firearm, the woman realised that if she interfered, he would kill her daughter, so she ran out of the hut screaming for help. The man fled.

Two days later, on Monday 26 June, Beatrice Phumeleni Ngubo and her boyfriend Amos Jimson Gxubane were walking hand in hand in St Charles Location on their way to work. Suddenly a man coming towards them pulled out a firearm and fired at them. He wounded Amos in the neck and Beatrice in the leg. The man then dragged Beatrice from the road, telling her that he wanted sex with her. He touched her genitals but ran off when he saw a vehicle approaching. Both Beatrice and Amos were taken to the hospital in Ixopo. Beatrice recovered, but Amos died from his wound.

In the early hours of the morning of 1 July, a man wearing a dark balaclava approached the hut of Siphiwe Zuma and his wife Annacleta in Tafuleni Location in the Donnybrook area. Siphiwe and Annacleta and their child were sleeping in the bed. The man kicked open the door and shot Siphiwe through the temple, killing him instantly. Then he grabbed hold of the screaming Annacleta and dragged her outside. He tried to kick her into submission, but she managed to break free and ran back to her hut. The man fled.

A week later, on 8 July, the killer was out and about again, this time selecting the kraal of Zanele Khumalo. She was alone. He entered her hut and immediately shot her once in the head. He did not want a repetition of the previous victim, who had managed to get away. Then he dragged the dying Zanele to the nearby plantation and raped her. Zanele was dead by the time he had finished.

One of the cases differed from the rest. The body of a naked woman was found in the Bulwer forest. Her legs had been spread-eagled and little wooden pegs had been knocked into the ground next to her ankles to keep her legs apart. One breast had been removed and her face had been 'scalped'. Small sticks and pieces of grass were found inside her vagina.

I deduced from this that the offender was sexually or socially naive. He felt safe in the forest, where he knew he would have enough time to explore the female body, which must have been a totally new experience for him. The mutilation of the breast and the grass inside the vagina indicated curiosity. It was not a large phallic object that had been inserted into the vagina, as one would find in other cases. Killers who do this tend to feel psychologically impotent. This one was not impotent, just childishly curious.

The fact that the victim's face had been removed indicated to me that he must have known her well and was scared that he would be linked to the crime when she was identified. Although the modus operandi differed from the other cases in the sense that the woman had not been shot, the victimology profile corresponded with the others and the woman was murdered in the same vicinity and within the same time frame as the other murders. So we decided to include the murder in the series. It is better to include a murder initially and then to discard it later, if necessary, rather than not include it at all.

On Thursday 27 July 1995, Beauty Zulu was on her way to work when she was approached by a man wearing a balaclava. He threatened her with a firearm and she tried to flee, but he grabbed hold of her and wounded her behind the ear. Then he fled. Passers-by responded to Beauty's cries for help and she was taken to hospital. It was here that she told the police that she had recognised her attacker as her neighbour, Christopher Mhlengwa Zikode.

But before he was arrested, Zikode attacked the hut of Locatia Madlamini Hlope in the early hours of 5 August. Locatia and her friend Cornelia Mahadebe Dlamini were asleep in the hut when Zikode forced his way in and demanded sex from both of them. He grabbed Cornelia and dragged her out of the hut, but she managed to escape and ran back inside. The women bolted the door. This infuriated him and he fired shots through the door, wounding them both. They survived. Zikode was arrested shortly after this attack but was released on three hundred rand's bail.

Although Zikode knew he was facing a trial for murder, he did not want to resist the urge to kill again after his bail hearing. This is common in serial killers. Not even the fact that they have been arrested and identified, nor the threat of a prison sentence, will prevent them from killing again and again. They kill because they enjoy it. During the early hours of Monday 25 September, Fikeleni Memela was sleeping in her hut in Seaford Location when Zikode forced his way in. Fikeleni threw a blanket at him and he ran away, only to return later. He shot her in the jaw, then raped her and shot her again in the chest. She died of her wounds.

I perused the dockets and then at 10 a.m. I met Mhlengwa Zikode, the Donnybrook serial killer. He was a tall, young Zulu man wearing prison greens and he was extremely shy. Inspector Morris, also from the Port Shepstone Murder and Robbery Unit, acted as interpreter. Zikode could hardly look at me when I spoke to him. Theo was sitting in the corner listening, since he was also fluent in isiZulu. Dionne had decided to sit in another office to write up the dockets. The interview was videotaped.

Zikode had been interrogated on three or four previous occasions by different members of the unit. I had read the notes and noticed that he often lied, contradicted himself and tried to implicate other people. The detectives followed up on the people he named as culprits, but found most of them were fictitious. Zikode was an ANC member and admitted to the political killings. It was my job to interview him about his background and to try to establish whether he had the psychological dynamics of a serial killer.

I would ask him a question, which the interpreter had to translate for him, and then I had to wait for Zikode to answer and for the interpreter to translate the answer. This was a lengthy process and I think it prevented me from sinking too deep into the abyss. It kept me anchored in the real world.

While waiting for my answers, I noticed Zikode's hands. They were large hands with long, slim fingers. It was difficult to believe that those hands had killed so many innocent people. He seemed ultra-shy and reserved. I knew I was slipping into the abyss when I sometimes felt empathy for him. But I was still comparatively new at this game and did not trust myself enough to let go and dive. I felt I had to keep reminding myself of the crimes he had committed, which was a mistake. Later I taught myself to let go of my role as a cop and to capitulate to that of psychologist when I faced a serial killer. I could revert back to being a cop as soon as I surfaced from the abyss. I was concentrating more on the content of what Zikode was saying than on the context.

I did not enter the abyss only when we were searching for a serial killer. I also entered it when I was interrogating one. I needed to find him there and to grab hold of his soul. He needed to feel understood before he would be willing to talk to us. All people respond to being heard.

Zikode had an interesting background. He was born in 1975, the middle child of seven siblings. His parents were poor. His father was paralysed and his mother collected firewood for a living. The family often moved around in KwaZulu-Natal to escape the faction fighting. Zikode had only one sister, who was fourteen years older than him. She was his main caretaker, since his mother had to work and take care of his younger brothers. For most of his young life, the only women Zikode ever knew were his mother and sister. He was a lonely child. His older brothers bullied him, and he spent most of his days alone in the veld attending to cattle. His father had forbidden his children to play with other kids, fearing they would have a bad influence on his offspring. Little did the man know that it would be his own son who would grow up to become a serial killer.

When Zikode was ten years old, his father died and his sister left the family for good shortly afterwards. He blamed his sister for the murders. He said it was her duty as his sister to introduce him to female company and to arrange girlfriends for him. He didn't attend school until he was fourteen years old. This was the first time in his life that he had had contact with people outside his immediate family.

Children usually start school at the age of six. Between the ages of six to twelve, they learn to socialise and to incorporate society's moral and ethical values. For Zikode it was too late. He could not relate to others and therefore had no qualms about treating them as objects to be used and disposed of as he wished. When Zikode was seventeen years old, he was expelled from school because he tried to recruit fellow scholars as ANC activists. The only employment he had was collecting firewood with his mother, being a truck conductor in Durban in 1994 and working as a labourer at the general trading store in Bulwer in 1995.

Zikode's mother and her two youngest adopted children lived in a hut on the hills of Donnybrook. Zikode had a room built of corrugated iron next to this hut. He claimed he had a girlfriend who lived in the kraal next to his. She was the daughter of his last victim, Beauty Zulu. The girl was interviewed and denied any relationship with him. She said they had spoken to each other a few times but that she had another boyfriend.

I asked Zikode if he knew the women whom he had killed. He said he knew them by sight. He would accompany his mother to the Catholic church on Sundays and select his next victim. He would note where the woman walked to after church and identify her hut. At night he donned his bala- clava and attacked the hut. He claimed that he was in love with these women. He seemed to have no idea that rape was wrong. He deemed it his right as a man to have sex with any woman.

In the case of Zanele Khumalo, he had shot and killed her before he raped her. The detectives asked him why he had had sex with a dead person and he replied that the body had still been warm. This confirmed the fact that people were just objects to him. All serial killers regard their victims as objects.

On one occasion, Zikode killed a woman outside her hut. He returned to his room and went to sleep. His mother came to wake him and informed him of the murder. He accompanied her to the scene, where many people had gathered in the meantime. When the mortuary van arrived, Zikode helped the attendants to lift the body into the van.

Theo had been present when Zikode's house was searched. He noticed pin-ups of women on the wall. Some were naked and some were semi-naked, but most of them were posing on a chair. The other detectives teased Theo when he took these posters down, but he regarded them as collateral evi- dence. Later, when the surviving victims were interviewed, they said that Zikode raped them over a chair before he tried to kill them. Similarly, Jeffrey Dahmer, the Milwaukee serial killer, had posed the bodies of his victims in positions that resembled those of the men on the posters he had pinned on his walls. Theo had remembered the lectures on collateral evidence, which I in turn had learnt from Roy Hazelwood.

As we had anticipated, Zikode pointed out the place where the mutilated body had been found in the Bulwer forest. He claimed that the woman had come from a certain kraal. The detectives made enquiries at this kraal but there was no missing adult woman. I found this strange. When I ended my interview with Zikode, I asked him if he had anything to add. He said that if he ever saw his sister again, he would not recognise her. We thought at one point that the body might have been that of the sister. His mother later denied that the body was that of her daughter, basing her denial on the vic- tim's dental features. The victim's identity was never established.

When we drove back to Himeville that afternoon, I was in a much more serious mood and didn't feel like calling the cows over the public address system.

We returned to Donnybrook the following morning and drove to Zikode's dwelling. We picked up his mother, Lydia, and drove her to Donnybrook. She was a naive old woman who had no idea of the horrors her son had committed. She corroborated most of what Zikode had told me about his childhood. When I asked her where the posters in his room came from, she told me she had found some magazines in the forest at a spot where some soldiers had camped and had brought them home. This was shortly before the sexual murders started. I believe those pin-ups were the catalyst that triggered the fantasy that had been brewing inside Zikode since his child-hood. If so, his mother had unwittingly lit the tinder that had erupted into a blaze and cost many women their lives.

Lydia Zikode had brought some food for her son and we took her down to the cells to see him. It was his twentieth birthday. I asked him if he wanted any message conveyed to the families of the victims, and he answered that it was his mother's duty to apologise to them on his behalf.

I returned to Pretoria that night, leaving Theo and Dionne behind. They had many difficulties in concluding the case. A major part of a detective's work starts only after the suspect has been arrested. Dionne had to struggle without decent transport in the muddy hills of Donnybrook. He was too far away to drive back to Port Shepstone every day and often had to stay over. He started to refer to himself as the mayor of Donnybrook and became popular among the locals. Fortunately, his work was done when violence and political warfare erupted in the area a few months later.

One problem that Dionne and the state prosecutors faced was the dis-covery of semen in the vagina of Fikeleni Memela, who was a woman in her fifties. The semen did not match Zikode's DNA. Dionne and the prosecutors went to the hut where Fikeleni had lived. They met her young grandson and asked him if Fikeleni had had a boyfriend. He denied this. Then they asked him if there had been a party at the hut the night the murder took place. He denied this too.

The prosecutors had a grave problem on their hands, for the defence attorneys could easily question Zikode's guilt on this charge and jeopardise all the other charges as well. Then the extraordinary occurred. It was established that the mortuary attendant had committed necrophilia with the corpse and it was his semen that had been found in the body.

Later, in November 1995, Robert Ressler returned clandestinely to South Africa for a week. A Japanese television company named Nippon had been granted permission to make a documentary film about the Atteridgeville serial killer. We kept this fact from the press and spent the week retracing our steps of the previous months. It was a busy and exhausting week, and completely different from my normal schedule. The film crew were very professional and courteous and treated us to a traditional Japanese dinner at a restaurant in Johannesburg. Frans van Niekerk and Cecile joined us, but Vinol couldn't make it. During dinner the film crew placed a small square box in front of Ressler and me. The box was then filled with sake, which I had to drink. I managed a few sips and then passed the box on to Frans, who I thought would be much better equipped to handle it. On the last day, I took Ressler and the Japanese to visit a cheetah breeding farm, since they had seen very little of Africa. They were enthralled.

I was deeply shocked when Dionne phoned to inform me that Zikode had escaped from custody. He was rearrested at Bushman's Nek on 8 November 1995 after breaking into yet another house. Luckily he had not killed anyone this time.

On 1 December I moved into my own house. I took a month's leave in order to settle in, and also to write my doctoral thesis. I had collected all the data and completed all the research, but I still needed to put it down on paper. I sat typing from dawn till late at night, and wrote the whole thesis in a month. All two hundred and fifty-four pages of it. I finished at about 4 p.m. on 31 December 1995. I was too tired to go out to celebrate, but I had a glass of champagne at midnight, toasted my beautiful new view and the New Year from my bedroom window, watched the firework displays and went to bed.

Zikode's trial ran from April to July 1997 at the High Court in Pietermaritzburg. The state prosecutors were Advocates Dorian Paver and Adelaide Watt. Zikode was charged with eight murders, five attempted murders, five rapes and one indecent assault.

I was not called to testify, but submitted a statement instead, which was read by Advocate Dorian during the court proceedings. In my statement I said that Zikode had the psychological mentality to fit the modus operandi of the killer. Since his father was paralysed and died when he was a young boy, he did not regard any man as competition, which would correspond with the fact that the killer quickly got rid of the males by simply shooting them to get to the females. The women represented his sister, whom he had adored and who had abandoned him. He was still subconsciously in love with her, as she fulfilled the mother role in the Oedipus triangle. He went to school only at the age of fourteen, when other children were entering puberty. He therefore missed out on the latency phase during which he was supposed to socialise. He acquired no empathy for other people, regarding them merely as objects. At the age of nineteen, when the murders commenced, he was in a retarded puberty phase. He experienced sexual urges, but he wasn't socially equipped to deal with them. He raped the women, who were substitutes for his sister, and he killed them because he was angry at her for rejecting and abandoning him.

During sentencing, Mr Justice Broome recounted the 'cold and ugly facts of the savage attacks on innocent people'. He also commented on the fact that Zikode had continued with his crimes while he was out on bail. The judge imposed life sentences on Mhlengwa Zikode for the rapes of the mother and her underaged daughter. He also sentenced Zikode to life for the woman killed in the Bulwer plantation, the murder of Amos Gxubane, the rape and murder of Zanele Khumalo, and the rape and murder of Fikeleni Memela. For the other crimes, the judge sentenced him to one hundred and forty years. When he was led out of court after sentencing, Zikode proclaimed his innocence, saying that he had been framed.

Sergeant Dionne van Huyssteen left the Service soon after this case and opened a bar near Port Shepstone.

FIVE

The Cape Town Prostitute Killer

Like one, that on a lonesome road
Doth walk in fear and dread,
And having once turned round walks on,
And turns no more his head;
Because he knows, a frightful fiend
Doth close behind him tread.

– Samuel Taylor Coleridge, 'The Rime of the Ancient Mariner', 1798

Prostitution has been called the oldest profession, and prostitutes have always been a part of the history of the human race. So have serial killers, but they managed to elude attention until the infamous Jack the Ripper killed five prostitutes in London between August and November 1888.

Since then, serial killers have often preyed upon sex workers. Roy Hazelwood, an ex-FBI agent specialising in serial rape and serial killers and a contemporary of Robert Ressler, taught me something very valuable. Prostitutes make easy victims because they are generally willing to go anywhere, to do anything with anyone. When investigating a serial killer case in which sex workers are the victims, one must ascertain whether the killer has a special preference for prostitutes or whether he has selected them just because they are easy prey.

The first week of January 1996 passed by reasonably uneventfully. I was looking forward to the new year and my head was filled with plans for expanding my unit. But by then I should have realised that trouble usually brews when I seem to sail in calmer waters.

The grapevine buzzed of a serial killer in Cape Town. By the grapevine, I am referring to detectives who mentioned to me over the phone that they had read about similar murders in a newspaper, or that they had heard someone discussing the possibility of a serial killer in a bar. In theory, all detective branches were supposed to let my office know the moment a serial killer was suspected to be operating in their region.

Unfortunately, this didn't always happen. I always tried to find the time to phone around to ascertain which direction the wind was blowing. Sometimes my journalist friends would tell me that they had noticed a particular trend in murders, and sometimes the SAPS photographers would inform me, for they attended most crime scenes. Until the SAPS installed a computer program designed to include all the details of serial killers' trademarks, signatures and modi operandi, we would have to rely mainly on word of mouth to link different crime scenes to one killer. Word of mouth indicated trouble in Cape Town.

In early February I embarked on my annual trip around the country to select detectives for my upcoming course. When I reached the Cape Town Murder and Robbery Unit, which was officially called the Peninsula Murder and Robbery Unit, Sergeant Piet Viljoen, whom I had assisted two years before with the profile of the Tamboerskloof rapist, confirmed that someone had been killing Cape Town prostitutes. Piet believed in me, since I had proved myself two years before. I collected most of the information I needed and returned to Pretoria to compile a profile.

The victimology report indicated that the victims were all streetwise sex workers who would defend themselves with knives if they suspected danger. They were cheap, but wise and selective, and they were mostly in their twenties. The killer had to be free to drive around at night to pick up prostitutes, and he also had to have free time during the day to preselect the remote spots on the farms where he dropped the bodies.

I surmised that he did not live with a wife, someone who would keep a watch on his movements, and that he had to be either a travelling salesman or unemployed. He possibly owned some kind of truck, which enabled him to drive around unobtrusively on farm roads. As none of the prostitutes had been raped, he was probably impotent. Although semen had been found in some cases, it would have been risky to ascribe it solely to the suspect, since the victims were sex workers after all. Unfortunately, it is difficult to establish rape with a sex worker, but the fact that the suspect tried to stage rape by leaving some of the victims in certain positions made us deduce that he wanted us to believe that they had been raped. I presumed he was intelligent since he was playing a cat-and-mouse game with the police. He definitely had problems in his relations with women, which probably stemmed from a bad mother–son relationship and possibly an Oedipal triangle.

I returned to Cape Town later in February and joined Piet's investigation team. Although Piet was only a sergeant, he had the attitude of a brigadier and ordered everyone around in like fashion. It worked and he got results. As he was having marital problems, he had moved into the men's bathroom on the ground floor of the Peninsula Murder and Robbery Unit in Cape Town. He believed the place was haunted and locked the bathroom door every night before he went to sleep. I have my own opinion regarding the phenomenon of ghosts and had encountered something evil in the building before. There were cells on the ground floor and a criminal had once hanged himself in one of them.

The detectives' official office hours were from 7.30 a.m. to 4 p.m. If we were at the office at 4 p.m., we would go to the in-house canteen, which was called XYZ, to have a drink. Piet would say he was going home, which meant he would walk down the passage and unlock the bathroom door. He changed his clothing and then returned to the canteen. No early morning traffic problems for him.

Piet had converted his office into an operations room. The investigation team had requested that all prostitutes report to the office to have their fingerprints taken. I do not think they expected the response they got. Hundreds of sex workers turned up to have their photographs taken and to be fingerprinted. Obviously, it would be easier for us to identify a victim if we had fingerprints. I missed this circus, but apparently it was quite something.

On the morning of my arrival, Piet assembled the investigation team. They were a diverse group. Some detectives from the Child Protection Unit had been incorporated to make up the numbers. I met Inspector George Lochner, who later took over the case when Piet was transferred. Poor George – if he had known then what problems would be awaiting him, I am sure he wouldn't have been so eager to join. Talmakkies had been allocated to another investigation and could not join the team. I asked that Inspector Div de Villiers be called in from the Stock Theft Unit, since he had worked on the Station Strangler investigation and had completed my course. I gave the team a quick lecture on serial killers and then we all left to visit the crime scenes.

At each crime scene I looked at the photographs, and then we all brainstormed to reconstruct the scenes. It had started to rain by then, and I think this contributed to the *esprit de corps* that developed among us. We bunched together in the cars, drove from one end of the Peninsula to the other, got out in the rain, opened farm gates, and reconstructed. The detectives were bright and eager to learn. When we returned to the Murder and Robbery offices, we all made a beeline for XYZ and warmed ourselves with Old Brown Sherry.

At 10 p.m. we assembled at the unit again and then hit the streets. The killer had a preference for Voortrekker Road as a spot to pick up his potential victims. Voortrekker Road is a long street that stretches from one end of Cape Town to the other, and runs through several suburbs including Maitland, Goodwood, Parow and Bellville. It is lined with shops and the suburbs are mainly middle class.

His victims were not sophisticated ladies of the night, but the outcasts of society. It was quite an experience talking to those girls. Most of them cooperated with us, as they needed our protection desperately. For the first time, they could conduct their business under police protection. To us, it was much more important to catch a serial killer than to make a few arrests for soliciting. Besides, we needed the information they could provide us, and it would serve no purpose to antagonise them.

Emergency telephone numbers were posted on every street corner, where they could easily be spotted by the sex workers. These posters had been sponsored by local businesses, as the South African Police Service didn't have the funds for them. The posters looked more like cartoons than a warning about a serial killer, but I guess they served their purpose.

The prostitutes who didn't have pimps worked in teams and kept notebooks in which they wrote down the number plates of the cars their partners got into. We generated a lot of information in this way – there were many prominent businessmen in Cape Town who shouldn't have been sleeping peacefully at night, since their number plates were among those that came up.

After midnight we revisited the crime scenes and kept observation. Most of the scenes were on remote farm roads. It was quite eerie sitting there quietly in the darkest hours of the night, waiting for a killer to strike. The call of a jackal pierced the silence and unsettled our nerves, but no one came.

Piet had called in all dockets with a similar modus operandi since 1992, and the following day we compared the facts in all the dockets. There were sixteen cases altogether. Except for one, all the victims were of the same race, and they were all sex workers between the ages of twenty and thirty. They had all been strangled; some were naked, some were only partially dressed and others were fully clothed.

Another victim was picked up by the killer on 23 March 1996, while I was back in Pretoria. Her body was found the next day in Brackenfell, which lies between Bellville and Kraaifontein. She was twenty-nine years old and was not a prostitute.

Like the other women, she had not been raped. We established that all the murders were linked – by the area where they were dumped, where the victims worked, how they were posed, or by the stabbings. When a killer tries to change something on a crime scene deliberately to throw the detectives off track, it is called staging. This killer was so good at staging that he should have been awarded an Oscar for his performance, but it also gave away a pattern.

We had figured out that the killer would cruise Voortrekker Road on a rainy night. He would proposition one of the many sex workers hanging about on the corners, and once she got into his car, he would pull into a deserted parking lot somewhere along the street and ask her to remove her clothing. After she had partially undressed, he would suddenly lash out and hit her in the face. As she slumped over in a dazed state, he would pull her onto his lap and strangle her with a piece of rope he carried in his pocket. The crime scene photographs indicated that most of the victims had been assaulted.

Once he had killed the girl, he would drive off to a remote, preselected spot and dump her body. Sometimes he just threw it out of the car, but at other times he positioned the body in order to try to throw us off the track. I supposed that the times when he simply threw them out of the car were when he didn't have time to pose them, or when he spotted an approaching vehicle. There were no street lights on the farm roads, so one could easily miss a turnoff or gate, especially on a rainy night, if one did not know exactly where to look. That was how we knew that he must have visited those spots during the day to preselect them. The fact that he staged so many crime scenes actually became his signature. That was the reason why I thought him intelligent. His actions were characteristic of a cunning and organised serial killer who planned his crimes meticulously. It was not the behaviour of a mentally disturbed person, or someone who could claim to be unaware of what he was doing.

The morning after we had worked through the dockets, the detectives took me to meet a sex worker named Sally. She worked in Sea Point and Green Point in Cape Town and had given us information about a man who was a regular client of hers. The man had problems with impotence. He was in his fifties and unemployed. His name had also been mentioned by some of the other sex workers we had interviewed. He drove a truck.

The reason we paid so much attention to Sally was that she had told me that the man had a fantasy about committing an indecent act with a Coke bottle after he had seen something similar in a movie. One of the victims had had a Coke bottle inserted into her vagina. Also, as it happened, the detectives had established that a man and a vehicle fitting the description of the suspect and his truck had been spotted in the area where that victim's body had been found.

Sally was an attractive woman in her mid-thirties. She was married and had a young son whom she dropped off at school in the mornings. She then conducted her business until it was time to fetch him from school. Although her son was unaware of her job, her husband was quite aware of it. He would wait in the room next door while she entertained her client in the bedroom. They were trying to save money to be able to afford a better life.

Sally was the proverbial prostitute with a heart of gold. She wanted to open a 'vetkoek' restaurant one day. When the detectives were hungry after looking out for the sex workers for hours on end, Sally would invite them to her apartment, where she and her husband cooked a huge meal for them. One of Sally's closest friends was a victim of the killer, so she did everything in her power to assist us.

The following day I interrogated a suspect and participated in the house search. We cleared him. In the meantime we had been doing some home-work on the name of the man Sally had given us. It appeared that this man suffered from blackouts. One of these apparent blackouts coincided with the time at which the woman with the Coke bottle was killed. He was dis-covered in a daze the day after the murder, claiming to be suffering from memory loss, and had been booked into Tygerberg Hospital.

I visited Tygerberg Hospital and explained our problem to the psychologist on duty. Psychologists are bound by an ethical code not to discuss their patients, unless a patient poses a serious threat to his own life or the lives of others. I was allowed to read his file. There appeared to be no medical or psychiatric problems with our suspect. I was reminded of the Station Strangler, who booked himself into hospital just before or after a murder.

That night I had to return to Pretoria again. The suspect was kept under surveillance. He was aware of this and led the surveillance team on a wild-goose chase. Then one night they kept watch until 2 a.m., decided he was not going to move, and went home. At 2.30 a.m., Piet got lonely in his bathroom and went for a drive. He passed the suspect's house and saw that the truck was gone. One of his last victims died that night. Unfortunate incidents like these happen, and it was typical of the killer to try to outwit us. That time he succeeded.

In March 1996 I presented my second Basic Investigative Psychology course in Pretoria. I was also frantically trying to arrange for Ressler and Thomas Müller from Interpol Vienna to visit South Africa in April to present an advanced course to all the detectives I had trained to date.

Anyone who has ever tried to take on the Red Tape Dragon will understand that this was a highly stressful time in my life. I won't go into the boring details – suffice it to say that the Red Tape Dragon almost succeeded in driving me nuts. I had also been invited to speak at the First European Homicide Convention at Bramshill in England and was trying to secure permission to go. It would take a member of the South African Police Service approximately three months to obtain permission to travel overseas.

On 29 March 1996 I met a wonderful man in Pretoria and fell head over heels in love. On 1 April there was another wonderful happening. My unit, Investigative Psychology, doubled its manpower, or womanpower, I should say. We were now two. Joining me was Elmarie Myburgh, a psychologist from the SAPS Institute for Behavioural Sciences, where I had worked before. Elmarie had completed honours degrees in psychology and criminology.

Her perfectionism compensated for my disorderliness. She started by organising the chaos in my office. Elmarie was twenty-six years old and had her head screwed firmly on her shoulders. She was strong-willed and eager to learn. I decided to take her along to Ressler's course in order to introduce her to the detectives. If they accepted her, she would be in. I couldn't afford to work with someone who did not get on with the detectives. Elmarie had grown up on a farm and had a no-nonsense attitude, although she could be quite moody if she wanted to be. I thought she would be able to handle the detectives and hoped they would be able to handle her.

On 3 April I drove the 1 600 kilometres to Cape Town. I had decided to go down a few days before Ressler arrived in order to put in some hours with the investigation team. I had finally secured the minister's approval for Ressler's course and all the arrangements had been made. By this time, Ressler and Thomas Müller were about to board their flights. Had I not managed to get the minister's permission, it would have cost me R80 000 out of my own pocket.

I signed in at the Peninsula Murder and Robbery Unit on my arrival in Cape Town, although I was dog-tired.

Piet had pulled our suspect in for questioning. I met him for the first time on Thursday evening, 4 April. Piet and I joined him in the office while the rest of the team stood behind the one-way mirror to observe. He had grey hair and piercing blue eyes.

I explained that I was a psychologist and a member of the SAPS and asked him whether I could interview him. He agreed. I made it clear that he should not regard the interview as a confidential doctor–patient relationship since a detective would be present. He said he did not mind and proceeded to tell me the story of his life.

His address was a boarding house in Parow, about two blocks away from Voortrekker Road. He slept in his truck, which was parked outside the boarding house, and only took his meals inside. His ex-wife paid for his meals. He was interested in cars and had been a mechanic for a racing-car driver who travelled all over the country, but he was currently unemployed.

His mother had been a strange woman who was interested in the occult. He hated his father, an alcoholic who had been abusive towards his mother. After his father's death, his mother took a young lover. He was terribly upset by this. He told me about his ex-wife and their children. At first he denied ever having visited prostitutes, although he claimed to have many girlfriends. I could not ascertain much from the interview, save the fact that he was upset by his mother's behaviour. He bragged about his sexual prowess to the detectives, but at the same time tried to convince me that he was a perfect gentleman.

The following morning his vehicle was fingerprinted and searched. The prints of one of the victims were found on the inside of one of the windows, and some makeup and several pieces of cheap jewellery were also found in the car.

Inspector George Lochner and I went to visit his ex-wife. While George was out of the room, I asked her some personal questions. I had to explain oral and anal sex to her and she was deeply shocked. She told us how she had checked the odometer reading of her husband's car. He would often tell her that he was going to buy bread around the corner. But then he would be gone for hours, and the reading would indicate that he had driven long distances. She said there were times when he claimed he had amnesia. But there was no medical substance to this claim.

The suspect was kept in custody, but we couldn't take him to court that morning since it was Good Friday.

That afternoon I fetched Ressler from the airport. I took him straight to the Peninsula Murder and Robbery Unit, where he met the detectives. He was very interested in the case. We had a few drinks at XYZ and then set off for the police training college in the neighbouring town of Paarl, where my course was scheduled to take place. We arrived quite late and discovered that there had been a mix-up with the bookings. I couldn't let Ressler sleep in one of the college dormitories, so I booked him into a guest house across the road. The man was used to five-star treatment, and I saw to it that he got it. The proprietor promised us discretion if the press managed to trace him.

On Saturday morning, 6 April, we joined the investigation team again and went to Sea Point, where Ressler met Sally. Apparently he scared the living daylights out of her when he told her that she could have been a victim as well.

For the rest of the afternoon I took him on a sightseeing trip around the Cape Peninsula. He spent most of the time telling me about the cases he had worked on. Whenever he opened his mouth, I learned from his experience. As we rounded a bend at Cape Point, we encountered several other cars that had pulled over to the side of the road. A troop of baboons was pestering the motorists. Normally I would have tried to drive past because baboons can damage cars, but Ressler found this all quite extraordinary – more fascinating even than the beautiful views I had shown him. So I pulled over and waited patiently until he had seen enough. Luckily none of the baboons approached us, but I had trouble convincing Ressler not to get out of the car.

On Sunday morning, 7 April, I was on my way to the Murder and Robbery Unit for another interview with the suspect, but my plans went awry when Div called to say that another body had been found. Ressler decided to wait in Paarl to meet the detectives who had begun to arrive for the course. Elmarie would be arriving with them.

I rushed to the crime scene. The body of a forty-nine-year-old woman was lying in the veld, on the same road as one of the previous crime scenes. Her body was badly decomposed and it was later established that she had died on 30 January. The poor pathologist arrived wearing a dress and high heels. She had been on her way to church when she was called.

The same pattern was evident as in the other cases. Like the previous victim, she wasn't a prostitute, but this wasn't enough to exclude these two women from our case. It was merely another ploy by the killer to try to mislead us. The fact that the bodies had been dumped in close proximity to the other crime scenes, as well as a number of other factors, proved that they formed part of the series.

We returned to the office after processing the crime scene. I questioned the suspect again, asking about his life. This time he mentioned that he had slept in his mother's bed until the age of sixteen. He had lost his virginity as a teenager to a woman about the same age as his mother and had contracted a venereal disease from prostitutes. The thought that he might have had sex with his mother crossed my mind, but I did not pursue this.

I spent hours talking to him. He told me that he would often drive to the Contermanskloof and Klipheuwel roads to get away from his wife. He would sit there, reading a book. I don't know if he realised the significance of this statement, but I am inclined to think that he liked taunting us with that sort of information. At one stage I told him that the prostitutes of whom he was a regular client had told us that he was impotent and that it took a long time for him to get an erection. He responded by taking my hand and telling me what a great lover he was, clearly trying to provoke me. He said he was going to sue the SAPS and take me to Paris with the money. He would buy me French champagne. He said I was a real lady and the type of woman he would like to date.

Sometimes I wondered at the strange situations my job got me into. How many women have had a suspected serial killer tell them he would like to take them to Paris? Years before, when I worked at the Pretoria Zoo, a gorilla made mating noises when he saw me, and this incident with the suspect reminded me of that episode. No wonder my love life was in a shambles.

I left the office to order him some coffee. When I returned, he was look-ing at some of the crime scene photographs. We had deliberately selected photographs that didn't reveal any evidence and put them up on the walls. I asked him offhandedly whether he had killed those girls. He turned around, looked at me slyly with his piercing blue eyes, and answered: 'I could have killed them, but then you would have to prove it, wouldn't you?' This was not the kind of remark one would expect from an innocent person, and it was the first time we had got anywhere near to a confession.

As I was leaving the office, he called me back. He said that he wanted to tell me a secret, but that I was not to tell the detectives. I looked him straight in the eye and reminded him that although I was a psychologist I was also a member of the South African Police Service and that whatever he told me could not be considered confidential. He squinted at me and said: 'Well, I won't tell you then.' I have often wondered if he wanted to confess at that moment, but if I had not reminded him of my status, the confession would have been gained by improper means. The suspect was taken to court on the Monday morning and released on bail.

The course was a strain on me. Ressler managed most of the lecturing and we all learnt a lot, but I was often so irritated and preoccupied by the killer that I would leave the class and phone the team. While I couldn't always concentrate, the detectives were very attentive, but at the end of the day they wanted to party. And party they did. They split into groups and took turns at taking Ressler and Thomas Müller to a different pub each night. I was tired and distracted by the case, so whenever I had time I would slip away to join Piet and his team.

Elmarie passed her initiation with flying colours. She was sociable and accepted the rough-and-ready 'take me as I am' attitude of the detectives. One night Andy Budke, who had worked on the River Strangler case, gave her Stroh rum to drink as an initiation. She downed it. I took her into the ladies' room, but she couldn't get rid of the vile stuff. She wanted to sit down, but I walked her to the hostel, which luckily was next door to the bar, and put her to bed. After that, she was one of the boys. I was reminded of the concoction I'd had to drink at Vlakplaas.

At the beginning of our working relationship, I was very protective towards Elmarie. I didn't want her to make the same mistakes that I had made. I also knew that even if the detectives were willing to accept you on a social level, it was not guaranteed that they would be willing to work with you. I knew that this would be another test she would have to face in the future, but I had a gut feeling that she would make it.

I joined the investigation team over the weekend. On Sunday morning, 14 April, as I was heading for the office, Div called me on my cellphone. Another body had been found – a thirty-year-old victim in a vineyard near Kraaifontein. She too was not a prostitute. We determined that the victim had been killed on Monday 8 April after the suspect had been released on bail. The fact that we had no manpower to keep him under twenty-four-hour surveillance frustrated us tremendously and we realised that the woman had died because of our lack of resources. Our surveillance team had been allocated other duties. We'd had to let the suspect go until we had enough evidence to charge him with murder, and Piet and his team also had to follow up on other leads.

During the time that the suspect was free, he walked around town dressed as an American Indian. He also attended a political rally of one of the right-wing parties and claimed that the politician General Constand Viljoen was Piet Viljoen's father. I think he adopted this behaviour to create the impression that he had lost his senses, so that he could claim mental instability if he ever went to court. Poor George Lochner had to sort out all these complications.

On 15 May, when I was back in Pretoria, another body was discovered next to Old Faure Road, which is on the way to Somerset West. This time the victim was a sex worker. The body was two days old. By this point, nineteen women had been killed by the Prostitute Killer.

Over the first few days of June 1996, my boyfriend invited me to join him and some friends to go scuba diving in Mozambique. It was the first time since I had joined the South African Police Service in 1994 that my cellphone was switched off. We spent three idyllic days scuba diving off Inhaca Island. I trusted Elmarie to handle any emergencies in my absence. Were it not for her joining my unit, I wouldn't have been able to take leave.

Aerial photos of the vast dunes of Mitchells Plain, where the bodies of the boys killed by the Station Strangler were found.

The train station in Mitchells Plain where Elroy van Rooyen was last seen alive.

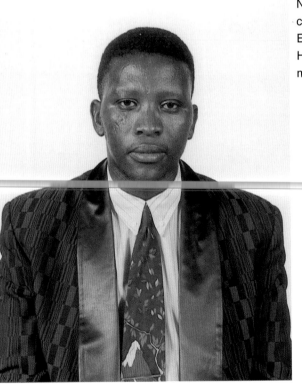

Norman Afzal Simons was convicted of the murder of Elroy van Rooyen in 1998. He was never charged for the murders of the other children.

Superintendent Vinol Viljoen and me taking a break. Vinol headed the Atteridgeville serial killer investigation.

Moses Sithole, the Atteridgeville serial killer. On 21 October 1996, he was charged with 38 murders, 40 rapes and six cases of robbery by the Pretoria Supreme Court. He was sentenced to 2 410 years in prison.

My mentor and boss, General Suiker Britz, commander of the Serious and Violent Crimes Unit.

Aerial photograph of Donnybrook in the KwaZulu-Natal Midlands, where Mhlengwa Zikode massacred members of the community.

Me amid the Phoenix cane fields, getting a grip on the mind of the killer.

Discussing the Phoenix case with Superintendent Philip Veldhuizen.

Observing the eleventh crime scene of the Phoenix serial killer, where a little purple flower had grown.

The crime scene in Bertrams, Johannesburg, of pyromaniac Norman Hobkirk's victim in August 1997. Superintendent Mike van Aardt was the investigating officer.

Nicolas Ncama, a serial killer who operated in the Eastern Cape, was arrested on 27 November 1997 and found guilty of three murders, one rape, one indecent assault and three thefts.

Stewart Wilken, alias Boetie Boer, pointing out a crime scene. He was charged with nine murders and four rapes and received seven life sentences.

Police vans overlooking Phoswa Village, a squatter camp on the outskirts of Piet Retief and the hunting ground of the infamous Saloon Killer.

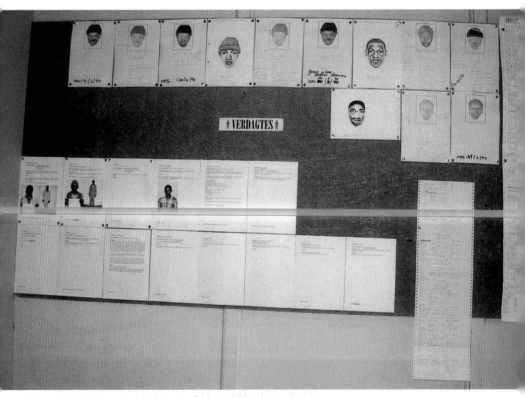

The operations room during the Saloon Killer investigation.

At this stage, I was experiencing considerable stress in my life. What had seemed to be the beginning of a new love fizzled out soon after we returned from Mozambique. He felt the relationship was getting too serious too soon. All the beautiful promises he had made turned into dust and it saddened me. The strain of getting Ressler and Müller to South Africa and running a course at the same time as an investigation was also getting to me. I was exhausted. The old longing for Mitchells Plain burned in my heart. As it turned out, our Cape Town suspect had caused trouble again, so on Friday 14 June I was on a plane before the ink on the authorisation forms had dried.

I went straight from the airport to Mitchells Plain. It was winter and very cold, but the wind lifted my soul and blew the cobwebs from my mind. I could feel the ambience revitalising me. My mental and physical energy returned.

I sat in the car and just watched the world of Mitchells Plain go by. Toothless mothers with their hair in curlers chasing screaming children down the road, the dogs dodging the traffic and the banter of the street brokers brought the familiar symphony to life once more. I was enthralled. I sat and listened and experienced. They still ignored the traffic lights. The gangs had painted new graffiti on the walls in some places, but the rest was as it had always been.

Piet had pulled our suspect in again on Saturday 15 June. The man was sitting in one of the offices and was not aware that I was back in Cape Town. George Lochner and I arranged that we would play good cop, bad cop. I was good cop. George went into the office and it wasn't long before we heard the suspect shouting at him. Then I entered the office and ordered George to leave. He acted his part, making a snide remark, and left the room.

Immediately the suspect warmed to me. He claimed that he didn't know why he had been brought in for questioning. He cried and held my hand. This time they had picked him up because he had put up an abusive poster in the window of the caravan he was living in. He had acquired the caravan since the last time I'd spoken to him and parked it outside the boarding house. The poster contained derogatory remarks about the detectives, including some of the officers. They had opened a case of crimen injuria.

He was more aggressive this time, but we managed to calm him down.

I expressed my concern about his blackouts and asked him whether he could have committed the murders while experiencing one. He said it was possible and that he would like to know about it. I suggested hypnosis as an option to unlock those forbidden memories. He agreed and declared himself prepared to be hypnotised.

I got the impression that he wanted to use hypnosis as a vehicle to make a confession. If he confessed to the murders under hypnosis, he could claim that he had committed them during a blackout. He said he could be suffering from Multiple Personality Disorder. The trauma of the murders could then have triggered the so-called memory losses. This would fit in very conveniently if the incident of the victim with the Coke bottle was taken into consideration, as he had landed up in hospital shortly after this, claiming to be suffering from amnesia. I saw through his ruse but agreed that I would arrange a hypnosis session with a specialist.

As we spoke, I almost succeeded in dragging this killer out of the abyss, but it seemed that just as we were about to break the surface, he would let go of my hand and sink back. It was very frustrating not only for me but also for Piet, who was waiting to catch us.

The psychological picture I had of the suspect was that he had been sexually abused by his mother as a boy. After all, he did sleep in her bed until he was sixteen, which is a very unhealthy situation. The rejection by an abusive father and a double-binding mother provided enough childhood trauma to qualify him as a person who could develop into a serial killer. He told me he loved his mother, but he considered her to be a prostitute. He experienced a double-bind, love–hate relationship with her. This is a dynamic where a mother behaves sexually and in a seductive manner towards her son, but rejects him as soon as he seeks intimacy. He could have killed the prostitutes because they represented his mother to him.

It was a classic Oedipus triangle. He was in love with the seductive but rejecting mother figure, hated the father figure, and felt mentally castrated by both. Since he had problems getting an erection, he did not kill the sex workers who were patient and kind towards him, as Sally had been. They represented the 'Good Mother'. He killed the ones who became impatient and who probably belittled him, as they represented the 'Bad Mother'.

He selected the cheapest prostitutes because they were freely available and would accompany him anywhere. To visit parlours would be dangerous because he could be recognised. Voortrekker Road, which was just a few blocks from his home, swarmed with sex workers at night.

He also must have felt that prostitutes deserved to die, because it was through one of them that he had contracted a venereal disease. He told me he would not pick up prostitutes because he didn't have money to pay for them. I replied that if he knew he was going to kill them, he wouldn't need money. He kept quiet after that. I classified him as a mission-motivated serial killer. He felt he had a mission to kill prostitutes, not because they were easy prey, but because their occupation had an intrinsic meaning for him – they reminded him of his mother.

Forensic hypnosis is not a party trick, so I decided to ask Professor Dap Louw from the University of the Free State to conduct the session with the suspect for me. He was an expert and had conducted forensic hypnosis sessions before. He also had experience as an expert witness in court.

But, by the time I had secured Professor Louw's services, the suspect had changed his mind again. This cat-and-mouse game was typical. He would trust me and hold my hand, but as soon as we were almost there, he would let go again. It drove George Lochner nuts. The suspect also had a love–hate relationship with George. Whenever he was in trouble, he called George, only to give him hell again later.

I returned to Pretoria on Sunday 16 June, and two days later I flew to England. I was met at Heathrow Airport and driven to a town close to Bramshill, a beautiful old mansion that was used as a training college for policemen. At the hotel I was met by Superintendent Phil Pyke, whom I had met the previous year in Scotland. Phil was in charge of Bramshill. He swept me off to the lawn where detectives from homicide branches all over Europe had gathered. I was pleased to see Ressler and Müller again, but too exhausted from the long flight to show much enthusiasm. The next moment a photographer gathered us all together to take a group picture. There I sat, in the clothes I had been wearing the previous morning when I boarded my plane in South Africa, suffering from jet lag, having my picture taken.

After the photo session I asked Phil if he would excuse me for a while so that I could take a nap. He was very sympathetic and had someone escort me to my room. I was hungry and ordered sandwiches from room service. When they arrived, I saw to my dismay that they had slices of roast beef on them. I had heard all about mad cow disease and had sworn off red meat by then, having seen too much decomposing flesh on bodies. I removed the beef, ate the bread and slept through the rest of the afternoon.

While I was in London, on 21 June 1996, the suspect was arrested after phoning the SAPS radio control unit. He had made an anonymous call, promising that more prostitutes would be found once the blue truck was in running order again. The conversation had been taped and it matched the suspect's voice.

He was sent to Valkenberg Psychiatric Hospital for observation and then transferred to Pollsmoor Prison. There he met up with Simons, the Station Strangler. Both claimed to be innocent. I can imagine how they must have convinced each other of their innocence. They even shared the same lawyers. Our suspect often fired his lawyers. He threw tantrums and refused to appear in court. As a result, his case was regularly postponed, and he spent more than a year awaiting trial.

During this time he wrote letters to several dignitaries in which he insulted me and the detectives. Once a killer is in prison, we carry on with other investigations and do not pay much attention to those who are behind bars. This infuriates them and they get jealous. I compare it to sibling rivalry. I had become the 'Bad Mother' to our suspect and he vented his anger in those letters. I chose to ignore them.

In September 1997 the state prosecutor, Advocate Anette de Lange, who had also managed Simons's case, decided to withdraw charges against our suspect. Although this was a huge disappointment to George, who had taken over as investigating officer by then, and of course to me, we respected her decision. The evidence in the case was too scanty.

Our suspect walked out of Pollsmoor Prison on 29 September 1997 a free man, after being an awaiting-trial prisoner for more than a year. I wondered if he remembered our date for Paris. I didn't think it a good idea to remind him.

Although George kept tabs on him, we didn't have the manpower to keep him under twenty-four-hour surveillance. But he was still regarded as a suspect. Three more sex workers died after his release, but George, Elmarie and I suspected this to be the work of another serial killer preying on sex workers. We dubbed the new case 'The Nightmare' to distinguish it from the Cape Town Prostitute Killer case. Both cases were investigated by George.

Sally moved to another suburb and became a madam with girls working for her. She no longer walked the streets. I think sex workers need to realise that one of their occupational hazards is the possibility of becoming the easy prey of a serial killer.

This serial killer slipped back into the abyss and there was nothing I could do about it, because in June, just before I left for England, detectives in KwaZulu-Natal informed me of another serial killer active in the region.

Eleven years after the Cape Town Prostitute Killer, when I had already resigned from the South African Police Service, another vicious prostitute killer became active in neighbouring Namibia, and their police service contracted my services. I had always been impressed with the conduct of the Namibian detectives. Some of the victims had been decapitated and the killer's anger towards prostitutes was red-hot. I worked with a local psychologist, who had identified a very good suspect as one of her clients in prison. I don't know if that case was ever solved. I was saddened when the family of my psychologist friend informed me later that she had passed away from illness.

SIX

Nasrec and Kranskop

The pang, the curse, with which they died,
Had never passed away:
I could not draw my eyes from theirs;
Nor turn them up to pray.
– Samuel Taylor Coleridge, 'The Rime of the Ancient Mariner', 1798

Seven months after the arrest of Moses Sithole, the Atteridgeville serial killer, the spectre of a dark force in Johannesburg reared its ugly head once again.

The two serial killers operating in this area before had been eliminated. David Selepe, the Cleveland serial killer, was dead, and Moses Sithole was in prison. But someone new had started killing women in the same area, using a similar modus operandi of strangling women with their own clothing. There were subtle differences between these serial killers, however. Sithole liked to tie up his victims and had a much more sophisticated fantasy involving bondage than David Selepe, who did not bother to tie them up. I wondered if this third killer was the mastermind I'd always suspected to be behind Selepe and Sithole's killings.

In mid-June 1996, just before I left for Bramshill, detectives in Kranskop in KwaZulu-Natal informed me that they had arrested a man suspected of being a serial killer. I checked the details of the case and confirmed that he was, indeed, a serial killer.

The suspect was Bongani Mteka. He had raped and strangled four women. The fifth victim managed to escape after he had raped her. Since he was securely in jail, I knew I didn't have to visit him immediately. I contacted Sergeants Tjaart Pretorius and Chris Dhlamini of the Newcastle Murder and Robbery Unit, who had both attended my course, and asked them to monitor the case and assist the investigating officer.

On 17 July I got a call from the Brixton Murder and Robbery Unit. They had a possible serial killer who had been murdering women in Johannesburg.

Several different police stations had recorded similar murder cases but, as usual, the lack of an efficient computerised system meant that the cases weren't linked until the press and public began noticing the trend. Only then were the case dockets transferred to the Brixton Murder and Robbery Unit.

Captain Piet Byleveld was the investigating officer. I made an appointment to meet him on the morning of 19 July. I was reluctant to return to Brixton after the hostility I had experienced there during the Cleveland case, but they now had a new commander.

Captain Piet Byleveld's reputation preceded him. He had been a Murder and Robbery detective for twenty years and was universally regarded as one of the most competent and experienced detectives in his field. I took Elmarie along to teach her how to draw up a profile as well as for some moral support.

Piet Byleveld was not at all what I expected. While detectives usually wear jeans or casual pants and shirts, he was dressed impeccably in a suit. I must admit, I was very wary of him and a little intimidated too. He was sitting behind his desk but jumped up as we walked in and shook our hands. I talked to him for a little while before I eventually looked into his dark eyes, whereupon I noticed a distinct twinkle. We both smiled.

Piet could be summed up in one word: hyperactive. He had a wonderful sense of humour, and although I often saw him exhausted and frustrated after that day, and while he lost a lot of weight during those investigations, he never ever lost his sense of humour. Piet took a liking to Elmarie as well and teased her endlessly.

We spent the whole week at Brixton, visiting the crime scenes and reading the dockets. I explained my theory about there being a mastermind behind Selepe and Sithole's killings to Piet, and he was open-minded enough to consider it. This was very encouraging. Piet called his case the Nasrec serial killer, because the Nasrec stadium, which was mainly used for soccer matches, was located in the centre of all the crime scenes. The crime scenes were dispersed roughly in a circle around Nasrec in the Johannesburg suburbs of Booysens, Maraisburg, Orlando and Mondeor. The Soweto Highway, the Western Bypass and the Golden Highway criss-crossed the area.

On 31 March 1996, the body of a thirty-two-year-old woman had been found in a part of a suburb that was still in development. The roads had already been tarred and streetlights had been installed, but no houses had been built. The date of death could not be determined, but she had last been seen alive about two weeks before her body was discovered.

The second docket we read was of the murder of a nineteen-year-old woman, whose body had been discovered on 1 May. She was found lying in the grass in the veld, and the outline of a mine dump was visible from the scene. The body was about a week old.

Gold was discovered on the Witwatersrand in the old Transvaal in the late nineteenth century, and within the boundaries of modern Johannesburg remain huge white mine dumps that look like small mountains. While the mine dumps were once on the outskirts of the town, the suburbs have since expanded around them and they stand there as monuments to a golden era.

On 3 May 1996, the body of a twenty-nine-year-old woman was discovered next to New Canada Road. The Consolidated Main Reef Gold Mine and a dam separated these two scenes. The body was still fresh.

The following day, on 4 May, the body of a fourteen-year-old schoolgirl was found in the veld next to the Nasrec stadium. She had gone missing on 29 April, and her body was discovered on the same day that she was killed. This crime scene was close to one of the previous scenes.

Three days after the schoolgirl was found, on 7 May, the body of a twenty-three-year-old victim was discovered next to the Western Bypass. She had been killed on the scene the night before.

Four days later, the body of another woman was discovered in the veld next to a taxi route. Her face was mutilated, and she had been killed the night before her body was found.

Seven days later, on 18 May, the body of yet another woman was discovered on the opposite side of the same road on which the previous victim had been found. She had last been seen alive the previous evening.

Six women had died at the hands of this ruthless killer within just one month. They had all been brutally raped, and the way that the killer had just discarded their bodies indicated that to him they were no more than objects to be left in the veld after he had vented his anger and sexual lust on them. These murders made me very angry, especially that of the young schoolgirl, who had been a bright student and would have had a wonderful future ahead of her.

Two weeks later, on 7 June, the body of a twenty-six-year-old woman was found next to the N1 highway interchange. She had been killed the previous evening. Her body was just opposite the spot where the body of an earlier victim had been found. What was amazing about these crime scenes was that both bodies were found in a little piece of veld between busy highways. Cars would have passed just a few metres from the crime scenes. But the women had not been dumped – they were killed on the spot where their bodies were found.

Three weeks later, on 30 June, the body of a thirty-five-year-old woman was discovered in the same area where the first victim had been found.

Another two weeks later, on 15 July, the body of a thirty-four-year-old woman was found next to the Golden Highway interchange. Her body was fresh. This crime scene was also right next to a busy highway, like two of the previous cases.

There were three other similar cases dating from 1995, but we didn't include these in our series since the DNA results of the semen taken from those cases didn't match the corresponding DNA of the ten cases we had.

With the help of Piet's team of detectives – Sergeant Paul Manamela, Inspector Lucky Ramaboa and Inspector Ronnie Masinga – we established that all the victims had been employed and that they had made use of taxis for their daily transport. It became evident that these women had been abducted by the killer on their way home from work. Most of them had lived in Diepkloof, a suburb of Soweto.

The daughter of Brixton Murder and Robbery's commander, Sergeant Riana Steyn, completed Piet's team. I referred to his team as The Pirates, for they were a motley crew. Piet was hyperactive and always impeccably dressed in a suit; Riana was a nervous, petite and pretty blonde; Paul was a young detective with a playboy image; Lucky was older and half-deaf; and Ronnie was also older and his hands always shook because of his diabetes. They were all very experienced detectives.

Elmarie and I got stuck into the profile and spent the next few days sifting through all the facts available to us at that stage. The cause of death in most of the cases was strangulation. In some cases, the killer had also tied the hands of the victims. Most of the women had been assaulted, probably by his fists, in order to subdue them. The murders were reported to the police by passers-by who had seen the bodies.

We classified the killer as an organised serial killer motivated by lust. The fact that the crime scenes were devoid of evidence and that those middle-class women would not have accompanied a derelict person pointed to the fact that the man must be quite presentable.

This time it was easier for me to find the killer in the abyss. The main characteristic that I picked up in my mind was his extreme anger. He was represented by a very vicious spot in the abyss.

The abyss is a dark place, so I have to feel my way around by trusting my instincts and intuition instead of relying on any of my other senses. I cannot see anything there; I can only feel.

If one could imagine a pitch-black hole of which the boundaries are unclear, one would have a fair description of the abyss. The atmosphere is filled with fear, and one has to rely on instinct when one moves. One never knows when one is going to stumble or where one is going, whether it is up, down, left or right. There is no direction.

One is alone, but aware of other beings within the abyss. One gravitates towards these beings, and when one moves into their orbit, one is guided by feeling. The feeling I got when I got closer to the killer was of red glowing anger. He did not like me and moved away, but he could still pounce at any moment. It was like being in a dark room with a vicious predator, and while he might be as wary of me as I was of him, I was also acutely aware of the danger.

Due to massive media interest and pressure, especially from the ANC Women's League, it was decided that Piet's team would be supplemented by other detectives in Johannesburg who had also completed my course. A press conference was arranged at the Brixton Murder and Robbery Unit for Friday 25 July 1996, where National Commissioner Fivaz explained that the team had been enlarged and he offered a huge reward for information leading to the arrest of the killer. He also released part of our completed profile to the press. I managed to stay close to the door and sneaked out as soon as he had finished to avoid being interviewed.

In the profile, we described the killer as a man in his late twenties to early thirties, since that was the age of most of the victims. He would be attractive, charming and sociable – the kind of personality that middle-class women would respond to. He would also be very intelligent and an excellent manipulator. Beneath this mask of a ladies' man would simmer a deep hatred of women. He would be the kind of man who demanded total submission from women. He would use a taxi as transport and might be a taxi driver.

Women were warned to be alert, to take notice of fellow passengers and to ensure that they were not the last passenger left in a taxi. They were advised not to walk alone on shortcuts but rather to move in groups. They were also told to inform their next of kin of their movements, especially of their expected time of arrival home, and to confirm that they had arrived safely. They were invited to report any suspicious behaviour directly to the Brixton Murder and Robbery Unit. Despite these warnings and pleas, information was not readily forthcoming and there seemed to be a reluctance on the part of the public to get involved.

Because of public pressure we hadn't been able to delay the press conference, but this also had an impact on the serial killer, whom I was sure would read the newspapers. He went covert. I could feel him slipping away from me inside the abyss. We found no more fresh bodies. The team continued to follow up on all available leads.

I completed the final touches to my doctoral thesis during this time and submitted it to my supervisor at the University of Pretoria. My examination date was set for 19 September 1996. I had to study eighteen books before that date, when I would face a panel of four professors who would evaluate whether I should be awarded the DPhil degree in psychology.

The professors were very friendly during the exam and the majority of their questions concerned my thesis. They concentrated less on the eighteen books, which I knew by heart by then. I illustrated some of the concepts in my thesis with slides, which they found very innovative and interesting. I am not sure how long the exam lasted, but to me it felt like seconds before I found myself outside the door again. I waited in the passage for my supervisor.

When he appeared, I asked him how it had gone. He frowned, but when he saw the expression on my face he answered: 'It went well ... Doctor.'

I was overjoyed. I had made it. I sped across to my father's office, but he wasn't there. I asked a secretary to phone him and tell him that Dr Pistorius was waiting for him, hoping that he would think it was my brother, but my father was in fact visiting my brother and immediately realised it could only be me. He rushed back to his office to congratulate me.

I drove to my mother's house and told her the good news. Then I left for the office where I told General Britz and my colleagues. Elmarie was in Pietersburg working on a single murder, but when I phoned her she immediately drove back to Pretoria to be there in time for the party. Many detectives had gathered at the canteen to congratulate me, but my eyes kept darting to the door for the arrival of my boyfriend. He arrived a little late – with a redhead on his arm. My elation shattered into pieces, but I managed to keep my cool and offered them a drink, whereafter I got completely sloshed. Before I made a complete idiot of myself, Elmarie guided me up to my office on the fifth floor above the canteen, where I slept it off.

I awoke in my office at about two the next morning feeling like hell and furious too. Back home, I ran a warm bubble bath and took a vow to steer clear of any personal relationships for a long time.

I returned to work and concentrated on getting the man out of my system by working extra hard, which was easy to do. One day, Elmarie was reading the fact file that I had received on Bongani Mfeka, the Kranskop serial killer, who was still in custody. She read that one of his victims came from Newcastle and she remembered that one of the Nasrec victims had been on her way to Newcastle when she went missing. We immediately phoned Piet and gave him the information. I was very proud of Elmarie. Piet set off to Kranskop to fetch Bongani and we hoped that he would be the Nasrec serial killer.

In June 1995, Bongani had killed Babazile Nompumelo near Jammersdal Farm in the Kranskop district. Three months later, on 31 October, he raped and attempted to kill Tholakele Ntombinhlophe in the same area. On 2 November he killed Nono Princess Shezi, and then sometime between 23 October and 3 November he killed Philile Happiness Masuku on a farm called Patience in the same district. He also killed Phumuzile Tholakele Phungula between 31 October and 8 November 1995.

Bongani refused to make any confessions while he was in Kranskop. On their way from Kranskop to Pretoria, Piet and his 'pirates' stopped at a picnic spot for a braai. Bongani was invited to join them. Piet did not put any pressure on Bongani – he asked him some questions about his life, avoiding the murders. Bongani warmed to Piet's fatherly approach and told him that he had committed the Kranskop murders. He also told Piet that he had murdered two women in the Johannesburg area while he was working on the mines. He was willing to point out the crime scenes. It was thanks to Elmarie's brightness and Piet's clever interrogation strategy that the murders of two women were solved in this manner, but Bongani's DNA did not match the DNA of the Nasrec serial killer.

It was only a year later, in July 1997, that I got the chance to interview Bongani Mfeka. Elmarie and I were rearranging Piet's office to make space for another serial killer case, and Piet brought up two prisoners from the cells to assist us. One of them was stockily built and very friendly and eager to help. The other man was tall and reserved. The two men helped us move the furniture and they cleaned the office. They washed everything, including the walls. I thought they might even wash the ceiling as well. I realised that any chance to get out of the cells for a while was eagerly accepted.

Piet was out during this cleaning operation, and by the time he returned later in the afternoon, the men had gone back to their cells. I asked Piet what crimes they had committed. Piet smiled and told me that the tall man was in for a phoney bomb scare. I asked him what the friendly man had done. Piet has a peculiar sense of humour. He told me the man who had been helping to put up crime scene photographs of serial killers all day long was Bongani Mfeka, the Kranskop serial killer. Bongani had not remarked on the photographs and seemed unaffected by them. The joke was on me.

Piet arranged an interview with Bongani for me. Unlike other serial killers, he did not murder the women shortly after he met them. He developed a relationship with each of his victims before killing them. He called them his girlfriends, although he also had a steady girlfriend and an infant son by her. Some of the relationships with his 'girlfriends' lasted as long as a year.

I asked him how he came to murder these women. He said he often walked with them in the hills and suddenly he would just have a feeling that it was time to kill them. He raped them and strangled them with their clothing. He said he felt as though it was a dream, and he could not remember the details of the murders. He didn't want the girlfriends any longer, but he also didn't want anyone else to have them. This is yet another example of a serial killer treating his victims like objects because of a lack of socialisation during the latency phase.

Like all serial killers, Bongani's father was emotionally absent when he was a little boy. He never had the chance to identify with a father figure at the beginning of the latency phase, which should commence at about six years. This is the time when children go to school, socialise and incorporate society's moral and ethical values, which marks the development of a conscience, or superego, as Freud called it.

Bongani identified with Piet as his father figure. He was extremely attached to him and wanted to please him at all costs. The development of his super-ego had been retarded, but it was nonetheless the late development of his conscience that caused Bongani to plead guilty to the murder of four women and the attempted murder of one woman at his trial two years later, on 15 July 1998 at the High Court in Pietermaritzburg. Piet and Riana attended the short trial. Bongani was given four life sentences.

On 8 October 1996, Piet discovered the body of another of the Nasrec serial killer's victims lying in the veld in Naturena, which was far away from the others and not among the suburbs. Her body was very badly decomposed and it was established that she must have been killed towards the end of May. The Nasrec serial killer had therefore killed seven women during May 1996, when Bongani was in prison. He was still at large.

Since no fresh bodies had been discovered, Piet's team was eventually disbanded and they returned to their units. The original 'pirate team' was all that Piet had left, but they still worked on the case daily.

In November 1996 I attended the trial of Moses Sithole, the Atteridgeville Strangler, whenever I had the chance. Elmarie assisted Captain Vinol Viljoen, and this provided her with the same kind of experience I had gained when I attended the Station Strangler's trial. It was vital for both of us to get acquainted with all the aspects of a detective's work. Once you become accustomed to court procedures, you are less nervous when your turn comes to stand in a witness box and testify.

I was burning the candle at both ends during this period. By day I would do my work, which included keeping tabs on the Nasrec case, writing new lectures and doing research, as well as planning the future of my unit and overseeing Elmarie's work, and by night I was listening to the detectives suffering from post-traumatic stress. Most of the detectives who frequented the head office canteen knew that I was a psychologist and they would often offload their burdens on me. I knew I couldn't help all of them, but I made time to see who I could. The process was highly irregular according to normal therapy practices. I met the detectives in a bar and spent the rest of the night simply listening to the horror stories they told me.

Many of them had been involved in the Vlakplaas Third Force atrocities. They had the sword of Damocles hanging over their heads, for if they were not granted amnesty at the Truth and Reconciliation Commission hearings, they would go to prison. Others were detectives who had had to investigate their own colleagues who had been involved in Vlakplaas activities. They not only had post-traumatic stress but also the additional burden of being ostracised by their colleagues. I had to deal with members of both groups. At first, these men were very reluctant to seek the help of other psychologists, and until I could convince them to accept my referrals, I listened night after night until the early morning hours.

I had taught myself to nurse a drink for an hour as I could never match them drink for drink. Every hour I would excuse myself and go to the bathroom to get rid of the liquor. In a way I felt I was trying to do my part in the reconciliation process, which was at its height with the amnesty hearings at the Truth and Reconciliation Commission. If I could be instrumental in relieving these men of some of their stress, I was doing my bit for the country, although it was strictly behind the scenes. My ex-boyfriend was one of the men to appear before the commission.

One night I realised that I was burning myself out. I needed my energy for my job, which was stressful at the best of times, and I had limited energy to spare. I managed to convince the men to go to private psychologists who were in a much better position to help them than I was. Some of them were referred to hospital for sleep therapy, some recovered and some resigned from the Police Service. I became careful not to let myself slip into situations like these. I had empathy for those men, for they had their side of the story to tell, but I couldn't give them any more of my attention, at the cost of our investigations.

I took a week's leave over the Christmas period and spent New Year's lying on my bed alone watching the fireworks from my window, as I had done the previous year. The isolation of the abyss was not far from my mind that night, but I refused to give in to melancholy. I reflected on the fact that I had worked on two major serial killer cases, I had trained many detectives and had succeeded in getting Ressler and Müller to train detectives too, I had added Elmarie to my unit, and I had made many new friends among the detectives. I also had a broken heart.

The Nasrec killer had entered a cooling-off period. For two years and two months we found no traces of his particular murders. Serial killers do experience cooling-off periods during which they willingly refrain from murder, or they are incarcerated and unable to commit murder, or they move to another place where they carry on undetected. Both Piet and I thought that the Nasrec serial killer was dead, but the crime scene photographs remained on Piet's office wall.

Then, in August 1998, Piet heard that a suspect had been arrested for raping a woman in the same area as the Nasrec murders. He had an instinctive feeling about this case and arranged for the suspect to be transferred to the Brixton Murder and Robbery Unit's cells. He took a blood sample from the suspect, without alerting him to the fact that he was investigating the Nasrec serial killer case.

Piet sent the blood sample to the Forensic Laboratory. On Friday 4 December, as I was walking along the beach in Knysna, Piet called me and informed me of the results. Twenty-five-year-old Lazarus Mazingane had been identified as the Nasrec serial killer suspect. Like his namesake in the Bible, Lazarus had risen from the dead.

The red glowing anger by which I had identified him in the abyss years before had died down but, like a Phoenix, he had risen from the ashes and was raging once more. Lazarus tormented my nights with terrible nightmares. Since he was already in custody, Piet had decided to postpone the interrogation until February 1999, when both of us returned from leave. But Lazarus refused any interviews, so I never met him face to face.

Later, the state prosecutors decided to postpone charging Lazarus until the trial of the Wemmer Pan/Hammer Serial Killer was completed. In 2002, Lazarus was eventually charged with seventy-three cases, of which fifty-one were murder charges. He was sentenced to seventeen life sentences and 780 years in prison.

SEVEN

The Phoenix Cane Killer

But soon there breathed a wind on me,
Nor sound nor motion made:
Its path was not upon the sea,
In ripple or in shade.

It raised my hair, it fanned my cheek
Like a meadow-gale of Spring –
It mingled strangely with my fears,
Yet it felt like a welcoming.
– Samuel Taylor Coleridge, 'The Rime of the Ancient Mariner', 1798

Long before Lazarus rose from the dead, another frightful serial killer had risen from the ashes of the cane fields in, coincidentally, Phoenix, a township on the outskirts of Durban.

During the winter of 1997 I experienced a lull in my work. I had just finished another course and had trained over a hundred detectives by that point. I had been promoted to assistant manager, which is the civilian equivalent of a superintendent or a major in the old ranking system. We were dealing with smaller consultations, including threats to the president and single bizarre murders. The administrative duties were frustrating me, and I was itching for a hands-on investigation.

Then, in June 1997, I received a call from Superintendent Philip Veldhuizen of the Durban Murder and Robbery Unit. The Phoenix detectives had found four decomposed bodies in the sugarcane fields in Phoenix. Philip had collected eight dockets by then, including cases with a similar modus operandi, that had occurred from 1994 to 1996 in the same area. While the bodies found in 1997 were badly decomposed and some were burnt, they were all women and they were all discovered in the same area. I informed General Britz of the circumstances and he gave Elmarie and me permission to travel to Durban for a week to establish whether a serial killer was at work. Philip needed a week to prepare the operations room before our arrival.

In the meantime, I had a strange personal experience. An old friend I hadn't seen for eighteen years contacted me, and on the spur of the moment invited me to meet up with him in Knysna, the quaint lakeside town where my father lived, so I said yes. That was the first time in the three and a half years I'd been working with serial killers that I opened up and talked to someone about how all the horror was affecting me. Although I did not divulge the particulars of the investigations, this man allowed me to metaphorically vomit all over his soul. He was kind and I felt safe and secure, like I did when I was still married. I was attracted to him. His strength percolated through my veins and the catharsis cleared me. I flew to Durban feeling refreshed and hoped a relationship would follow from this.

Upon arriving in Durban, Elmarie, who had driven there by car, picked me up at the airport and we went to the mortuary. The bubble of dreaming about a new relationship burst as soon as I walked inside. Anyone who has ever entered one of these places recognises the smell – one can almost taste it.

The pathologist had almost completed the post-mortem when we arrived. The victim was lying on her back. Her stomach had been cut open and detectives were standing around holding intestines to be weighed. Her skull had been removed. Maggots were still crawling on the floor. The pathologist sliced her leg open and removed the femur, which then had to be ground to provide the forensic specialists with DNA material. I had attended many post-mortems before, but this was an exceptionally rude awakening to the reality of my life, especially after three idyllic days spent walking in the cool, misty Knysna forests and strolling on Wilderness Beach in the company of my new potential boyfriend. It was Elmarie's first post-mortem, and only the third body she had encountered, but she handled it well.

We returned to the Durban Murder and Robbery offices. I was impressed by Philip's preparations. For the first time, I walked into an operations room that was already set up. Photographs of the victims were lined up on one wall and aerial photographs of the cane fields on another. Crime scenes were clearly marked. Elmarie and I had our own offices allocated to us. The dockets were in order, statements had been retaken and extra sets of photographs were ready. I was very proud of the men.

Later that night, Elmarie and I consulted with the Port Shepstone Child Protection Unit on another case, and it was 9.30 p.m. by the time we booked into our hotel. I had a bath and then settled down in bed, reading through all the dockets before falling asleep.

The next morning, after a quick meeting with Director Naidoo, the media liaison officer, Superintendent Allan Alford of the Durban Murder and Robbery Unit took us to the crime scenes. Allan had just completed my course the previous week. He and Philip were a great team. Philip was lean and abrupt and ran the Comrades Marathon. He had red hair and a reddish beard. Allan had dark hair and was huge. Both were introverts, but once they relaxed, they could really party. They were both hard men, but they became fiercely protective once they decided to 'adopt' you. Elmarie and I were both adopted. The *esprit de corps* I was experiencing by now among the detectives was so different from their rejection a few years before, when I worked on the Station Strangler, Cleveland and Atteridgeville cases.

Two of the forensic specialists from the Forensic Laboratory in Pretoria had also driven to Durban and they accompanied us to the crime scenes. Allan had arranged for some of the Phoenix detectives to point out the exact spots to us. I liked to spend time at a crime scene even if the body had been removed. I needed to retrace the steps of the killer, and the scene of the crime was a place where I could get into his mind. These were the places where they acted out their most secret fantasies, and I believed that the atmosphere remained laden with emotion, waiting for me to tap into it. Elmarie was on the ball as usual. At each crime scene, she handed me a clipboard with the notes as well as the photographs taken at the scene. She then managed to lure the detectives away, leaving me by myself.

I was alone at the first scene. This was not the scene of the first victim, as we didn't visit them in chronological order. I found a rock to sit on and then just opened my mind to any thoughts that might intrude. My senses are usually very alert. I picked up on the wind again, the same peaceful wind I had found at the Station Strangler, Cleveland and Atteridgeville crime scenes. It was like a familiar friend. I began reconstructing the steps and movements of the killer and a narrative formed in my mind.

We moved on to the next scenes. Later, Elmarie told me that, at the third scene, Allan had asked her what I was doing sitting there alone. She told him I was meditating, whereupon he just said, 'Oh.' We visited six crime scenes that day before returning to the office. Allan waited patiently at each crime scene for me to finish 'meditating'.

That night I retired to my hotel room early while Elmarie joined the others on the beachfront. The Gunston 500 surfing competition was on and there were fifteen thousand people on the Durban beaches. She knew me well enough by then to realise when I needed time out. I relaxed in a hot bath and tried to calm down. But the killer was inside my head. I was amazed at how fast this had happened. I had scarcely mentally met him that day at his exhibition, and already he was moving in on me. I couldn't wait to get back to the crime scenes the following morning. Elmarie got in slightly after dark and read all the dockets that night – what strange bedtime stories we shared.

The next day, we returned to the crime scenes. To the others it might have seemed that I was doing exactly what I had done the previous day, but they were unaware of what was going on in my mind. The killer had taken over. I was thinking in the first person singular.

People would often ask me what I feel when I sit next to the spot where a body has lain. If a body has decomposed on a crime scene, there is usually a black stain on the soil, caused by bodily fluids and insect activity. Additionally, the odour can often still be detected, and sometimes there are still maggots or their shells left behind.

This was what I found at the scene of the eleventh body. The detectives had cleared a pathway through the cane and around the spot where the body had been found. I crouched down and found a rock to sit on. I stared at the black scar on the ground in front of me. From the photographs I could work out exactly where her face had lain. I was surprised to see that a small purple veld flower had grown there. To me it was beautiful.

I reconstructed exactly what the killer had done to her. I said a prayer and got up. Allan led me a little further into the cane field so that I could experience what it would feel like entering and walking through a pristine sugarcane field. It was a strange experience. The sugarcane was five to seven feet high. The leaves caressed my face as I walked and made a rustling noise that blocked all other thoughts from my mind.

Now I knew how the killer's mind worked. While he walked with the victim on the footpaths, he would make small talk to gain her confidence. Then it seemed as if the cane fields just invited him in. The moment he entered the cane with the victim, all rational thoughts were blocked from his mind by the rustling noise, and the murderous urge automatically took over.

When we reached the office, I started writing with urgency. For the first time since I had started compiling profiles, I wrote in the first person singular. I described his general modus operandi as if he was telling it himself. Then I tackled each crime scene separately and, still writing in the first person singular, I described the subtle changes that crept in, how his fantasy developed, the mistakes he made, how he tried to correct them and how he improved.

This man had a fantasy about bondage. He would knock the victims senseless with a blunt object, and the closer to death they were, the more of their clothes he took off. He then turned the victim over onto her stomach and sat on her backside, tying her hands behind her back with rope or strips of clothing. After this he turned around and tied her feet closely together and then he plaited a harness for her head. He used three pieces of clothing for this. Then he committed a sexual deed with the victim while strangling her. Afterwards, he picked up her clothing and either scattered it in the cane fields or took it along with him.

There was no need for me to reconstruct the first crime scene. He had taken two young girls the first time, and one had escaped. I interviewed her, and what she told me confirmed what was already in my mind. She also gave a description of the man. I am usually not concerned with the killer's appearance, but rather with what's inside his mind. An identikit was drawn up based on the girl's description, and by the end of that day, I had a face to match the man in my mind. We still needed a name, though.

I was amazed at the speed with which I picked up on the killer, but I knew it was because I'd had such a cathartic experience the previous weekend. I appreciated the man who had been brave enough to enter my mind and extract my pain, and I attribute a major part of my capacity to draw up this particular profile to him.

That Wednesday night, after I had started writing, I got a call from Captain Piet Byleveld, who had some very disturbing news: there was a serial killer operating in the Wemmer Pan area in Johannesburg. I promised Piet I would report at Brixton the following Monday. I knew that now I would have to open my mind to the thoughts of both the Phoenix killer and the new Wemmer Pan killer. Having two serial killers in one mind was going to require the utmost self-discipline and concentration to keep them apart. I knew my mental capacity was up to it, but I didn't know how I was going to handle it physically.

On Thursday afternoon, Philip ordered us to attend a braai on the beach in Amanzimtoti. General Suiker happened to be in KwaZulu-Natal at the time, so he joined us that night. The detectives were honoured, and I could sense that the general was very proud of us. Elmarie and I left early, but I heard that the others stayed on into the early hours of the morning.

The next day, everyone was at the office on time. I had to interview the sister of victim number ten. She had brought her little boy and the daughter of the victim along with her. The two toddlers played in the offices and passages while we spoke, their laughter ringing in our ears. We kept them out of the operations room, where the grisly photographs of the victims adorned the walls. I felt hopeless watching the daughter, knowing that the only thing the mighty SAPS could protect her from now was seeing the photograph of her mother's decomposed body. After the interview, Elmarie and I decided to drive back to Pretoria.

It was a six-hour drive, and as darkness set in, so did a certain playfulness. I suppose it was relief, or perhaps our way of de-stressing. But we passed the time by making silly jokes and telling each other stories about our childhoods.

I reported to my own office on Monday morning, walking into a mountain of paperwork. I phoned Piet. He was going to be held up at the High Court all day, but we agreed that Elmarie and I would go to Brixton the next day.

On Tuesday we walked into the Brixton Murder and Robbery Unit – and total disarray. Piet was his usual disorganised self. Some of the dockets hadn't even been transferred to Brixton yet and we had no operations room, so the four of us had to squeeze into Piet's overcrowded office.

Piet had a peculiar way of getting rid of stress. He would take a sachet of Grandpa headache powder with a Coke before nine o'clock each morning, and when the going really got tough, he liked to walk into his office and kick all the dockets that were lying on the floor. Poor Riana would then have to restore order to this chaos. No wonder she was always so nervous. Piet was carrying over a hundred dockets at the time, including the two serial killer cases of Nasrec and Wemmer Pan. Because he was such an excellent detective, a lot of other people's messes tended to get dumped on him. He always remained cheerful, though.

We organised ourselves an operations room by playing musical offices with the other detectives. We then worked through the chaos of moving furniture, with two landlines and two cellphones ringing at the same time, along with interference from the press – the stress of which was alleviated by some Old Brown Sherry we had discovered.

By Friday we had our operations room fitted out, with Nasrec occupying one wall, Wemmer Pan another and a huge map of Johannesburg on the third. Some people might think us abnormal to be proud of an office decorated with wall-to-wall photographs of decomposed bodies, but to us these were normal working conditions. Piet's wife had even given us some lace curtains, which added a soft touch to our décor. It was on this day that we were assisted by Bongani Mfeka, the Kranskop serial killer.

On Monday I was on a flight to Durban again. Seven more bodies had been found by police dogs in the cane fields during my absence. Some of them were fresh, which meant that the killer was unperturbed by the fact that we knew about him. Elmarie stayed on at Brixton to work on the Wemmer Pan profile.

I arrived at Durban airport with a splitting headache. Philip and Allan were waiting for me. They took me to my hotel and invited me for a drink. I explained about the headache, but they pleaded that it would be just one quick drink. We went to one of Allan's haunts, The Red Dog. I settled for a brandy and Coke, and Philip and Allan stuck to their usual rum.

Two hours later I still had the headache, but I was glad I had gone to the pub. Both men were experienced detectives, but that night I realised that they had truly understood what I'd taught them in my courses. The theoretical knowledge wasn't as important as the fact that they had managed to get the killer into their minds. Not the way that I could – not his fantasies – but enough to understand him. For the first time in twenty years, they were hungry for a hunt again.

On Tuesday I declined to visit the new crime scenes. I didn't need to. I looked at the photographs, recognised his work, and started working on the profile immediately. Philip and his team had traced an old docket in which a man had committed a rape similar to the ones we were investigating, but the suspect had been released due to lack of evidence. I asked them not to tell me anything about this man since I didn't want the profile to be influenced.

By Wednesday afternoon I had the complete picture of the person we were looking for in my mind and most of it on paper. I felt confident that hearing about the other suspect wouldn't influence me. I read the old docket and agreed that it seemed like our man. Philip then handed me a photograph and some personal particulars of the man before he went to the mortuary.

I took the notes to my own office and trembled when I looked at them. The face that we were searching for was looking back at me. As I have said, I was never concerned with what the killer looked like – only with his mind. But then I read the man's personal details. He used the name Agmatir Twala, which meant nothing to me. I paged through the documents and suddenly my blood turned to ice. I think I stopped breathing – stopped living – for a few seconds. The man's full name was Sipho Mandla Agmatir Twala.

Mandla was the name David Selepe, the Cleveland serial killer, had called his partner. I grabbed the photograph again. Could this be the man I had been looking for these past three years? Instinctively, I had always felt that Selepe hadn't worked alone and nor had Sithole, the Atteridgeville Strangler. Someone else had to be behind them in the abyss. Piet believed me, and although we'd considered that the Nasrec killer could be the mastermind, it was at that moment that I believed I had in my hands the face and name of the man who could reveal the truth. I couldn't wait for Philip to get back.

The policemen and mortuary attendants at the Phoenix police station were on strike at the time, so Philip and the other detectives had to attend to the post-mortems themselves. Philip had been phoning every few hours to give me a progress report so that I could fill it in on the profile. When he finally called after my big discovery, I was so excited I could hardly talk. He didn't seem very excited, though. I realised that he literally would have been covered in blood, guts and maggots while he was talking to me, so I knew I couldn't expect him to be excited about anything at such a time.

We decided to release part of my profile to the press by the end of that week. I predicted that the Phoenix killer would be a Zulu man between the ages of thirty and forty, a local resident in the Phoenix area who was well acquainted with the sugarcane fields, and a man with at least a high-school education. He would be a loner with no friends and would earn his living by dishonest means. I said that he would be single and that he wouldn't use a car in the crimes. The full profile was more than fifty pages long, but that was as much as I was prepared to release to the press.

The press always seem to have the attitude that the investigation team owes them a profile. But this is a misconception. The profile belongs to the investigating officer, as it is their aid. It is an instrument by which they can eliminate suspects and concentrate on those who fit the profile. To release an accurate profile and too many details about a person one is close to apprehending could always provoke him to run.

I returned to Pretoria once again and accompanied Elmarie to Brixton. She was making great progress on the Wemmer Pan profile. Philip drove up to Pretoria that Thursday, bringing the forensic evidence. I met him at the SAPS dog school. They had found the nineteenth body and three condoms on the scene. He told me to be ready to fly to Durban by the next Wednesday for the arrest. It is difficult to contain one's excitement at a time like that. Only Elmarie, General Suiker, the investigation team and I knew we were going to make an arrest. I couldn't wait. How the attitude of the detectives had changed towards me by then. Finally I had been accepted into the brotherhood.

On Monday Philip phoned me from Durban. They had found the wrong Twala. I asked him if he still wanted us to come down. He confirmed that they were still looking for the right man and he was sure they would find him by Wednesday. This was a gamble I was prepared to take.

Elmarie and I arrived in Durban at 9 a.m. on Wednesday 11 August 1997. We went straight to the Durban Murder and Robbery Unit and waited. At 11 a.m., Inspector Bushy Rambhadursingh reported that they had located the house of the right Twala.

Our excitement soared. Suddenly everyone jumped into gear. Philip applied for a search warrant and a warrant of arrest. The Internal Stability Unit had been assigned to assist us. They would be the uniformed men with the guns ready to protect us, as the house was in KwaMashu, a township where violence was rife. Philip also phoned the forensic specialists in Pretoria, who had a car ready and packed on standby, and they left immediately, driving through the night.

Elmarie and I were issued with bulletproof vests. Elmarie was also issued with a semi-automatic rifle. I declined, settling for my own 9mm. At 9 p.m.

we checked into the hotel. We got some strange looks from the other patrons but were too tired to care. We had to carry two heavy bulletproof vests and a semi-automatic rifle, as well as each of our suitcases and briefcases, up two flights of stairs.

At 2.30 a.m. we all met outside the CR Swart Headquarters in Durban. Philip briefed everyone and then we set off for KwaMashu. While we congregated at a certain spot, Philip, Bushy and one or two other detectives went ahead to the house. We waited for about fifteen minutes. The adrenalin was pumping. It was agony. We didn't even know whether the suspect would be at home. But we were so close. Then the call came. He had been arrested and we could move in.

We drove closer but still had to get out and walk to the house, which was situated on a hill. There are no formal roads, streets or numbers in a squatter camp. The shacks are built close together and in a disorganised way, and tend to be made from corrugated iron and mud. A bullet could travel through several houses and no one would know where it came from. I remembered the lesson I had learnt from Barry during the Station Strangler investigation.

My heart pounded against the heavy bulletproof vest, and the forty-five cigarettes I had been smoking per day at the time didn't help me very much when I climbed that hill. It was still pitch-dark. Again, as on that night in Mitchells Plain, only the dogs were awake.

We arrived at the hut. In the torchlight I could see a man sitting outside. He was handcuffed. I moved into the hut. Philip and Allan were silently hugging each other and then turned to include me. There were no words to describe what we felt. It was a sentimental moment between the three of us. At times like those I feel that colleagues can be closer to each other than families could ever be.

I focused on my surroundings. It was a three-roomed house built of mud and wattle. The killer lived in the first room. My eyes immediately searched for collateral evidence. There were two women's watches lying on the floor next to his mattress, and the room was filled from floor to roof with items of female clothing, as well as a few umbrellas and some ligatures lying around. It seemed like Aladdin's cave to me. Philip ordered the suspect to come inside, and he sat on a tiny bench. He looked up at me and I saw the candlelight reflected in his eyes. They were wild, animal-like, fearful and accusing. They penetrated my soul. 'I know you,' I thought, 'and you know me too.'

Philip had sent Agmatir's family down to the vehicles. He asked Elmarie and me to take them back to the office and start interviewing them while they finished the house search and took Agmatir to the district surgeon. Detectives always take a suspect to the district surgeon for a physical check-up to prove that he was not assaulted during the arrest.

We arrived at the office at about 4.30 a.m. I interviewed the suspect's mother with the help of an interpreter, and one of the team members, Inspector Lloyd Arjunan, took notes for me. Elmarie interviewed the sister with the help of Inspector Shane Suklal and Sergeant James Mbikwana. Then I interviewed Agmatir's brother-in-law with the assistance of Sergeant Mike Goge. We secured important background information on the suspect.

I changed into a suit, actually dressing up to meet the serial killer. Philip had returned in the meantime and had also changed into a suit. We wanted to convey a message of professionalism and seriousness. Since he had been caught and released before, we wanted him to know that this time it was the end of the road for him.

Elmarie and I met Philip in the operations room and filled him in on Agmatir's background. Philip then told me the suspect was all mine and that he wanted an acknowledgement of guilt within fifteen minutes. I was caught off guard. I knew I had to interview him, but since that morning things had been so hectic that I'd had no time to prepare myself mentally. I stalled for a few minutes by asking someone to buy me some cigarettes. He returned too soon.

I entered the interrogation room. Agmatir and the interpreter, Captain Kwyema, were waiting for me. Philip warned the suspect of his rights again, introduced me as a psychologist and left. I had been waiting for this face-to-face meeting for such a long time. I offered him a cigarette, which he took, and then lit one for myself. We sat there smoking silently, just looking at each other. I then did a quick mini mental test on him to ascertain his mental state. He was quite well orientated.

I told him that I was a doctor of the mind and that I knew his mind and his heart like my own. I asked him if he believed me, and he nodded. Then I said that I was going to tell him a story. I recounted his sexual fantasy in precise detail, using the third person singular. He listened silently. When I had finished, I asked him if I knew his heart. He looked into my eyes and nodded. I asked him if he recognised the man in the story. He answered: 'It is me. I am the man. I killed the women in the cane fields.' He also said that there were one or two points in the story with which he did not agree.

I realised that he had just made an acknowledgement of guilt and was about to incriminate himself. I stopped him and asked him if he would be willing to tell his story to Superintendent Veldhuizen. He agreed. I left the interrogation room and entered the operations room next door. Everyone was watching me, but no one spoke. I looked for Philip but he wasn't there. Allan couldn't tolerate the suspense any longer and asked me what had happened. I so badly wanted to tell him, but I had an obligation towards Philip, so I just winked at Allan and left the room. I found Philip in one of the other offices. I told him what had happened. He seemed pleased. We then returned to the operations room and I could finally tell the others. They were elated.

I realised then that I had spent three-quarters of an hour in the interrogation room, during which time I had smoked fifteen cigarettes. Philip, Elmarie and I returned to the interrogation room. Philip warned the suspect again of his rights and asked him if he wanted to tell him something. He began by telling his story.

Philip then handed Agmatir a piece of the pink string we would use to tie up official documents. Agmatir commanded the interpreter to turn around and proceeded to tie up his hands. He then tied his feet, and the interpreter's eyes grew large as Agmatir slipped the string around his neck. He turned the interpreter around to show us how he had done it, seeming very proud. I just sat on a chair and watched. We untied our detective quickly. When he explained how he had made the gags he'd put in the victims' mouths, both Philip and the interpreter showed genuine interest. Agmatir's attitude changed. He was now the expert, commanding the undivided attention of two experienced detectives. He became quite scientific and enjoyed his moment of glory.

After the interrogation, Agmatir was sent with an independent officer to point out the scenes, and we went to The Red Dog to celebrate. The drink flowed and we were all euphoric. In truth, there are no words to describe the feeling. Elated, exhilarated, excited, exultant – none do justice to that feeling. Then I phoned my boyfriend. He had shared the sadness caused by the killers, and now I wanted him to be part of the joy of catching him. Although he was six hundred kilometres away, he felt very close at that moment, and he understood my joy just as he had understood my horror some weeks before.

There was a mechanical rodeo bull in the club. While the others were watching the news on TV, I sat on the bull. I was quite alone. I prayed and thanked God for helping us to catch the killer. I prayed for the souls of the victims, their families, and for the killer and his family. I thanked God for my life and my job and my colleagues and for keeping my mind reasonably sane through all of this.

Elmarie and I left the party early. A few of us – including Philip, Allan and Bushy – had realised that night that the team would be breaking up the next day. We didn't want to spoil the younger ones' fun, but we were getting quite melancholic. I was certainly in no mood for drunken sorrow and decided to leave. I needed time out.

I returned to the hotel and went straight to bed, but I couldn't sleep.

During my interview with Agmatir, he'd told me that he had killed the women because they reminded him of his girlfriend who had aborted his baby. He said it had almost killed him and had certainly broken his heart.

While he spoke, I could feel myself sinking into the abyss. I would feel sorry for anyone who had lost a baby, but there was turmoil in my heart. I could not deny my emotions, for they were very real and overwhelmed me, but on the other hand, I felt my logic rebelling fiercely against my feelings. Abandoning all reason, I decided to dive into the abyss, come hell or high water, and without any mental oxygen bottles to keep me alive. I felt myself sinking into the killer's eyes and through to his soul. It was a cold and bitterly lonely place. There was no wind or sunlight there – only intense pain. I felt it, all of it. Then, slowly, I resurfaced, and I could feel myself breaking through the barriers, drifting up once again, seeing the sunlight and breathing the clean, pure air. It must have been during that time that I smoked all those cigarettes.

I reflected on this experience while lying in my hotel bed. I felt strong but exhausted. I buried the experience inside my soul. I knew it would return to haunt me later, but I also knew I had learnt from it. I had survived.

On the Friday we continued with the interrogation process. Agmatir had pointed out one of the crime scenes correctly. By 3.30 p.m. he had been sent to a magistrate for a confession. Unfortunately, the courts closed at 4 p.m.

and it was somehow conveyed to him that he had to have an attorney present. He didn't want a lawyer, however, and therefore returned without making the confession. Philip was disappointed. By this time, Director Bala Naidoo had confirmed the arrest to the press. A funny thing about the press is that they phone you when you are busy, but they don't phone when they should. Neither Philip nor I got any calls from them.

On Saturday morning we brought Agmatir in again. Philip asked him again if he wanted an attorney. He said he would only talk to us if he didn't have to sign any official documents. I asked him if he was prepared for another psychological interview, and he agreed. This time, he told us that he had watched while we were retrieving body number eleven. He went back the next day to see what we had done and saw that we had removed the body. I asked him why he had left the bodies concentrated in one area. He replied that he'd wanted the police to find them all at once so that the families of the victims could be notified. He said he wanted to stop killing, but that he could not resist it.

Elmarie and I flew back to Pretoria that Saturday afternoon and the suspect appeared in court on the following Monday. He was not granted bail.

Back at the office, we concentrated on the Wemmer Pan case again. Elmarie was pouring her heart and soul into that profile. She would ask my advice now and again but didn't want me to read it yet. She wanted to present me with the final product, and I was happy to let her. Meanwhile, I concentrated on other cases. There were three other cases that could involve serial killers. I asked the detectives I had trained in the relevant areas to monitor the situation and to keep me updated.

I phoned Robert Ressler and gave him the news about Twala. He pronounced it a world record. It had taken us six weeks from identifying an operative serial killer to arresting him. The profile was 99 per cent correct. The only mistake I had made was with Agmatir's level of education: he had only primary education and not secondary. Ressler was very complimentary and his usual friendly self. It felt good to report a success to him. He had taught me well, and it was good to know that I had surpassed my mentor.

Two weeks after Agmatir's arrest, I measured my own stress level. I was shocked at the result. I was dangerously close to a heart attack. The experience I'd had when I interviewed Agmatir started to haunt me. During the numberless hours before daybreak, I would wake from nightmares. I was physically exhausted. Allowing a serial killer to enter your mind and allowing his perverted sexual fantasies to cloud your own psyche causes mental damage that can become permanent.

I was seeing less of my boyfriend, mainly because of work commitments on both sides, and there was no one else I could talk to. I became moody at the office and withdrew into myself. I increased my vegetable intake, drastically cut down on liquor and went to bed early, only to wake from the nightmares. I bought myself expensive new bed linen, thinking it would chase the dragons away, but it didn't. Maybe I'd just wanted new linen. I couldn't give up smoking entirely, but managed to cut down to twenty cigarettes a day.

Sergeant Nkomozulu, who had interviewed Mandla in prison in 1995, did not recognise the photo of Agmatir as the same man.

Over the next few weeks, my work continued at a steady pace. Elmarie had almost perfected the Wemmer Pan profile, but every time she considered it done, a new docket would be added to the group and she would have to readjust everything. Her frustration and patience levels rose and fell accordingly. Luckily, I knew what she was going through. The SAPS did issue her with a brand-new car, though, which caused a brief smile for a day or two.

The Wemmer Pan killer had been attacking couples who were making out at the Wemmer Pan dam in Johannesburg. It seemed that the recreational spot – with its dam, trees and mine dump – was the ideal place for couples to meet after work for a quickie before they went home. Some of them were married and conducted their illicit affairs there. The killer would approach the couples and confront them. His usual method was to shoot the man, rape the woman and then shoot her too. Sometimes he let the woman go, and some of the men escaped too. He would also rob his victims of clothing, watches and cash. The first incident occurred in April 1996, and by September 1997 he had twenty-six victims on his scoreboard. He did not discriminate between races, with black, white, Asian and coloured people among his victims.

One night he moved from the Wemmer Pan area into town. Catherine Lekwene and her boyfriend Samuel Moleme were walking along a road when he shot at both of them, killing Samuel and wounding Catherine in the knee.

He then dragged her into the veld and raped her. That same night, a few kilometres away, he shot and killed Sarah Lenkpane and her boyfriend while they were making love. Then, in the early hours of the following morning, he met a young couple on their way home: fifteen-year-old Lelanie van Wyk and her nineteen-year-old boyfriend, Martin Stander. He shot them both.

It was during this time that the Psychological Society of South Africa held its annual congress in Durban. I was invited to participate in a panel discussion. The keynote speaker was Dr David Canter, a professor at the University of Liverpool in the United Kingdom. He had worked on the Railway Ripper case, among others. I was eager to meet him and to discuss a research programme he had embarked on with Dr Mark Wellman, my contact at Rhodes University. The deputy minister of safety and security, Mr Joe Matthews, and the deputy national police commissioner, Mr Morgan Chetty, had also been invited to the conference. Commissioner Chetty had asked me to contribute to his speech, which I did.

On the morning of 9 September 1997, before I flew to Durban, Elmarie and I went to Brixton. Later that afternoon my boyfriend arrived. Things hadn't been going well between us recently, and for a while we had lost touch. We went to a coffee shop and had a heart-to-heart talk. I should have realised by that stage that something was very wrong with me, for I looked at him and felt dead inside. There was no emotion in me. No joy, no anger, nor any bitterness. I thought I was just tired.

I realised I was going to be late for my flight when Elmarie frantically called me on my cellphone. My boyfriend rushed me back to Brixton and phoned the airport to confirm my booking. He hugged me, gave me a kiss and told me to look after myself. I realised then that no one else would do so. Elmarie would usually drive when we shared a car, but we had just half an hour to get to the airport and Johannesburg peak-hour traffic was awaiting us. So, she asked me to drive. I made it to the airport on time and handed my gun and keys to Elmarie. To say that the traffic was accommodating would be a nice way of explaining my driving that day.

Philip met me at Durban airport. I had an urgent need just to get to my hotel and sleep, putting the disturbing events of the afternoon out of my mind, but things don't happen that way in the SAPS. Philip told me my every wish would be his command, which was funny because he completely outranked me, but he also mentioned that members of the Durban Murder and Robbery Unit and the previous commander, Colonel Vlaggies Roux, as well as Bushy and Allan, were at the office. It was pouring with rain and only 7 p.m.

I have always had a soft spot for Colonel Vlaggies, who had since retired. I never forgot his support during the River Strangler investigation in 1995. I was very fond of the other detectives as well. They were all my friends. I told Philip we could go for a quick drink but that I wanted to be at my hotel by 9 p.m. He delivered me to the door of my hotel at midnight. In hindsight, I think it was a good idea not to have gone to bed earlier, because I wouldn't have been able to sleep. That night, no nightmares visited me.

The following morning I put on one of my best outfits and dressed up my hair. The face staring back at me in the mirror was old. There was no life in my eyes, no sparkle of emotion, just death. Philip fetched me and took me to the conference centre for the Psychological Society congress. I had a quick interview with a journalist and then took my place on the stage. I was seated last. The chairman, Dr Saths Cooper, introduced the guest speakers. Dr Canter spoke, followed by the deputy minister, Mr Matthews; the deputy national commissioner, Mr Chetty; and then another psychologist.

There were about four hundred people in the audience. I kept my eye on Philip most of the time, feeling secure in the knowledge that there was an able detective and a valued friend close to me. He made funny faces at me most of the time. I was exhausted, but I knew I was just a member of a panel and only had to answer some questions from the audience.

Then I heard Dr Cooper telling the audience that he had saved the cherry on top, the person that everyone was waiting for, for last, and introduced me as a speaker. For a few seconds I was stunned. Everything I would have wanted to say about my work I had written into the deputy commissioner's speech. There were four hundred people waiting for me to say something. I managed to reach the podium and apologised for the fact that I was unprepared. Then I just told them about my work. I remember mentioning that I was a bad example of a psychologist because I didn't manage my own stress levels very well. I paid tribute to the detectives' hard work and dedication, and then somehow it was all over. The audience applauded and the deputy commissioner shook my hand.

I managed two more press interviews and then Philip took Dr Canter, Mark Wellman and me to a restaurant for lunch. I knew this meeting with

Dr Canter was important, but I could not concentrate on a word he said. At one stage he smiled sympathetically at me and said I needed a sabbatical. He invited me to come to England. I smiled and thanked him. The lunch went on for an hour and a half, and I can remember nothing except Canter's kindness.

Mark dropped Canter off at the conference centre, and then Philip took Mark and me to the airport. My flight was due to leave at 6 p.m. They had a drink, but I stuck to Coke as I had another splitting headache. Mark assured me that he was on top of the negotiations with Canter and told me to take a break. His flight left first, but Philip waited patiently with me. I felt bad because I knew he had a family to go home to. He promised me he would take the next week off, as the Phoenix case had also taken its toll on him.

My flight was delayed for two hours. I sat at the airport hardly registering a word Philip said, although I knew that he was trying his best to cheer me up. When I boarded the plane, I recognised a woman who had attended the conference. She kept staring at me, so I guess I was not a very pretty sight.

Someone placed a pillow behind my head and I slept until we landed. Elmarie, as supportive as ever, was waiting for me. When she dropped me at home, I told her to keep the car and not to pick me up the following day, which was a Thursday. I spent that day cleaning my house, since my charlady had not turned up, and then I went back to bed.

On Friday I went to work, and then I went to see a doctor. The doctor told me that stress had brought on an attack by a brain virus and that I was burnt out. She prescribed a week's rest. I went to General Britz and explained my situation to him. He was very understanding and ordered me to take the week off. I refused to go to a clinic. I decided that I would rather rest in my own home where I felt safe and secure.

It is difficult to explain this kind of stress. I did not blame my work for it, nor the developments in what was left of my private life. I still loved my work and couldn't wait to return to it, but unfortunately all romantic inclinations would have to be sacrificed. This was a sad state of affairs for a childless, divorced woman of thirty-six. The tears that I cried were for opportunities missed, not only by me, but also by those who professed to care for me.

Fate seemed to have dealt me a hand of cards from which I could not escape. My dreams of living a normal life, of being a wife, faded into a mist of pleasant memories, which I will always cherish. Maybe the dreams would return one day. I knew that at that time my life was the SAPS, and I appreci-ated the friendship of the detectives.

I thought a lot about Mitchells Plain during that week. I wished that I could have spent the week there. I knew I would have been accepted anony-mously as a changeling and that no pretences, title or rank would influence the residents' attitude towards me. I considered the possibility of just board-ing a plane and fleeing, but I knew then more than ever before that if I escaped to Mitchells Plain, I would never return. I was physically tired and mentally exhausted, my brain was burning, but I was not beaten yet. I refused to take the prescribed sleeping pills, which would not chase the nightmares away in any case.

That Saturday, I felt a little better and called my boyfriend. I explained I was home and asked if he wanted to see a movie. He said he was busy that afternoon. I asked him if he was working. He answered that he was getting married. Apparently I was never available, so he had reconciled with his previous girlfriend. I wished him good luck, terminated the call, smashed my glass of wine against the wall, and crumpled down and cried my heart out.

Word had spread that I was ill, although General Britz had told everyone that I had the flu. My cellphone rang at all hours and the detectives expressed their concern for me. I thought it ironic that so many men expressed their concern in genuine friendship, but that the man who had professed his love for me had abandoned me.

It was time for me to get back to work.

Sipho Agmatir Twala was charged with seventeen counts of rape, sixteen counts of murder and one count of attempted murder. I testified at his trial. On 31 March 1999 he was sentenced to an effective 506 years in prison.

Years later, Philip, Allan and Bushy had all retired from the SAPS. Philip started working as a tour guide, travelling across Africa, and then became a diving instructor on the north coast somewhere in KwaZulu-Natal.

EIGHT

Lenyenye, Pyromaniac, Wemmer Pan/Hammer and Eastern Cape

About, about, in reel and rout
The death-fires danced at night,
The water, like a witch's oils,
Burnt green, and blue and white.
– Samuel Taylor Coleridge, 'The Rime of the Ancient Mariner', 1798

The belief in witchcraft is embedded within many cultures all over the world and it has existed in Africa for centuries, surviving well into the modern era with its accompanying technological advances. In the early 1990s, witches were hunted and burned nightly in rural villages in the Northern Province (later Limpopo province).

Inyangas and sangomas are traditional healers who mainly use plant and animal products to make medicine or potions (called *muti*) for healing physical and psychological ailments. A few of these traditional healers are witch-doctors as well, who use human body parts in their concoctions. In traditional African cultures, some believe that an individual's misfortune or success is brought on by witchcraft. In a case where tragedy has struck an individual, the villagers will call for the help of the sangoma to divine the identity of the so-called witch responsible for the misfortune, or they might hunt down the witch themselves. Witches will be approached at night and are stoned or beaten to death, or else tied up and thrown into their huts, which are then set alight. The last documented execution for witchcraft in England was in 1682, but it remains rife in South Africa.

A person who experiences tremendous success – whether it be an exceptionally good harvest or even a successful modern business venture – may also be suspected of having used witchcraft in the form of muti to secure this success. This person could have consulted a witch-doctor, who would have used human body parts to concoct the muti. The ingredients may be 'harvested' by the witch-doctor, the client, or by someone paid by the witch-doctor. The most commonly used body parts include the eyes, nose, lips and ears, as well as the hands, genitals, intestines and organs such as the heart. It is believed that the younger and more virile the victim, the more potent the medicine will be. Because the body parts have to be removed while the victim is still alive, the victims are often left to bleed to death in a place where their bodies are likely to be discovered. This way, the client is assured that the victim is dead, as survivors may seek revenge or try to retrieve their body parts.

A person who works for a witch-doctor, or a witch-doctor himself, who kills people with the sole purpose of harvesting ingredients for muti, cannot be regarded as a serial killer. The person who works for the witch-doctor is being paid for the killings, so it may be more fitting to compare them to an assassin. The witch-doctor might also sell muti for financial gain. Neither the witch-doctor nor his hired help would have a deep, subconscious, psychological reason for killing – not like a true serial killer.

Although a serial killer's primary motive is one of psychological gain, there have been some who have procured a minor financial gain as a secondary bonus from the killings. Sometimes, the killer's true motive can only be established once he has been apprehended.

In the early 1990s, before I joined the South African Police Service, a serial killer named Moses Mokgethi murdered six children in the township of Mohlakeng near Randburg in Gauteng. He pulled out their teeth with pliers and also removed their hearts, livers and genitals. Mokgethi might well have been classified as a muti killer who worked for a witch-doctor – he was paid three hundred rand for each body part. His seventh victim, a five-year-old girl, managed to escape.

In 1993 Mokgethi kidnapped three toddlers, including the little girl who escaped, and took them into the bush, where he extracted their teeth with pliers. He then raped the little girl twice in front of the other two. She managed to run away while he was strangling the others and alerted the villagers, who returned to the scene to find the mutilated corpses of the other two children.

The children were discovered in the same area in which the bodies of two other children had been found in 1992, as well as two more before them in 1991. The fact that Mokgethi was sexually aroused by the torture and murder of his victims qualified him as a serial killer who obtained a secondary financial gain from his murders.

Shortly after I returned to work after my week's rest in September 1997, I ventured into the heart of witchcraft country.

'Mpumalanga' means 'place where the sun rises' and it was the new name given to the old Eastern Transvaal region. The province is as beautiful as its name. Captain Thinus Rossouw of the Nelspruit Murder and Robbery Unit in Mpumalanga had informed me of the possibility of a serial killer in the province, as well as the possibility of another in the neighbouring Northern Province. I had finally recovered from my exhaustion, my nightmares and my broken heart, and I felt that both Elmarie and I could do with a break from the city, so I invited her to join me on the Mpumalanga trip.

Sergeant John Engelbrecht of the Nelspruit Murder and Robbery Unit had once investigated the murder of a farmhand. The elderly lady who the farm belonged to didn't want to stay there alone after the murder. So she appointed John as custodian to keep an eye on her property while she moved to town. It was to this luscious, evergreen farm that Elmarie and I were escorted after we arrived at the Nelspruit Murder and Robbery Unit on 15 September. The farm was situated between Graskop and Bosbokrand in the middle of the gumtree plantations, about a two-hour drive from Nelspruit.

When we arrived at the farmhouse, I could hear a fire already crackling in the hearth in the lounge, but the first thing that caught my eye was the huge, old coal stove in the kitchen. The coal stove had to be heated up before one could have hot water for a bath. Elmarie had grown up on a farm, but to me this was a novel experience. John was going to stay over with us, and the R5 semi-automatic machine gun he took out of the boot of the car reminded us that violence can disturb even the most idyllic of settings at any time.

Elmarie and I lay down on the carpet in front of the hearth and indulged in the books that the owner of the house had left behind. John made himself comfortable in one of the easy chairs and read a book about birds.

Early the next morning, we woke up to the sound of rain pelting against the windowpanes. It is usually very hot in this province, so the cold weather that came with the rain was unusual for mid-September. The grounds resembled a misty fairy garden. The trees were huge, old and covered in ivy, and the soft leaves of the ferns glistened invitingly in the rain. It reminded me of that secret garden I had treasured as a child. Fish ponds were scattered across the lawn, one of which had a Madonna statue placed next to it. Cute vervet monkeys played tag in the trees and heckled us as we got into our car to go to work.

Africa is not only dust, thorn trees and red sunsets. It is also green and jungle-like, and I love all of it.

Thinus joined us in Graskop. On our way to the scene where several human skeletons had been found in a plantation, we passed many of the scenic spots that make Mpumalanga one of South Africa's top tourist attractions. One of them is God's Window – a magnificent view of the Blyde River Canyon, which was formed millions of years ago. The Pinnacle, a solitary thirty-metre-high quartzite rock sticking out of the escarpment like a thumb, is also in this canyon. There are also several cascading waterfalls in the area. It seemed to me that God was in a benign mood when creating this part of Mpumalanga.

Because of the rain and the mist, we weren't able to see much of the scenery. Then, upon arrival, we couldn't get to the spot where the bodies had been found because of the muddy condition of the plantation roads.

The Forensic Unit had already removed the skeletons to try to establish whether the cause of death was natural or due to violence, and whether all of them had died at the same time. If they had all been massacred at once, this would point to political or tribal violence as opposed to the work of a serial killer. The Forensic Unit had to establish the sex and age of each victim and also had to try to determine whether any body parts had been removed, to see if they were killed for muti purposes. This would be impossible regarding internal organs, but might be possible regarding limbs. The victims could also have been illegal immigrants killed by xenophobic locals, or they could have been victims of a witch hunt. Since only skeletal remains were found, we lacked the forensic evidence to determine whether or not a serial killer was responsible.

When we returned to the farm that evening, Thinus decided that he would also stay over. I was still very much intrigued by the old coal stove, so we stopped at a roadside café on our way home to buy some flour. I decided I would treat the others to crumpets that night. Elmarie also bought a bag of marshmallows. She made us a chicken *bredie* for supper – a mixture of chicken, vegetables and spices – and while the others were relaxing in front of the fire in the lounge, I made a batch of crumpets. This process took much longer than I'd anticipated, but eventually I served everyone the small pancakes.

Elmarie, Thinus and I played cards while John read his book, and we toasted the marshmallows over the flames in the hearth. The rain sifted down outside, enveloping the mysterious garden in a soft blanket of grey and green. I could hear the fire crackling beside me and the rain falling outside at the same time. An ambience of camaraderie had settled among us – the *esprit de corps*. We knew one another well enough to relax into peaceful cohabitation. This is the kind of familial support one finds among a close group of detectives. I found it as heartwarming as the fire inside the old house and as refreshing as the rain outside in the fairy garden.

The next morning, we set off for a small settlement called Lenyenye in the neighbouring Northern Province. Lenyenye used to be part of the old homeland of Lebowa, which became a self-governing state in 1972. The homeland policy was devised by the National Party regime to segregate white and black races. Black people were divided into groups according to their ethnicity and then allocated areas from which each group had apparently originated. These areas became self-governing states, and four of them even gained independence. One of the main problems with this policy, however, was that it was a decision made *for* people instead of one made *by* the people themselves. These patches of land were reincorporated into greater South Africa after the African National Congress won the election in 1994, but the evidence of the poverty that had scorched the land for decades was still apparent.

Lenyenye had a big brick building several storeys high that housed the general administration of the area, including the local Murder and Robbery Unit. The houses close to this building were made of bricks, and fenced yards lined the streets. As one moved away from the main building, one found township shacks and kraals with mud huts dotting the landscape.

Sergeant Patrick Mogoboya filled us in on the murders in his area.

On the morning of 1 April 1996, seventeen-year-old Elizabeth Masilane and her aunt, thirty-five-year-old Maria Masilane, were walking on a footpath in the veld. The path was just a few metres from the main road, but the grass was quite high on the day the murder occurred, shielding the pedestrians from the view of passing traffic. Their bodies were discovered side by side later that day by two schoolboys. Maria died of a fractured skull and Elizabeth's neck had been broken. Both women had been raped.

Two days later, on the evening of 3 April and not too far from the first scene, fifteen-year-old Drose Masia was walking towards the local shop at about 7 p.m. She took a shortcut through the veld but never completed her journey. Her battered body was discovered the next day. She too had been raped and her neck had been broken.

A year later, on 17 March 1997, eighty-two-year-old Nkakareng Rammalo was chopping firewood. Her fully clothed body was found in the veld. She had been raped and her neck broken. Five months later, on 6 August, sixty-seven-year-old Mmangwako Mathole was also chopping wood in the veld. When she did not return later that day, her concerned family asked the local chief to organise a search party. Her fully clothed body was discovered in the veld. She too had been raped and her neck had been broken.

It was clear to me that the suspect had changed from attacking young women to attacking defenceless elderly women. Where he had taken a risk in the first three murders by killing the victims in more accessible areas, he had since become more careful by attacking older women alone in the veld. It is always a tragedy when a woman is raped and killed, but I am always affected most by children, who still had their lives yet to live, and the elderly, who should be granted dignity and respect.

The local community had already arrested several suspects on their own accord and, in a vigilante outburst, had severely assaulted some of them before handing them over to the detectives. None of them were the serial killer, however. Sometimes suspects are pointed out by a sangoma's divination. These men are then brutally attacked and taken to the police, only to be found totally innocent of the crimes of which the community has accused them.

In a preliminary discussion on the profile, I described the killer as a local man who had grown up in the area, but who might often be away working as a migrant labourer. The murders were committed during periods when he returned home to visit his family. He would be young – in his early twenties – and sexually inexperienced. He would not have a vehicle, mainly because he couldn't afford one, and was used to walking long distances. I predicted that he would have low impulse control, indicating a frustrated and volatile personality.

144

He did not have a sophisticated fantasy like the Phoenix killer. He used a blitz attack to overpower his victims, and it was likely that he broke their necks before he raped them in order to eliminate any resistance. He would have grown up in a poor family and was probably physically abused as a child, which would have caused a need for power and revenge towards adult women.

The killer did not strike again, however, and after my trip to beautiful Mpumalanga, my mind became occupied by many others. I did not enter the abyss with this one, although I believed he would strike again if he had not died in the meantime.

Soon after my return from Mpumalanga, another killer moved in to occupy my time and mind. This one derived perverse pleasure from setting the bodies of his victims alight.

Humans have always been fascinated by fire, an element rich in diverse symbolism, representing warmth and passion at one end and hell and destruction at the other. A subcategory of pyromaniacs are pyrophiliacs, who are sexually aroused by fire. It is a very rare sexual disorder, also called a paraphilia, and pyrophiliac serial killers are so rare that I found it hard to believe that two separate men could both be pyrophiliacs and both be committing the same kind of murders at the same time. Again, this totally discredits the theory that after a serial killer has been arrested, no similar murders would be committed in the same area.

Captain Mike van Aardt of the Jeppe Detective Branch in Johannesburg had been a cop for several years. Mike reminded me of the typical 'experienced detective' one would typecast for an American movie. He was solid, intelligent and meticulous – one of those men who just refuses to give up. Mike was confronted by a difficult problem: two of the many murder dockets he had on his hands corresponded with each other, but he also had the sense and experience to realise that something was amiss. He phoned me and made an appointment to see me on 25 September 1997.

Mike brought the two dockets with him. The first murder occurred on 30 August 1997, when the charred body of thirty-five-year-old William Crichton, an assistant in a local hardware shop, was found in a park in Bertrams, Johannesburg, a low-income, racially mixed suburb. A burnt-out mattress was found lying on top of William's body.

Just four days later, on 3 September 1997, the charred body of sixty-nine-year-old Clarence Pretorius was discovered in his room in an old-age home across the same park. Clarence's bed and mattress had been set alight. His room had a door leading to the outside of the building.

Corresponding factors in these two cases were that both victims were of the same race and gender, both cases included indications of sexual interference and both victims had been burnt. A brick was also found on both crime scenes. One victim had been strangled and the other's throat was slit. Both murders occurred in the early morning hours before sunrise, and, in both cases, a mattress had been set alight. The mattress found on top of William in the park had come from a nearby rubbish dump.

I classified the crime as the work of a serial killer – disorganised and visionary-lust motivated. The murders had been spontaneously committed in one area, and although the victims corresponded regarding their race and sex, they just happened to be at the wrong place at the wrong time. Both victims were vulnerable: William because he was drunk and Clarence because he was old.

William had been on his way home after drinking at a bar and had taken a shortcut through the park when the killer spotted him. Clarence, on the other hand, had had the habit of waking up early in the morning and walking outside in the garden to smoke a cigarette.

The murders were more deed-focused than process-focused. The actual murder of the victim and setting him alight was much more important to the killer than any meticulous planning or attempt to conceal the bodies. The fact that both victims were found with their pants pulled down and their underpants removed indicated a sexual motive as well. The killer could have sodomised the men, although the autopsies couldn't confirm this. It was more likely that he stood and masturbated while watching the fire burn the victim.

I profiled the killer as a male between the ages of twenty-five and thirty-five, but probably twenty-seven years old. Research has indicated that arsonists are usually between the ages of fifteen and twenty, but when the arson is directed against another human, they are usually older than twenty-five. I predicted that the killer would live in the vicinity of both murder scenes and that he wouldn't own a car. He would probably live with a parent who had little control over his comings and goings.

These characteristics are generally found with disorganised serial killers.

These killers are mentally unstable, although not necessarily mentally ill, and therefore can't hold down a job. As they have no source of income, they are unable to afford transport or their own accommodation. They can't really afford entertainment either, and will rather buy a bottle of alcohol to drink alone in a park than visit a pub.

This killer would be single and would likely have homosexual tendencies. He would be unemployed and might receive a disability grant. His previous employment record would be erratic and would include skilled or unskilled labour. He had probably spent time in prison for theft, arson, indecent assault or sodomy (which was a crime under South African law until 1998). Clearly he was criminally sophisticated, having left virtually no evidence on the crime scenes. Apart from sexual arousal, fire also has the functional role of destroying evidence. The killer would have nocturnal habits, probably sleeping through most of the day. He would have unhealthy eating habits and would be negligent regarding his personal hygiene.

His family would describe him as temperamental with unpredictable violent outbursts, a loner with low self-esteem and very secretive. His aggression would often be self-directed and he would have attempted suicide. He would take no responsibility for his own actions and would regard himself as a misfit who should never have been born. Arsonists, and especially pyromaniacs, have these kinds of personality traits. They are also cowards and do not select victims who could pose any threat to them.

The killer would not have the interpersonal skills to initiate or maintain any long-term intimate relationships. He would have no money to pay for the favours of homosexual prostitutes, so he would either hustle his own body to earn money or he would overcome his victims in a blitz attack and force sex on them. He would definitely be sexually aroused by fire.

During his childhood, this killer would have grown up in a family atmosphere where the mother figure played a dominant role, which she cleverly masked with submissiveness. The father would have been emotionally absent and probably an alcoholic or a criminal. The mother would be overly possessive of her son and would castrate him mentally. She would treat him like a boy although he was already an adult male. The killer would have suffered from enuresis and would probably still be wetting his bed as an adult.

Psychoanalysis regards bed-wetting and fire-setting as well as cruelty to animals as a child's revenge and mental self-defence mechanism against parental abuse, be it physical, sexual or emotional. The killer was probably sent to an institution as a young boy, where he would have been sexually molested or sodomised. He would often have played truant and run away from school as well as from home. To compensate for his fragile ego, he would fantasise about power, fixating on the power of fire, since it is so totally destructive.

I warned Mike that the killer would strike again very soon since he was on a roll.

At the end of September, a similar murder was committed in Pretoria West. The body of fifty-year-old Alex Landsburg was discovered in his burnt-out apartment. As with the other victims, Alex was naked and there were indications of sexual interference. There were multiple knife wounds on his body. Clothing had been thrown over him and set alight, and his bed had also been set on fire. The detective investigating this case, Inspector Claasen, pressed the redial button on Alex's telephone and reached a woman in Kimberley, who told him that her son had phoned her and admitted to killing a man.

The woman's son was identified as twenty-six-year-old Jan Adriaan van der Westhuizen. The mother informed the detectives that her son had never known his biological father. He had been sent to reformatories as a child and had left school in Grade 11. He had run away thirty-five times and had complained of being sexually assaulted in the reformatories. He was unemployed and had been arrested for car theft and sentenced to a term in prison. His mother also told the detectives that he had a fetish for fire. He had poured petrol over himself while he was in prison, setting his left hand and his head on fire. He had then escaped from the hospital, and was on the run from the police at the time the murder was committed. He had indicated to his mother that he was on his way to Durban.

Mike and I alerted Philip Veldhuizen of the Durban Murder and Robbery Unit, and Jan was arrested in Durban on 21 October 1997. Mike brought him to me the following day.

During the interrogation, Jan admitted to Mike that he had killed Alex. He said that Alex had picked him up in a bar and taken him to his apartment. Alex had tried to have sexual relations with him, which triggered the memory of his sexual abuse as a boy, leading him to snap and kill Alex. Jan denied having anything to do with the two murders in Bertrams, Johannesburg. I found this hard to believe. The crime scene photograph of Alex's charred naked body and burnt bed seemed a carbon copy of Clarence's. The only difference was that one of these scenes was in Johannesburg and the other in Pretoria, but these two cities are only fifty kilometres apart. On the other hand, the scenes of Clarence and William were scarcely three hundred metres apart, the main difference being that one was indoors and the other outdoors.

Jan remained unrelenting in his denial of the first two murders. He agreed that he fitted the psychological profile and acknowledged that the profile had been based on the first two murders. He even admitted that he often hung around Bertrams. He realised that if he was found guilty of the murder of Alex, he would probably receive a life sentence and that admitting to the other two murders wouldn't really make a difference to the amount of time he would spend in jail. But still he denied his involvement.

A month after the interrogation session, on 20 November 1997, Jan escaped from the Pretoria West police station, where he had been kept in custody. A motorist unwittingly picked him up as he was hitchhiking from Pretoria to Johannesburg. Jan told the motorist that he was unemployed, so the motorist gave him his business card and promised to try to find a job for him.

Later that night the motorist had a conversation with his father, who mentioned the escape of a suspected serial killer. The motorist realised the description of the suspect matched that of the hitchhiker and contacted the police. The following Friday, Jan called the motorist and asked if he had managed to organise him a job. The motorist asked him to meet him at a certain garage. When Jan recognised the police waiting for him, he threw his arms up in the air.

Mike brought him to me a second time. There was no change in his attitude. This time he admitted to Mike and me that he was a professional hustler who made money by selling sexual favours to men. He still denied killing William and Clarence.

Mike decided to return to Bertrams to try to obtain more information. The problem with Bertrams was that many of the people who lived there were involved in some kind of criminal activity and were generally unwilling to volunteer any information to the police.

But Mike persisted. A year later, in May 1998, he traced the name of a twenty-seven-year-old male, Norman Hobkirk, who had killed a man with a brick in the same area in 1992. The victim had not been burnt, but he'd been assaulted with a broken glass bottle and his pants had also been pulled down. The suspect had not been in prison when the murders of William and Clarence were committed and was in the habit of walking around Bertrams during the early morning hours before dawn. He lived with his father close to the murder scenes and made his living as a burglar. He was arrested for theft shortly after Clarence's murder and was in prison awaiting trial when Alex was killed. Mike booked Hobkirk out of prison and brought him to me for interrogation. He confessed to the murders of Willam and Clarence. Hobkirk was convicted with a life sentence for each of these murders and another twenty years for the first murder. Jan Adriaan van der Westhuizen was sentenced to thirty years in prison.

I will always find it eerie that two people could both suffer from such a rare sexual disorder as pyrophilia and that they committed carbon-copy murders. There was always a possibility that Van der Westhuizen had read or heard about the two murders in Bertrams, since he moved around in that area, and that the pyromaniac element triggered a fixation in him, urging him to commit a copycat murder.

While I was working on the pyromaniac killer case as well as the profile of the Lenyenye killer, Elmarie was still assisting Captain Piet Byleveld at the Brixton Murder and Robbery Unit with the profile of the Wemmer Pan killer. This killer had not struck since July 1997.

Then, on 4 November, I received a call from one of the very first detectives to complete my courses, Sergeant Derrick Norsworthy of the Port Elizabeth Murder and Robbery Unit. Derrick told me that a serial killer operating in the Eastern Cape had been identified. The suspect was Nicolas Ncama. He had killed his own stepdaughter, among other women. Since none of the detectives working on the case were trained, I requested that Derrick be involved in a supervisory role. I did not want to impose myself on an investigation unless I was requested to do so by the investigation team.

Two weeks later, on 21 November 1997, Jessie Duarte, then minister of safety and security for Gauteng Province, informed me that she had been receiving complaints about a serial killer attacking tailors with a hammer in central Johannesburg. Within a day, the caseload from several detective branches had been transferred to the Brixton Murder and Robbery Unit and poor Piet, who already had the Nasrec and Wemmer Pan cases on his hands, had to sort out the mess. We decided that Elmarie would continue with the Wemmer Pan case while I would draw up the profile of the Hammer Murderer.

The dockets transferred to Piet indicated that fourteen cases had been reported since January 1997 of a man attacking male tailors in their shops with a hammer. Ten of these assaults were committed during and after August 1997. The attacker would enter a tailor shop where a man was work-ing alone. He assaulted the victim with a hammer and then grabbed cash or clothing before leaving the store. Some of the victims died, some survived but were left with brain damage, and some made a full recovery.

I profiled the suspect as a man between the ages of twenty-five and thirty who was able to speak isiZulu and English. He would probably stay in one of the nearby hostels and was well acquainted with the Jeppe area, where the attacks had taken place. Since most of the attacks had happened in the morning before lunch, I predicted that he could be a shift worker who worked nights. He would have committed the murders when he came off duty and before he went home. I predicted that he earned a salary, as although he stole some money, he did not take large amounts, even though the tills often contained significant sums of cash. His salary would not be big, however, and he wouldn't own a vehicle.

I suggested that he could have been in prison before, and he appeared to have a criminal sophistication because of the lack of fingerprints on the crime scenes. I predicted that he had probably once worked for a tailor who had treated him badly.

The killer was bitter and revenge-motivated. He could not control his aggression. He felt that he had been a victim in life, and he had no internal locus of control. He would probably assault his wife and would not tolerate any resistance. The killer was cold-hearted and had absolutely no respect for human life.

Piet had organised a stakeout one Saturday morning, but despite our pleas the local newspapers blasted the story about the Hammer Murderer on their front pages that particular morning, foiling the whole operation. Journalists had interviewed surviving victims and published the locations as well as the exact modus operandi used during the attacks. I was absolutely livid. This meant that a confession – as well as any pointings out of the crime scenes – could be challenged in court since the accused could protest that he had confessed under duress and that he'd pointed out the crime scenes that he'd read about in the newspapers.

This was exactly the kind of irresponsible journalism to which I vehemently object. The journalists and their editors were totally ruthless and had no respect for the lives of the surviving victims. Publishing their names and addresses meant that the killer could have found them and killed them because they could identify him. In addition, the journalists were interfering with and obstructing a police investigation, instead of assisting us and playing a responsible role in community policing. I wished that members of the public would overcome their naivety and start boycotting this kind of journalism. Surviving victims and family members of victims should realise that by discussing the details of a murder with journalists, they are seriously jeopardising the chances that the suspect might be found guilty in court. They can always sell their stories as soon as the case is closed and the killer is behind bars.

In the meantime, Nicolas Ncama had been arrested on 27 November 1997 by detectives in the Eastern Cape, and I was asked to assist in the interrogation. I met the team under the leadership of Superintendent Andrew Middleton and Captain Deon Marais at the Port Elizabeth Murder and Robbery Unit on 1 December. I sensed a slight hostility among them, but they were all polite, and they discussed the cases with me.

Seven weeks earlier, on 13 October, a policeman, Inspector Zanto of KwaDwesi in the Eastern Cape, had discovered the body of his fifteen-year-old daughter, Sonja, in a ground-floor apartment. She had been raped and strangled with an electrical cord. It was established that her stepfather, Nicolas Ncama, was the last to be seen in her company and that he had a key to the apartment. Ncama was immediately identified as a suspect.

Captain Deon Marais then established that Ncama had a cellphone. He traced Ncama's sister-in-law, Nomonde, who informed him that her female lodger, twenty-six-year-old Nompumelelo Mpushe, had been missing for some time. Ncama had stayed with them until he was asked to leave.

Deon traced the murder docket of Nompumelelo to Sergeant Tommy Jafta of the East London Murder and Robbery Unit. Nompumelelo's body had been discovered on 12 September 1997 in the bushes near the Fort Jackson station, wrapped in a plastic bag. The cellphone belonged to her. Ncama's wife, Sonja's mother, then handed a firearm belonging to her husband to Deon. Deon traced the firearm's ownership, establishing that the legal owner was Constable Gloria Ngcizela, a twenty-six-year-old woman whose body had been found on 28 May 1997 at a bus stop in Bityi, about thirty kilometres from Umtata. All the detectives in the different cases were drawn together to form a task team.

Ncama was also suspected of being involved in the murder of Cynthia Ndlaku, the wife of a United Methodist minister in KwaZakhele. She had been raped and murdered on 16 December 1996. Ncama was an understudy of Mr Ndlaku and had worked on the electricity in their house the afternoon before the murder.

After the counselling session, one of the detectives sceptically asked me what use I could be to them. I told him that I'd had some success in the past and that if they would give me a chance, I would see what I could do. We didn't discuss the issue further and went out for supper. Later, when I was alone in my hotel room, I devised a strategy for the interrogation session.

Ncama was very religious and had wanted to become a Methodist minister. I decided to use this. I didn't want to misuse religion in the interrogation, but if Ncama was really so religious, I expected that he would feel extremely guilty about the murders.

By the time I interviewed Ncama, he had already confessed to murdering Sonja and Nompumelelo to Tommy and Deon, but he had not confessed to Gloria's murder.

The following day, Derrick Norsworthy sat in while Ncama was brought in to talk to me. I asked him how he was feeling, and he replied that he felt very lost. I asked him whether he felt so lost that not even God could find him. Ncama immediately opened up to me and related his life story. I didn't even need to introduce the concept of guilt because he did it himself. He felt so bad that he wanted to commit suicide. He felt that the community would never forgive him.

He requested that Derrick be replaced by Deon since he knew Deon better. People normally don't want to divulge secrets in front of strangers. Derrick obligingly excused himself and Deon took his place. Deon had scarcely sat down when Ncama said that he wanted to tell us about Gloria's murder. Deon warned him that he was about to incriminate himself and reminded him of his rights. Ncama waived his rights and told us how he murdered Gloria.

He explained that the main object of his anger was his brother's wife, Nomonde. His brother had been a Methodist minister whom Ncama had adored. The brother had previously been married to a wonderful woman, but he'd had a relationship with Nomonde. When Nomonde fell pregnant, she forced the brother to divorce his wife and marry her. He could not remain a minister under these circumstances, which upset Ncama tremendously.

The brother later died in a car accident. Ncama felt that his brother's wife was responsible for his idol's fall from grace. He said he had wanted to kill her, but he could not kill the mother of his brother's children. He had killed his stepdaughter because his wife had belittled him and threatened to divorce him. Thereafter he moved in with Nomonde until she chased him out. He killed Nompumelelo and Gloria, who were both his girlfriends, because they too had belittled him and reminded him of his brother's wife. He denied killing Mrs Ndlaku, the minister's wife.

After his confession, I warned the detectives that Ncama might attempt suicide in prison. We left the offices and went to the beach to have a celebratory braai. The detectives had given me a chance and I had secured a confession for them. Their hostility evaporated and was replaced by elation.

While the men were making the fire, I walked along the beach and watched the waves. Ncama had crept into my mind within a short space of time. Andrew Middleton gave me a lift to my hotel as soon as the sun had set. I did not feel like partying that night.

I visited Ncama while he was awaiting trial in prison the following year, and he asked me to write a message in his Bible. I wrote 'Keep the faith', for that was all he had left. Here was a man who had converted to Christianity, but who still committed murders because his 'pride as a Xhosa man had been tarnished by a woman', as he put it.

Nicolas Ncama was eventually found guilty on three counts of murder, one rape, one indecent assault and three thefts. He was found not guilty of the murder and rape of Mrs Ndlaku, as there was not sufficient evidence to link him to this crime.

I took a vacation from 16 December 1997 and went to Knysna. I had to exorcise the ghosts of the weekend I had spent there with my then boyfriend that

July. I visited the huge tree hidden deep in the Tsitsikamma Forest and the beach where he told me that he had fallen in love with me. I recovered my heart.

Two days before Christmas, Piet Byleveld phoned to tell me that he had arrested the Wemmer Pan serial killer. I was overjoyed and wished him speed in catching the Hammer Murderer as well.

An astonishing revelation still awaited us.

Acting on information, Piet had waylaid a suspect at a taxi rank. Through his interrogation of the suspect, Cedric Maake, a thirty-four-year-old Pedi man, Piet established that Cedric was not only the feared Wemmer Pan Murderer, but the Hammer Murderer as well. When he had gone quiet in Wemmer Pan after July, he had carried on with the Hammer murders from August to November.

And we'd thought that fate had dealt Piet a heavy blow when he was allocated the Hammer case as well. Piet eventually had over a hundred cases against Maake, including murder, attempted murder, rape, and illegal possession of firearms and ammunition. The victims numbered more than sixty, including men and women of all races. When Piet asked Maake why he had committed the murders, he answered only that he did not like people.

Elmarie was more accurate in her profile on Maake than I was. She also predicted that he would be in his thirties and said that he would be living in La Rochelle, which he was. She said he would be a gardener, while he was actually a plumber, but she was correct in surmising that he had no fixed employment and much free time during the day. Both of us profiled him as an organised, mission-orientated serial killer. The motive for Maake's killings remains open to speculation, however, since he never told anyone why he did it.

Maake's court case ran from April 1999 to March 2000. This court case would effectively take Captain Piet Byleveld – one of the most experienced Murder and Robbery detectives in the country and a man fast becoming a legend in his own lifetime, like Commissioner Suiker Britz – out of the field for a year. Piet was eventually promoted to superintendent late in his life and was acclaimed as the best serial killer investigator in the South African Police Service, having solved five serial killer cases. I made a fuss of this in the press, for he deserved the recognition. Piet Byleveld passed away on

24 May 2017 at the age of sixty-seven, due to cancer. Years later a television series, loosely based on his life, called *Die Byl* ('The Axe') was filmed.

Maake was found guilty of 27 out of 35 counts of murder, 26 out of 28 counts of attempted murder, 41 out of 46 charges of robbery with aggravating circumstances, one count of attempted robbery, 14 out of 15 counts of rape, one count of assault with grievous bodily harm, three counts of illegal possession of a firearm, and one count of illegal possession of ammunition. He was sentenced by Ms Justice Geraldine Borchers on 16 March 2000. The cumulative sentence was 1 835 years and three months in prison. This includes 27 life sentences.

I returned to Pretoria from my vacation on 31 December 1997 and spent New Year's Eve lying on my bed alone, watching the fireworks through my window as usual. Another romance had failed dismally. I recalled New Year's Eve of two years earlier, when I had just moved into my new home. I seemed to have set a pattern of spending this night alone on my bed watching the fireworks. I felt very distant from the revelry of the rest of mankind.

NINE

Stewart Wilken, alias Boetie Boer

The very deep did rot: O Christ!
That ever this should be!
Yea, slimy things did crawl with legs
Upon the slimy sea.
– Samuel Taylor Coleridge, 'The Rime of the Ancient Mariner', 1798

Serial killers are not born serial killers, but develop as a result of deeply ingrained pain and unbearable rejection that took place during a specific psychosexual developmental phase, which causes a fixation in their subconscious. This triggers revenge fantasies as a means of restoring the psychological imbalance, and these fantasies are then realised and acted out on innocent victims.

It is tragic that these killers avenge their misery on people who had absolutely no part in causing their initial suffering, except that they subconsciously remind the serial killer of his first tormentor.

I do not measure a serial killer's notoriety by the number of victims he has killed. I measure it by the intensity of his anger and psychological agony that resounds in me as we meet in the abyss. This should not be interpreted to mean that I do not have profound empathy for the victims and their families, nor that I think serial killers should receive mercy or be released on parole. Which brings me to a case that really punched me in the gut.

On 31 January 1997, Sergeant Derrick Norsworthy of the Port Elizabeth Murder and Robbery Unit arrested a thirty-one-year-old male named Stewart Wilken, alias 'Boetie Boer'. He is perhaps the most notorious of all South African serial killers to date. Although Boetie Boer was one of the worst sadists I have ever met, there was also an innocence in him to which I responded. He was both victim and aggressor.

Boetie Boer was born on 11 November 1966 in Boksburg in the old Transvaal. He was barely six months old when his father abandoned him and his two-year-old sister in a telephone booth, as he no longer wanted to be burdened by his children. Apparently, Boetie's mother did not know what had happened to them. The children were found by a domestic worker who took them home to her male employer. He accepted the children into his home. This was not an act of benevolence, but one of greed. The more children this man had in his house, the more money he could claim from welfare. Boetie's sister disappeared shortly after this, and he didn't know what happened to her.

Boetie spent two years in the house of this man, where he was subjected to severe cruelty. He had to eat out of dog bowls, and the man burnt his genitals with cigarettes. The man committed bestiality with his dogs and Boetie was forced to perform fellatio on him afterwards. He was underfed and infested with vermin. The neighbours, a Mr and Mrs Wilken, took pity on the wretched little boy and adopted him as their own son. They gave him the name Stewart Wilken. He called himself Boetie Boer, meaning Brother Boer. Sometime during his childhood, the Wilken family moved to Port Elizabeth.

As a young boy, Boetie was terrorised by his peers, who teased him about the fact that he was adopted. He assaulted one of his teachers on this account. Boetie was also sodomised by a deacon at the age of six. His adoptive mother related that he would often bite her and other children and that he was a very sickly but aggressive child. She would often punish him by locking him up in a cupboard in his room.

He was sent to a reformatory for wayward children where he was repeatedly sodomised and locked up naked as punishment. He started smoking marijuana at the age of eight. He often ran away from the reformatory, but eventually returned to complete Grade 11. He was discharged from the army after four months after a suicide attempt.

Boetie married his first wife – who already had a daughter – and their own daughter, Wuane, was born on Christmas Day in 1986. A second daughter followed a few years later.

Boetie's first wife related that after the birth of their second daughter, he had only wanted to have anal sex with her and that he would force her into severely uncomfortable positions to have sex. He accused her of prostitution and blamed her for his murderous anger.

They divorced and she was awarded custody of their children. Although

Boetie tried to visit his children, he was often refused visitation rights by his ex-wife, who would phone the police as soon as he set foot near her house. Boetie then got involved with another woman of a different race, claiming that he never wanted to have sex with a white woman again in case she might be his lost sister. His girlfriend became ill and died, and in 1990 Boetie married another woman of a different race, whom he accused of prostitution as well. She already had two sons, and two daughters were born out of her union with Boetie.

Boetie later recounted that he would leave the house after a fight with his wife and walk the streets looking for a prostitute. He hated prostitutes and considered it a sin that they charged money for a gift they had received from their Creator. In his opinion, they did not deserve to live.

On the evening of 2 October 1990, Boetie picked up a sex worker, twenty-five-year-old Virginia Gysman, who charged him fifty rand for sex. She accompanied him to the playground of a nearby primary school, where he had sex with her and then forced her to have anal sex as well. When she complained of the pain, Boetie strangled her with a piece of her clothing. He said he ejaculated while he strangled her. He left her naked body in the playground.

On 10 January 1991, the urge to kill again was uppermost in Boetie's mind. He left home to hunt for a suitable victim, finding thirty-seven-year-old Mercia Papenfus, also a sex worker. She went with him to St George's Park, which is about four kilometres from the hotel where he had picked her up. She demanded that he pay her first. Boetie was enraged and strangled her immediately. Thereafter he committed necrophilia on her body. He left her uncovered body in the park.

Nine months later, on 21 October 1991, Boetie diverged from his previous pattern and selected an underage boy who prostituted himself. He took the boy to St George's Park. He sodomised the boy and he ejaculated as his hands wrestled the life out of his young victim. He left the body under a tree in the park.

Two years elapsed during which Boetie apparently did not kill anyone. Sometime between June and September 1993, the urge to kill struck again, and Boetie, who had acquired a taste for young boys, decided to take another one. He met an underage boy on Main Road and they walked about seven kilometres to Target Kloof, an undeveloped ravine in Port Elizabeth. The boy was not a prostitute but a street child. Boetie sodomised the boy and strangled him. This time he hid the body of the boy, since he was not a prostitute. When he returned later to point out the scene, he could not remember exactly where he had left the body.

Another two years passed during which Boetie continued with his life as a fisherman. He loved the sea and he loved his job. He would often compare the sea to a moody and mysterious woman.

On 27 July 1995 Boetie met forty-two-year-old Georgina Zweni, a sex worker, and took her to Prince Alfred Park, which was closer to the hotel where he picked her up than St George's Park. He had sex with her, but it left him unsatisfied, so he sodomised her. When she protested, he strangled her with a piece of her clothing. Afterwards, he stuck a knife into her vagina and ripped it open. He then cut off her nipples and ate them. He stabbed her in the stomach as well, and left her naked, mutilated body in the park. He threw her clothing into a fish pond.

On 29 September 1995, Boetie decided to visit his daughters from his first marriage. He had heard rumours that their stepfather was molesting Wuane. He also thought that the children did not have enough to eat and that his ex-wife had turned to prostitution for an income. Nine-year-old Wuane, an impish black-haired child, told her father that she wanted to run away from home. So Boetie took his daughter's hand and they started walking. He wanted to take her to Happy Valley, a park filled with fantasy fairy-tale figures that are illuminated at night. As a child Boetie had often played in this park, and as an adult he had lived like a hobo in the dense bushes behind the park.

Halfway to the park he boarded a taxi with little Wuane, eventually leading her to his hideout in the dense bush. He said he inspected her vagina and found that she was no longer a virgin, whereupon he strangled her in order to save her from the same kind of life that he had. He then removed her clothing and covered her body with a tarpaulin. He often returned to the spot and spread her clothing out on the ground, talking to her as if she were there, still wearing the clothes. He would sleep next to her decomposing body at night.

A case of a missing child was opened after Wuane's disappearance, and although Boetie was the last person seen with her, no charges were brought against him.

On 25 May 1996, Boetie picked up twenty-two-year-old Katriena Claassen, a sex worker. He took her to the beach, where he had sex with her. He pushed a piece of plastic bag down her throat to prevent her from making a noise and strangled her. Ironically, he left the body next to a wall on which the graffiti 'You should not steal' was written. He later told us that the act of prostitution was stealing money from men.

Between May and August 1996, Boetie picked up another underage street child and took him to Fort Frederick, an old historical fort situated in a park. There is an undeveloped ravine covered in dense vegetation leading from the park. The boy agreed to masturbate Boetie, whereafter he told the boy to remove his clothing. He sodomised the protesting child, who threatened to report him to the police. Boetie strangled the boy with his belt and hid the naked body under a bush in the ravine.

On 22 January 1997, the day he was due to appear in court on a charge of indecently assaulting his stepsons, Boetie went to visit friends. He met twelve-year-old Henry Bakers, the son of the family he was going to visit, in the road. Boetie and Henry walked towards the open veld. Boetie claimed that Henry told him that he had a girlfriend and asked Boetie's advice on how to have sex with her. Boetie led Henry to the veld near Algoa Park.

He informed Henry that he had learnt about sex when he was six years old and told Henry to remove his clothing, which the boy did. Boetie committed fellatio on Henry and told him to lie on his back. He sodomised the boy and strangled him while he ejaculated. He then hid the body and Henry's clothes in the bush nearby. His thinking was that he had saved the boy from his abusive parents and sent his soul to God, as he had done with his own daughter's soul.

Another case of a missing child was opened, and, as with Wuane, Boetie once again featured as the person last seen with the missing boy. The Child Protection Unit was handling both cases at that stage. They had no hard evidence that Boetie had anything to do with the disappearance of Wuane or Henry, and he even offered to help them search for the children. The case was then brought to Derrick's attention, since he had been trained in the investigation of serial homicide.

On 31 January 1997, Boetie was brought to Derrick's office for an interview. Derrick allowed Boetie to sit on a chair, facing a photograph of Derrick's own beautiful toddler. Boetie could also see Derrick's certificates on the wall.

Derrick confronted Boetie almost immediately, telling him that he knew he had killed the children and that he also knew that Boetie returned to the bodies to fantasise and commit necrophilia. The innocent eyes of Derrick's own little girl bore down on Boetie, affecting him just the way Derrick had intended. Boetie realised that he had met his match. He admitted to killing Wuane and Henry, even telling Derrick that he had gone back to Henry's body that very same morning to commit necrophilia.

Later that evening, Boetie pointed out Wuane and Henry's crime scenes. At Wuane's crime scene, there was nothing left but a skeleton. Boetie could not find her panties and crouched down on all fours, scratching around in the dirt like a dog. At Henry's crime scene, they found the boy's decomposing, maggot-infested body.

When they got back to the office, Derrick sat Boetie down on a chair and confronted him again, saying that he knew there were more bodies. Boetie asked if Derrick wanted to know about all the twelve people he had killed.

Over the next few months, Derrick and his colleagues spent a lot of time searching for old murder dockets pertaining to the cases Boetie had told him about. Boetie told Derrick that he would rub vinegar and butter on the soles of the boys' feet after killing them so that the police dogs wouldn't find the bodies. He admitted that he had returned to two of the boys' bodies to commit necrophilia. He would also insert rolled-up newspaper into the anuses of the boys to prevent the maggots from crawling up the orifices. He returned to Wuane's body only to talk to her. He also said that when he strangled his victims, there came a moment when their eyes would bulge and their tongues would protrude from their mouths. He called it the 'jelly-bean effect' and said it was at that moment that he would ejaculate.

Boetie told Derrick that he had been a bystander on two occasions when the bodies of the prostitutes were discovered in the parks. He watched the policemen processing the scene and learnt from the experience. One of the policemen had asked him if he knew anything about the murder and he had answered that he was only a passer-by.

Boetie refused to see me or allow me to interview him. He had read an article about me and decided I was a major bitch who was out to get him. Eventually, in February 1998, he was charged with nine murders and four counts of rape. The other three murders he claimed responsibility for could not be traced. The state prosecutor was Advocate Leon Knoetze and the defence counsel was Advocate Alwyn Griebenow and attorney Gideon Huisamen. Mr Justice Chris Jansen presided.

Boetie had given a statement to Advocate Griebenow in which he described the sex and the murders in the most explicit detail and the crudest language imaginable. This statement was read out in court. I am sure that Boetie not only had an erection when he wrote it, but that it also aroused him when it was read in court.

I was called to testify for the State and to give an explanation about the general characteristics of serial killers and how Boetie fitted into the pattern. I also had to explain how Boetie's particular modus operandi – including the sodomy, the cannibalism and the selection of victims – related to his early childhood fixations. But when the time came for me to testify, the State was of the opinion that they would not need my testimony to prove their case. Immediately, the defence called me as their witness. I think they thought my explanation could be used as mitigating circumstances. Boetie could not understand why I was suddenly testifying on his behalf, but he greeted me cordially. As a professional psychologist and an expert witness, it is my belief that I testify in court to advise the judge on certain issues of which he does not have expert knowledge. My testimony is always unbiased and as close to the facts as I can keep it. I will not colour it to suit either side, be it prosecution or defence. Nothing can ruin a professional's reputation faster than showing bias in court.

I was sworn in and began my testimony. Ten or fifteen minutes in, Boetie put up his hand and requested that the judge call a short break, as he wanted to go to the toilet. The judge pointed out that I was testifying and asked if he could wait. Boetie insisted that he had to go to the toilet that very moment. The judge granted him five minutes. I caught his eye as he descended the stairs to the cells below and I knew he was not going to the toilet. My suspicion was confirmed when Boetie indicated to Derrick on his way down that he was going to masturbate. It often happens that serial killers become extremely aroused in court when the details of their murders are discussed.

Both Dr Tuviah Zabow, the forensic psychiatrist from Valkenberg Psychiatric Hospital, and I advised the judge that there would be no chance of rehabilitation for Boetie. He should never be granted parole.

Boetie was sentenced to seven life sentences on 23 February 1998. In two cases, there wasn't enough indisputable evidence to prove that he was responsible for the murders. One was a prostitute in the park and the other was the little boy in Target Kloof, where Boetie could not point out the correct crime scene.

Boetie's wife attended court every day and they were reconciled. He sold his story to a magazine and gave his wife the money to buy an apartment for herself and their children. His ex-wife, the mother of Wuane, and his adoptive mother did not attend the trial.

But Derrick always had something up his sleeve. He managed to trace Boetie's biological mother and sister before the end of the trial, although he withheld this information from Boetie during the trial. It was very difficult to explain to this woman that her long-lost son was a notorious serial killer whose horror story had just been published in a popular magazine. She was deeply shocked, but asked Derrick to convey her love to Boetie and to assure him that she had never abandoned him. His sister had been reunited with the mother soon after the children disappeared, and the mother had also had another daughter.

Derrick and I visited Boetie in prison a month after his sentencing. I wanted to interview him for my research and he was very friendly towards me this time, but we kept him in handcuffs since his temper was so easily aroused and he had little control over his impulses. He did not seem to mind the cuffs. He started out in his crude manner, but when he saw it had no effect on either Derrick or me, he became a little more civilised. Twice during the interview Boetie asked to be excused and left the room to masturbate. I do not think he did this on purpose – I am more inclined to think that he genuinely could not control himself. At least he didn't do it in front of me. I regarded it as a sign of respect that he asked my permission to leave the room.

Although Boetie is not stupid, I found myself treating him like a child. I had developed a particular understanding for this man whom everyone called a monster. Although he had even killed his own beloved daughter, I could still clearly recognise the abused and rejected little boy in his eyes and face. It was to this child that I responded when I interviewed him. This should not be interpreted to mean that I felt sorry for him or that I condoned his actions in any way.

At one stage I asked him if he bit his victims. He said he bit them on their breasts and vaginas, using crude words in his answer. I did not respond to his crudeness and asked him if he bit them anywhere else on their anatomy. He dropped his head and glanced coyly at me. I wondered why he was suddenly so shy when he had shown no scruples about using profanities in my presence just a moment before. He softly and shyly answered that he also bit them on their toes.

Boetie had only one question for me at the end of the interview. He asked me why I had not picked him up in my mind earlier so that he could have been arrested sooner. He said he was tired of murder. I had no answer. Although he was tired of murder, it was not enough for him to give himself up, refuting the myth that serial killers want to be caught.

I often get the feeling of an unknown serial killer inside my mind, but it is vague and undefined. It feels as if someone is stirring up the mud inside the abyss and many murky images are unsettled in the process. I cannot attach an identity to the killer, nor can I identify the race or gender of the victims. I just know that somewhere someone is killing people, and I have no means of stopping it.

A few months later, Boetie's psychologist called me from St Albans prison and informed me that things were not going well. I flew down and Derrick and I visited him. We were late and Boetie had already been locked up for the night, but the wardens gave us access. Boetie was standing bare-chested in his cell. The grid door was locked, but the solid door remained open. He explained that the ghosts of the victims, including that of his daughter, haunted him at night and that the walls of his cell were oozing acid. We calmed him down and asked him to trust his therapist, who would address his hallucinations. I asked the wardens to keep only the grid door locked at night and leave the solid door open. I also asked a warden to buy him a poster of the sea to put on his wall, to stop the oozing acid. At some stage I believe he was transferred to a prison closer to his biological mother so she could visit him.

In my opinion, an interesting switch had taken place. Boetie had been a passive victim of emotional, sexual and physical abuse as a child. As an adult he identified with the aggressor and did to others what had been done to him. But when he was imprisoned, he could no longer vent his anger and suffering and reverted back to the role of the passive victim, allocating the role of the active persecutor to his victims.

The credit in this case must go to Sergeant Derrick Norsworthy of the Port Elizabeth Murder and Robbery Unit. Derrick was very young when I initially selected him for my course in 1994, but I recognised a potential and brilliance in him, and these were put to the test with the arrest of Boetie Boer. Derrick reacted on his gut instincts and immediately recognised Boetie as a serial killer when he saw him. He did not play games, but courageously jumped into the abyss and within minutes had confronted Boetie with the fact that he had returned to the bodies of his victims to commit necrophilia. Boetie immediately realised that he had met his match in the mind game he was playing and confessed.

Were it not for Derrick's sagacity, Boetie Boer would have continued murdering sex workers and children, and were it not for Derrick's compassion, Boetie would not have been reunited with his biological mother. The venture into the abyss left Derrick much wiser and more mature and he earned my respect and that of his peers.

TEN

The Saloon Killer

Alone, alone, all, all alone,
Alone on a wide, wide sea!
And never a saint took pity on
My soul in agony.

The many men, so beautiful!
And they all dead did lie;
And a thousand thousand slimy things
Lived on; and so did I.

– Samuel Taylor Coleridge, 'The Rime of the Ancient Mariner', 1798

Not all serial killers are motivated by lust. Some find their pleasure in sense-less, seemingly motiveless killing. Captain Danie Hall of the Secunda Murder and Robbery Unit called his case the Saloon Killer because the weapon that was used was a .22 rifle, nicknamed a Saloon. By April 1998, when I started working on this case, sixteen people had already been killed and ten people wounded. The killer operated in the Piet Retief area in Mpumalanga.

The town of Piet Retief was named after one of the leaders of the Great Trek, the migration by the Boers in the 1830s to escape British rule in the Cape and Natal colonies. The region of Piet Retief is bordered by the Pongola River in the south, which separates it from KwaZulu-Natal, the Drakensberg in the west, and the Kingdom of Swaziland to the east. In the early days, Piet Retief was regarded as a frontier district and the first settlers were harassed during the 1870s by the Anglo-Zulu wars to the south and the Swazi uprising to the east. The Zulus and the Swazis had been fighting each other since 1750. In 1876 the settlers purchased 12 820 hectares of land from the Swazi king Umbandini, and by 1884 Piet Retief was declared a town in what later became the Transvaal province.

In the late 1990s, Piet Retief was a typical quaint rural town, dominated by a church and one main road, called Church Street, of course. Twenty-five per cent of the white community were of German stock, descendants of German artisans from the Hermannsburg Missionary Society in KwaZulu-Natal who settled in the nearby Lüneburg district in the late nineteenth century. They planted the plantations that resulted in the area being referred to as the Black Forest of Africa. The Germans needed wagons to transport their timber, so they also became expert wagon makers.

Even after Mandela's release and the 1994 elections, clear racial divides still existed in South Africa. On rare occasions interracial marriages occurred, but definitely not among policemen and women. Although black and white detectives did not socialise together, they worked as a team, with white detectives relying heavily on the black detectives whenever they had to infiltrate the townships situated on the outskirts of the predominantly white towns. The township outside Piet Retief was called eThandakukhanya, which means 'we want a clean place'. Behind the formal settlement lay the informal squatter camp of Phoswa Village. Dwellings were built of clay, mud, corrugated iron, hardboard and sometimes bricks. The roads were dirt, unnamed and disorderly. Only a few houses had numbers painted on them. The village, about ten kilometres across, sprawled up the hill.

There were many shebeens or bars in the village. Usually one room of a two- or three-roomed dwelling served as the bar. The woman of the house would be the shebeen queen and her children usually slept in an adjoining room while she served her clientele. Patrons also sat outside to drink.

Khonzapi Qwabe owned such a shebeen. On the evening of Friday 13 June 1997 it was business as usual. Khonzapi was sitting in her kitchen with her friend Aaron Mtshali next to her. Her daughter Thandazile had just informed her mother that she was tired of serving the guests and had gone to the other room to go to bed. It was already past eleven o'clock.

Khonzapi and her friends were discussing the shooting incident that had occurred earlier that evening. Two men and a woman had been shot on a road leading to Kempville, a suburb situated two kilometres from Phoswa Village. The first woman, Nomsa Ndlangamandla, had been walking along a footpath at about 7.30 p.m. when a man approached her and shot her without warning, wounding her in the arm. As she fell to the ground, she heard another shot behind her. The same man had killed Sitende Dhlamini, who was walking just behind her. Then the man walked past Ashton Sheick and shot him in the back. He survived.

News travels fast in a rural community. Mandla Ngwenya, who was in the shebeen, joined the group in the kitchen. They were all shocked by the meaningless attack on the three people. Khonzapi looked up to see a man named Vusi Khumalo enter the shebeen. She knew Vusi, who was a regular client, but he was followed by an unknown man wearing an army coat and a black balaclava over his face. Without warning, the stranger produced a .22 rifle and shot Mandla in the stomach. He then pointed the rifle at Aaron and shot him two centimetres above his left eyebrow, killing him instantly. Khonzapi leapt to her feet and demanded to know why the stranger had shot her two friends. He swung the rifle in her direction and shot her, also two centimetres above the left eyebrow.

Drunken clients rushed out of the shebeen and into the night. Vusi and the stranger also left the shebeen. Mandla fled as well, only to die later in hospital. Thandazile came out of her room and stumbled over the bodies of Aaron and her dead mother. Being only twelve years old, she could not comprehend the situation, nor did she know what to do about it. In a state of denial, she went back to bed. A little later she stared into the face of the man who had shot her mother. He and Vusi had returned to the shebeen. He told Vusi he had found another person he was going to kill. Vusi took Thandazile by the hand and led her out of the shebeen, before going back inside. Thandazile crept back into the house and thought she saw Vusi and the other man having sex with the corpse of her mother. After they left, she hid under her bed, where neighbours discovered her the next morning.

Vusi Khumalo was arrested the next day by Danie and his colleagues. At that stage Danie thought he had caught the man responsible for the shooting of the three people on the road to Kempville, and one of the two men who had shot a nightwatchman and robbed a store in Commondale, thirty kilometres south-west of Piet Retief, earlier that month. Vusi denied being the killer or that he knew who the other man was. He was charged with raping Khonzapi and denied bail. He was kept in custody, awaiting trial for rape. Danie's hopes were dashed. Vusi's brother mentioned to him that Vusi and a man called Lucky shared his house. But Vusi denied knowing Lucky.

A month later, another man was shot on the same road in Kempville, but the local detectives did not alert Danie. He would only trace this docket, nine months later, in April 1998. Danie was based at the Murder and Robbery Unit in Secunda, about two hours' drive from Piet Retief. The detective branch at Piet Retief often investigated murders in their precinct without alerting the Murder and Robbery Unit.

On the night of 5 September 1997, Lucky Mbuli and his girlfriend were sleeping in their hut in Phoswa Village. They both woke when someone rattled the window. Lucky stormed outside and chased the perpetrator down to the river, where the man shot him in the chest. He managed to stumble back in the direction of his hut, but the perpetrator caught up with him and shot him again. This time the wound, slightly above the left eyebrow, was fatal.

Danie realised that Vusi was not the killer, because he was in custody when this incident took place.

Yvonne Nkambule lived in another mud hut, without electricity or water. On the evening of Thursday 25 September 1997, Yvonne, her boyfriend, his friend and her sister had just finished dinner. After washing the dishes in a plastic basin, Yvonne opened her front door, picked up the wash basin and stepped outside to throw the water out. The next moment her sister and friends heard a loud noise. 'It sounds as if someone is playing cricket,' said Yvonne's boyfriend. Then the door burst open and Yvonne stumbled in, clutching her chest. 'I'm dying,' she said as she fell into her boyfriend's arms. A few moments later she was dead. Yvonne had been shot on the left side of the chest, as had Lucky.

An hour and a half after Yvonne was killed, Paulo Manana and his friend Jacob Ngobesi had just alighted from a taxi and were walking along the road behind Phoswa Village. They suddenly became aware of a man walking behind them, who called to them and told them to hand over their possessions. Paulo and Jacob didn't understand what the man meant. The man then started shooting at them with a .22 rifle. In a state of fear, the two friends, who had no means of defending themselves, picked up stones and threw them at the man. He fired more shots and they ran away. The man shouted that he had run out of ammunition and disappeared into the trees. A few moments later he reappeared and shot at them again. Paulo's left hand was wounded and Jacob was shot in the stomach, but both men managed to escape.

The following night, 26 September, Bongani Mlipha and a friend were walking along a dirt road next to the Welverdient plantation, close to Phoswa Village. They had been gambling at the Lunch Box, a tavern in Piet Retief. A man appeared from the trees and fired at them. He shot Bongani two centimetres above his right eyebrow. Bongani's companion fled, but left his hat and shoes behind on the crime scene.

Later that same night, the Piet Retief charge office got an anonymous call about a body lying next to the road at the abattoir. The abattoir was about a kilometre away from the spot where Bongani was killed. Members of the uniform branch found the body of Amos Nkosi. He had been shot in the left side of his chest.

Danie and his colleagues were called in and managed to trace the clothing found at Bongani's scene to a man named Lala, who initially told them that he did not know the man who had shot at them. Then he implicated another man, who was brought in for questioning. This man admitted that he had shot Bongani, but told the detectives that Lala had given him the weapon. He also implicated other men. Eventually it was established that none of them could point out the right scene, they all had valid alibis and Lala's original story about the attacker being a stranger was the truth. None of the men were pointed out at an identity parade and they were all later released.

Again, Danie's hopes were crushed. He still did not have the killer. One of the men had told the detectives that he had been talking to a man named Lucky at the Lunch Box tavern earlier on the night Bongani was shot.

Shortly before these men were arrested, Danie had called me for help. But when he arrested Lala and his companions, we felt it was unnecessary for me to go to Piet Retief.

For three months the killings stopped. Then, in January 1998, they started again, following the same pattern as the previous year. The men arrested in Bongani's case were still in custody.

First, on the night of 14 January 1998, a shop in Phoswa Village was broken into and the nightwatchman, Ambriose Ntalinthali, was found killed with a shot in the right side of his chest. No one had seen anything. Two more men were shot in January as they were walking along the road to Kempville. Another, Fanie Malinga, was shot in February as he was walking on a road in Phoswa Village.

On the night of 5 February, Nellie Mdluli and her friend were sitting inside their hut in Phoswa Village when the door burst open. A man with a .22 rifle entered and shot Nellie two centimetres above her left eyebrow. She died instantly. A month later, on 6 March, the body of Rebecca Manana was found next to the road in Phoswa Village. She had also been shot above the right eyebrow.

Three days later the killer moved to the farms about twenty-seven kilometres south-east of Piet Retief. Sometime during the night of 9 March, he entered the kraal of Babili Ndaba. He kicked open the door of Babili's hut and shot him in the left side of his chest. Then he took a bowl of porridge and a tin of fish and ate his meal outside the kraal wall.

He moved on, reaching the kraal of Johannes Nhleko at 8 p.m. Johannes heard someone moving about the kraal but was too frightened to go outside. No shots were fired, but the killer stole a chicken and two loaves of bread.

By half past ten he had reached the neighbouring farm and entered the kraal of Andries Mthimkhulu. He kicked open the door of Andries's hut and fired a shot, but no one was injured. He shot at Andries's dogs, killing one of them. Then he went to the hut of the neighbour and kicked open the door. He felt underneath the pillow of the sleeping grandmother for money, but did not find any. He pointed the rifle at the owner, but before he could shoot, the grandmother had woken and, in a drunken stupor, she chased the perpetrator out of the hut. He fled into the night.

On Saturday 4 April 1998, several people made complaints about a man who had threatened them with a rifle on the farm at Goedetrouw, which is five kilometres east of Piet Retief. By 7 p.m. he had killed Elphas Mbuli and by 10 p.m. he had wounded Zweli Nkosi. Elphas Mbuli had been seen at the Lunch Box tavern before his death.

After these threats and attacks, the Piet Retief Detective Branch realised that the situation had spiralled out of control and they called Danie in again. He phoned me.

I spent two days at the Secunda Murder and Robbery Unit, making summaries of the dockets. I immediately noticed the similarities in the wounds. Six people had been shot above the left eyebrow and two above the right eyebrow. Five people had been shot in the left side of the chest and two in the right. That afternoon I could tell them that the suspect had military training. I suggested that he might have been trained as a sniper. The witnesses had described him as wearing an army uniform and a black balaclava.

I was sitting in an office with Inspector Jan Hattingh, who had been the investigating officer in some of the cases. We were discussing the possibility of the suspect being an ex-soldier when suddenly a man entered the office. He was wearing an army coat and had a black balaclava over his face. He was nervous and hid behind the door. In those few seconds my heart stopped. Jan and I stared at each other in silence. Then one of the detectives came in and led the man out. We both jumped to our feet and called after him. We explained our hypothesis about the serial killer.

The detective burst out laughing. The man in the coat and balaclava was one of his informers who had been called in to identify suspects in another office. They didn't want him to be recognised and so had dressed him up in one of their coats. A strange and disturbing coincidence.

The next morning Danie, Jan, the Secunda Murder and Robbery commander Superintendent Koos Fourie and I set off for Piet Retief. As we drove around Phoswa Village, I thought that it looked like a hybrid between Donnybrook and Lenyenye. The huts were the same as in Donnybrook, but they were not scattered into different kraals. Also, they were not as tightly clustered as in Phoenix. The atmosphere in all the squatter camps remained the same, however. White people were regarded with suspicion. Only the children smiled and waved at us. We waved back. I thought of the detectives' children, both white and black. Their fathers worked together in teams, often relying on each other for their lives, but at home races were segregated and their children did not play with each other or go to the same schools. This would start changing under the new regime, but change had not yet reached these informal settlements.

I returned to Pretoria and got to work. I came up with a profile of a man who had been trained as a sniper. As a boy he must have been severely rejected by his parents. This caused a basic distrust and paranoia in his personality. Psychologists would diagnose it as paranoid personality disorder. As a boy he would have had a secret hiding place in the forest where he could dream in solitude. He would be the hero in his dreams. As a young man he found the army the perfect setting for his fantasy. Here he could be trained to become the dangerous soldier who has no feelings for others. This was the realisation of his childhood dreams. At last he could be someone who commanded respect. His rifle became an extension of his personality.

Somehow he had been discharged from the army, which led him to develop a grudge. He had the delusion that civilians were the enemy. The black adult civilians he killed represented his rejecting parents. Whenever he felt offended by anyone, it would reactivate the pain of the little boy inside him. This was incompatible with the image of the dangerous soldier, and the only way he could re-establish the equilibrium was by killing some-one – anyone. Killing restored his power and his bruised ego. Firing the rifle made him feel omnipotent, regardless of who the victim was.

The fact that the suspect had been described as having a clean-shaven head and a preference for uniforms supported my hypothesis that he was a soldier. He would hide his weapon in a secret place in the forest where no one could touch it. It would not be in his home. The hiding place would remind him of the secret place he had enjoyed as a boy.

The hit-and-run modus operandi and the fact that he stole survival items such as tinned food, shoes and batteries from shops also indicated army tactics. The fact that he attacked kraals, shot at civilians and then stole food reminded me of terrorist behaviour during the Angolan War. Our suspect had either been a member of the South African Defence Force, or he had been a member of SWAPO or Umkhonto we Sizwe (MK), the ANC's mili-tary wing. Many former MK soldiers could not find employment in the new Defence Force and were disgruntled. Some became outlaws. Danie had traced two cases in the Piet Retief district where .22 rifles had been stolen from farmers. One of these rifles had a telescopic sight.

Inspector Danie Reyneke, whom I had met during September 1994 when I attended the Murder and Robbery course, had completed both my courses. He was disappointed that he had never worked on a serial killer investi-gation since his training in 1995. He was stationed at the Vryheid Detective Branch, which is close to Piet Retief, but in the province of KwaZulu-Natal. Danie Hall agreed that he would welcome Danie Reyneke onto his team. I phoned Reyneke and told him about the investigation. He was very excited.

I told the detectives that the suspect might be named Lucky and that he might hang out at the Lunch Box tavern. It might be the same Lucky who shared the house with Vusi. We didn't want to show Vusi's brother the identikit in case he alerted Lucky. I suggested they keep the house under observation. Vusi had been released on bail by then.

During the two weeks that I worked on the profile in Pretoria, Danie

Hall had to set up an operations room at the Piet Retief Detective Branch. The investigation team would be launched officially on 4 May 1998. He had two rooms at his disposal, but little else. I requested extra crime scene photographs, aerial photographs, bulletin boards, a television and video recorder, and maps. Superintendent Koos Fourie and Danie set out to obtain all these items, which was quite a task when restricted budgets are taken into consideration. Reyneke's commanders agreed that he could join the team on 4 May, on condition that Mpumalanga province paid for his accommodation.

Detectives in the USA and UK have often remarked that it must be easier working for the South African Police Service, since one police force serves the whole country. They often have difficulties with different forces operating in the same or neighbouring regions. The dispute over who was going to pay for Reyneke's accommodation when sixteen people were already dead seemed petty to me. Danie Hall was also experiencing problems in getting Captain Rudi Neethling of the Belfast Detective Branch, who had also been trained, onto his team. Eventually Danie said that he was prepared to cut his field team by two members in order to get Reyneke and Rudi on board.

I brought matters like this to the attention of General Britz. I wasn't happy doing this, because it made me feel like a little girl telling her father about her brothers' naughtiness. On the other hand, when men act like children, they should be treated as such. Although I understood their budgetary concerns, if I could not make them realise the seriousness of the case, then higher command would have to force them. At least the top structure of the South African Police Service understood what a serious threat serial killers were to a community. The SAPS had made a commitment towards community policing, and most of us took this commitment to heart. I do not wish to criticise the SAPS, but I am not blind to the faults of individuals.

At 7 a.m. on 4 May I reported to the operations room in Piet Retief. Danie clocked in a little later as he had some chores to finish in Secunda. The two of us spent the whole day trying to get the logistics in order. The station commander at Piet Retief assisted us with stationery and by 4 p.m. we had four hardboard bulletin boards from the local hardware shop, but they were still unpaid for. There was no sign of Reyneke or Rudi – their commanders evidently were still having problems releasing them from their stations. Danie and I stayed at the office until 6 p.m. preparing the operations room.

Early the next morning I phoned General Britz and shortly afterwards all hell broke loose. He had the reputation of having the temper of a lion and he certainly donned the lion's skin that day. A few commanders felt his wrath, and I felt sorry for them. Superintendent Koos Fourie had also arrived, as well as Director Blighnaut, who spent three hours wishing us well and promising us all the support we needed. By 6 p.m. Rudi and Reyneke were there. A handful of detectives from the Piet Retief Detective Branch were seconded to us. One of them, Sergeant Jabu Thela, knew the Phoswa Village area well. The team was now assembled, and we all went out for a beer.

The next day we visited the crime scenes. Sergeants Jabu Thela, Paul Masibuko and Dennis Nkosi accompanied us to Phoswa Village. They drove in one car and we followed in Reyneke's car, which had tinted windows. We did not want the killer to spot us. Thela pointed out the crime scenes but we did not get out.

We did, however, get out when we reached the farm scenes where the killer had attacked kraals. I prayed at Babili's kraal. His hut had remained undisturbed since his death. It was a typical Zulu hut made of wattle and mud, with a thatched roof. In the middle of the hut was the fireplace where food was prepared. The porridge pot was still standing in the ash. Babili's sleeping mat was lying on the floor, but its owner would never return. The kraal had been abandoned. There were plantations and trees close to the kraals and I sensed the wind playing among the trees. It seemed as if it was just observing me. I tried to entice it out and invited it to touch my soul, but it would not.

On Friday General Britz visited us in Piet Retief and then I followed him back to Pretoria in my own car. That day the wind blew in all its fury. It stirred up dust storms on the plains, it rushed through the plantations and almost swept my car from the road. I opened my window and welcomed it into my soul. I opened up to the serial killer and ventured the first few steps into the now familiar darkness of the abyss. My mind was devoid of thoughts. A moodiness settled in.

I reached my house at half past three that afternoon and fell onto my bed. I was mentally exhausted and fell asleep at once, but troubled dreams tortured me. My cellphone woke me half an hour later and I felt disorientated. It was a detective informing me of a possible serial killer in Kroonstad. The victim was a seven-year-old girl. I immediately phoned Elmarie and asked her to inform Inspector Thinus Oosthuizen of the Vanderbijlpark Murder and Robbery Unit. He was the investigating officer in the Orange Farm serial murder case. Vanderbijlpark was about 150 kilometres from Kroonstad and his killer had been quiet for several months. Elmarie had been working on his case.

The darkness of my mood continued. Why did serial killers have to come at us three or four at a time? I ran a bath and tried to cleanse my mind. It didn't work. I went to bed and dreamt I had to walk through a field up to my ankles in maggots. Then I had to dive down a deep gorge into a raging river and swim.

On Saturday I lay on my bed, watching the wind wreaking havoc outside. Winter had settled over the land and over my heart. I felt overwhelmed with work. How could I manage an active serial killer in Piet Retief, another in Empangeni, testify in the Kranskop and Cape Prostitute cases, select detectives for my course, and attend important meetings on the training of detectives – all at the same time? I also thought of Elmarie, who had several serial killer cases and serial rape cases to manage. I was concerned about her workload. She had not seen many bodies and had reported no nightmares, so I presumed her mental health was still intact.

The fact that I had a killer in my head again did not lighten matters. I had entered the abyss by now and was living in darkness. A friend invited me to a movie that Saturday night. I enjoyed the company and for a few hours my mind was diverted from the killer.

On Monday morning I drove back to Piet Retief. Inspector Vivian Bieldt, an expert on victim identification and identikits, followed in his own car. We reached Piet Retief at noon. The detectives had assembled most of the surviving victims, who were able to assist in drawing up identikits as Vivian set to work. Danie had to attend the High Court in Pretoria for two weeks and Rudi had taken over command of the investigation.

One of the surviving victims told us that he had seen the man who had shot him walking on a certain road in Phoswa Village that weekend. We were excited that the suspect was still in the vicinity. With the help of Sergeant Thela and his informers, a house had been identified as that of the suspect. Two brothers lived in the house and both of them had weapons, but we did not know their names.

It would have been difficult for any of our team members to keep the house under surveillance because the detectives were too well known. We did not want to endanger the lives of civilians either. We decided to call in the help of the Defence Force.

An appointment was made for members of a highly trained covert unit of the Defence Force to visit us. In the meantime we organised a police helicopter to fly over Phoswa Village to take aerial photographs. The photographs were developed immediately, but to our dismay they did not reveal the exact location of the house, although they gave us a good overall view of the squatter camp. Somehow, Superintendent Koos managed to arrange a flight in one of the forestry companies' aeroplanes the next day. Danie Reyneke boarded the plane with his camera and an hour after they landed we had our aerial photographs.

Sergeant Thela had visited a prison where he interviewed the criminals who had been arrested in connection with the housebreakings in which the .22 rifles were stolen. The information that he obtained was that a .22 rifle was given as compensation to one of the gang members, Dumisani, who had accidentally been shot by another gang member. Dumisani had not been charged with the housebreaking and was still outside. Another of the gang members was a youngster, and he had been released with a warning. His name was Lucky Masibuko.

The suspects we were therefore focusing on were Lucky Masibuko, Dumisani and the two unidentified brothers who lived in the marked house.

On Thursday evening three soldiers arrived. We briefed them and it was decided that they would return the following week with a team who would set up their own squatter hut close to the marked house to observe the two brothers. The army team selected were trained snipers. We had to keep in mind that our suspect was likely to be a trained sniper himself and that he had no scruples about shooting anyone who confronted him. The main task of the army team would be to observe and gather information, but if they were involved in a skirmish, they would have to defend themselves.

During the week, some squatters set up huts on private ground next to Phoswa Village and a battalion of Defence Force members was called in to assist in their removal. On the one hand this complicated our investigation, because we were looking for a suspect wearing army clothing and suddenly Piet Retief was swarming with men in army uniforms. On the other hand, it helped us because it provided a cover for our army lads to move into Phoswa Village, although they would pose as civilians, and we thought it would also account for the fact that a police chopper had flown over the area. The suspect's paranoia was a factor we always had to keep in mind.

In the meantime Vusi was picked up again and interrogated. He still denied knowing the person who had accompanied him to Khonzapi's shebeen the night of the shootings, but confirmed that he had taken Thandazile out of the hut so that she would not be killed. We released him.

I returned to Pretoria again on Friday afternoon and spent the weekend in bed with flu. On the following Wednesday morning, I woke up at quarter past three in the morning. The wind was howling outside and the killer was active in my mind. I switched on the light and sat in front of the heater smoking cigarettes. I could feel him, and he was extremely angry.

I went to work at seven that morning in a foul mood. I phoned Rudi, who told me that the victim who had pointed out the house to us had in the meantime pointed out another man as being the killer. The man was picked up and brought in for interrogation and his house was searched. It turned out that he was an old Zulu man who was employed as a street sweeper. Some items of army uniform were found in his house but it was quite possible that he had picked up this clothing in dustbins in the course of his work.

Rudi and I were unconvinced that this man was our sophisticated killer. He did not remotely fit the profile or the identikits. Unfortunately, he was pointed out by the victim at an identity parade, so the team had to take him to court and charge him. They decided to charge him only on the one case and not to oppose his bail.

Sergeant Thela, Paul and Dennis had in the meantime traced Lucky Masibuko. We thought this was our lucky break. Lucky was very short, which did not match our description of the suspect. Danie Reyneke took Lucky to Vryheid, where young Thandazile had moved to live with her family, and she pointed him out in an identity parade. Reyneke was overjoyed. He thought we had caught our man, until Thandazile was asked if this was the man who had accompanied Vusi on the night of her mother's death. She answered no, she had only pointed him out because she knew him as a friend of her mother's who had attended school with her. So, Lucky Masibuko was not our suspect either.

When Rudi related these developments to me, I was not surprised. I had the killer in my head that night, and I knew that he was furious, but that he was still undetected.

I asked Rudi what other information they had secured. He said there had been a report that weekend of a woman being raped by a man in one of the plantations. The man had told her that he had left his hut in Phoswa Village and moved into the plantation because he knew the police were looking for him. He had seen the police helicopter. He also said he still had to kill a few people before he fled to Swaziland. This interested me, but I did not comment on it to Rudi. Our suspects at that stage were the two men in the hut and Dumisani. We did not know if the hut was still inhabited while we waited for the army team to arrive. We did not want to arouse any suspicions by driving around in the vicinity of the hut.

I was agitated by the fact that the team had picked up suspects without checking out their backgrounds first, as too much police activity would alert the killer. We had all agreed that a suspect's background would be checked before he was picked up. I also knew if they had picked up the right suspect he would not have confessed to anything, and without finding the rifle we would have no evidence. But I also knew that I could not interfere with their investigative methods. Rudi reassured me that he had told the team 'not to burn the food in haste', as he put it, meaning that they should not try to rush the arrest. He managed to calm me down.

I tried to analyse my feelings. I knew I had no reason to be annoyed with the detectives. I trusted them and they knew what they were doing. General Britz was also pleased with their progress. The source of my irritation must therefore lie elsewhere.

I was often called eccentric by the detectives and one of the reasons was that I had a large tablecloth covering my desk, reaching down to the floor. Under my desk I had several large pillows, and whenever I needed time out, I would creep into my little private enclave to think. That morning I sat under my desk, hiding from the world, and waited. It came to me that the irritation was not mine. It belonged to the killer. I tuned into his feelings. The fact that I had identified the source of my irritation did not alleviate it, however. It remained my mood for the rest of the week and it affected my colleagues. When Elmarie needed documents to be signed by me, she slipped them under the tablecloth, not saying a word. I would sign and pass them back out.

I had worked out that for the months of May, June and July I would be away from home more than half the time. I still had to fit in a visit to Empangeni to assess the situation with their serial killer, and I had to go to Cape Town from 29 June to 10 July to present my course. The fact that I had to arrange for someone to live in my house when I was away, that my garden was full of weeds, and that I had friends and family whom I would have liked to see, seemed not to be taken into consideration by the top structure of the Service.

I was swamped with administrative duties as well. Where other people find the prospect of going overseas exciting, I regarded it simply as more work. I had been invited to Liverpool by Dr David Canter and to France to lecture in September and October respectively.

By Friday lunch time my mood was dangerous. My cellphone rang and it was Frans van Niekerk informing me of the possibility of another serial killer on the East Rand. Three children had been found murdered. I thanked him for the information and called General Britz. It was impossible for Elmarie or me to be in more than one place at the same time. I had been promised more personnel, but there seemed to be no chance of this being realised. There was no way either of us would be able to go to the East Rand within the next week because we both had to travel extensively to select detectives for the course.

General Britz told me that he had discussed my situation with the high command of the Detective Services and again promised to do something about my lack of personnel. I switched off my cellphone and crawled back under my desk, where Elmarie found me an hour later. She enticed me out by telling me that the detectives were having a braai in the tearoom. I locked my office and followed her. The detectives had set up a gas braai on some newspapers and were cooking meat. None of us seemed to have the time or the inclination to go out into the veld to have a braai. Fortunately I had cut down on drinking or I might have indulged severely that afternoon.

On Friday evening I acknowledged to myself that my personal life was in a sorry state. There I was at thirty-seven, sitting in front of a heater in a tracksuit on a Friday night, where friends would be out on normal dates going to dinner and the movies. I felt isolated and very sorry for myself. Since my divorce in 1994, my two relationships had not lasted longer than five months in total. Five months of romance in a total of forty-eight months was not a healthy situation. It seemed as though I always fell in love in winter, and come spring, the relationship would be history. It was winter again and by coincidence the song 'It Was Only a Winter's Tale' was playing on the radio. I switched it off and went to bed.

Another nightmarish night passed, during which I dreamt I was being chased by a killer whale. I spent Saturday morning taking care of housework, buying a few groceries and watering the garden. It was good to do normal chores, like a normal person. Elmarie came by and promised to fit in a visit to the East Rand during the following week. Although I could not share my emotions with her, she remained a pillar I could lean on when it came to the distribution of work. She knew her job well by then and I knew I could trust her. She did not have the same kind of intuition regarding serial killers that I did, and was more interested in the investigative side than the psychological aspects of our work, but she worked very hard and very well.

The following week I drove down to Piet Retief again. Ballistics experts had found that the .22 rifle stolen during a burglary at a certain farm matched the rounds and ammunition that we had found on our crime scenes. The 28s gang had been involved in this burglary. The team concentrated on rounding up members of the gang. We were careful not to let them know that we were seeking a serial killer, and brought them in on the charge of burglary. One of the gang members was identified as Wonder. Wonder seemed a likely suspect, since he had always wanted to join the army or the police, but he eluded us.

I flew to Empangeni in KwaZulu-Natal two weeks later. The Empangeni Murder and Robbery Unit had discovered the bodies of six women and a child and needed me to determine if a serial killer was at large. Inspector Coen Maritz was one of the very first detectives I had trained. Coen was salt of the earth. He was big and steadfast as a rock.

A mortuary attendant had noticed that several of the bodies he had received had their hands tied, and alerted the cops. Coen and I spent a day visiting the crime scenes. There was a link between most of the seven cases. The last crime scene we visited was in a pine plantation. Walking into the woods felt like entering a fairy garden. The pine needles made a thick, soft carpet beneath our shoes. We stood quietly listening to the utter silence of the woods. The wind gently caressed the trees, but made no sound at all. The experience calmed my troubled soul. I never realised one could hear silence.

That night the detectives arranged a braai on the beach and I watched the ocean in the moonlight. At times like these I wondered about the meaning of my life. No matter how hard we try to make a difference, to combat crime and prevent the innocent from falling prey to the evil, the waves still follow the tides, exactly as they did a century ago and exactly as they will in a century's time.

I compiled a profile for Coen, but I had to leave him to go back to Pretoria. I had faith in Coen, although I felt bad not having more time to spend with him. His case was as important to him as any of the other fourteen serial killer cases I was dealing with at that stage.

I was scarcely home for a week when I had to drive down to Paarl in the Cape to present my course. It was midwinter, and cold, wet and raining. Elmarie and I were proud of the detectives we had selected. Director Leonard Knipe, who had been in charge of the Station Strangler investigation, attended most of the lectures, and I was pleased that our relationship had grown amicable. Detectives working on current and earlier cases attended the course. There were representatives of the Saloon Killer case, the Nicolas Ncama and Pyromaniac cases, the Lenyenye case, the East Rand and Orange Farm cases, the Phoenix case, the Wemmer Pan/Hammer case, and the Prostitute Killer and Pinetown cases.

On that first Sunday some of us visited Mitchells Plain. We bought ice cream at my favourite café and the woman behind the till remembered me and spoke to me as if I were still living there. It warmed my heart. Some beautiful new graffiti adorned the prefab walls in AZ Berman Drive. Mitchells Plain was happy and my house still stood in the same spot. I might have been imagining things, but it seemed as though the motorists were adhering to the traffic lights. I hope I was wrong. I love the disorganised chaos of the place.

I spent a lot of time in the company of Superintendent Chappie Krugel, commander of the Middelburg Murder and Robbery Unit, and with Superintendent Koos Fourie, commander of the Secunda Murder and Robbery Unit, who was overall in charge of the Saloon Killer case. During breaks Koos and I would phone the team in Piet Retief to be updated. It was frustrating not being able to be there.

On the evening of Tuesday 30 June, Koos, Chappie and I returned to the hostel at 11 p.m. after a night out on the town. I was in a strange mood and asked them to wake everybody up because I wanted to lecture there and then. Both men thought I was mad and asked me why. I told them that I suddenly had the killer in my head and that since he was present he might as well lecture to the detectives himself. But they refused to wake the others.

The next morning Danie Reyneke phoned me. They had arrested Wonder the previous evening at 11 p.m. I was so relieved that the Saloon Killer had finally been arrested that I did not take the time to analyse the feeling I'd had at exactly that time.

It was a very stupid mistake.

For the rest of the week I relaxed and spent the evenings socialising with the detectives. We went out on the Friday and Saturday nights and generally fooled around as a bunch of detectives do when they are on a course and far from home, visiting pubs and wine farms. I was happy and I drank some fine red wine.

On the morning of Sunday 4 July, Koos, Mike van Aardt and I were filling up with petrol at Paarl police station when my cellphone rang. It was Reyneke. The Saloon Killer had killed a person on Friday night and another on Saturday night. Obviously, it was not Wonder. There was no mistake that the killer was still on the loose, since both victims had been shot above the left eyebrow.

A raging storm broke inside my soul. Koos found me later. I had crossed two busy roads and was walking aimlessly in the veld. I couldn't remember how I got there but realised that I was on my way to Mitchells Plain, about thirty kilometres away. Koos loaded me into the back of the Combi. I was very confused, very hurt, and experiencing extreme anxiety.

I phoned General Britz, but he had gone on a hunting trip. I grabbed a pen and my notebook and tried to make sense of the mess. I could not differentiate between my feelings and those of the killer. Once I started writing, I realised that I was right about the feeling that I'd had at eleven o'clock on that Tuesday night.

The killer was angry. He was not angry at being arrested – he was angry because someone else had been arrested. Either he knew Wonder personally or information had been leaked by someone in the team. In any case, he knew about the arrest and he was furious. I had made the fatal error of being so pleased with the arrest that I had not interpreted his feelings correctly. I had relaxed my mental hold on him, which was a mistake.

How dare I relax and enjoy myself with friends while he was still out there in the cold and miserable, hellish abyss? While I was writing, I entered the abyss again. The path to this killer was familiar by now and I reached out and grabbed him firmly. I promised myself not to leave him again until he was out of the cold. I felt guilty about those victims – it was my fault they were killed. Later in my life, when I finally went for therapy, I realised how the symptoms of post-traumatic stress rob one of rational thought processes, but at that stage, I was firmly caught in its dragon-claw grip.

While I was writing, Koos turned around and looked at me. I can imagine what a sight I must have been – sitting there, dishevelled, crying, shaking and writing. He smiled at me, which made me feel more secure. I was safe with these men. I knew that the killer did not have this security. Although Mike and Koos were quiet, I appreciated their presence and protectiveness. This *esprit de corps* formed the foundations of the brotherhood and strong friend-ship I knew I could always rely on in any one of the men or women that I have trained. They would not let me fall and they would not fail me.

Mike and Koos drove me to a cosy restaurant at Constantia Nek where I met my stepbrother, whom I had not seen in years. I sat in front of the fire sipping hot Glühwein. The detectives kept their distance, leaving my brother and me to reminisce about our childhood. It was good to see him. The fire, the wine, my brother and the two big detectives protecting me warmed the chill in my heart. I could not afford to break down, although I knew that I had received an almost fatal wound.

I regained enough strength to complete the course. On the last day, Mike heard that he had become a father. I gave the class the rest of the day off. They all had to report back at 6 p.m. for the certificate ceremony. Some of us, including Director Knipe, went out for a drink to celebrate the birth of Mike's baby. Mike was packed off on the first available flight home.

When we returned to the hostel at a quarter to six, I experienced a severe anxiety attack. I phoned my mother, but I was crying so much that the only words I could get out were: 'They are killing me, Ma.' I was not referring to the serial killers inside my head, but to the detectives. I felt I could not abandon them by retiring, but I also knew that if I stayed I was going to lose my mind. My mother calmed me down and reminded me that I was about to make a speech.

I ran down the passage and into the recreation room. Everyone had already gathered and the speeches had started. Big Daan Botha was standing at the door. He took one look at my face, placed his huge arm around me and whispered words of encouragement in my ear. For the second time in a week there was a big, burly, protective detective ready to catch me. I delivered my speech, thanking them for their dedication and their love. Once we had dispersed, I walked out into the rain and sank down beneath a palm tree.

My heart was breaking. The detectives had bought me a beautiful wooden cat. I hugged my cat and could almost hear it purr. My heart opened and the pain drained out like the pouring rain around me.

Very ugly monsters surfaced from my subconscious. I was mourning for Elroy van Rooyen, the little boy whose body we discovered on my birthday back in 1994. I worried that if I had only started mourning the Station Strangler's victims after five years, how many victims would I still mourn in the future? I mourned for the pain of the victims' families, missing their loved ones. I mourned, too, for the torment of the serial killers, for Stewart Wilken hallucinating in prison, for the hours of sleep I had lost and the nightmares that I was riding bareback by then. I mourned for the boyfriends who had deserted me and all the love I had inside me. I mourned for my family and friends whom I did not see often enough. I mourned for my house, where I hardly touched base any more.

Most of all, I mourned for myself, for the detectives were killing me with their kindness. I knew I had finally reached the point in my career where I had to get out in order to save my own sanity, but still I could not let go. I knew the detectives would be able to catch serial killers without me – they always could – but I would miss them so much.

> *I looked upon the rotting sea,*
> *And drew my eyes away,*
> *I looked upon the rotting deck,*
> *And there the dead men lay.*

> *I looked to heaven, and tried to pray;*
> *But or ever a prayer had gusht,*
> *A wicked whisper came, and made*
> *My heart as dry as dust.*

I closed my lids, and kept them close,
And the balls like pulses beat;
For the sky and the sea, and the sea and the sky
Lay like a load on my weary eye,
And the dead were at my feet.

The cold sweat melted from their limbs,
Nor rot nor reek did they:
The look with which they looked on me
Had never passed away.

An orphan's curse would drag to hell
A spirit from on high.
But oh! more horrible than that
Is the curse in a dead man's eye!
Seven days, seven nights, I saw that curse,
And yet I could not die.

– Samuel Taylor Coleridge, 'The Rime of the Ancient Mariner', 1798

Koos found me in the rain and led me to my room. Automatically, I packed my belongings and then I went to bed. They woke me at 5 a.m. and bundled me into the back of the Combi. Koos and Chappie had organised that two other detectives would drive my car back to Johannesburg. Again, they took care of me.

Elmarie had to stay a day longer in Paarl and would drive back the following day. I spent most of the day sleeping on the seat of the Combi underneath my duvet while Koos and Chappie shared the driving. I had crawled back into the abyss and was generally unresponsive.

It felt so good sleeping in my pure white bed in my own safe home again.

Back at work I realised that the symptoms of my post-traumatic stress were getting completely out of hand. I was losing control and didn't want to become a pathetic woman who needed mollycoddling all the time. I fell back on my childhood resilience and I knew I was going to survive, although this time it was going to be hell to get through.

Years before, when I was still new in the Service, I had met a wise man. He had predicted this would happen to me and invited me to call him whenever I needed him. I decided this was the time and set about trying to contact him. This man is like a wise old magician who appears and disappears in the mist. I will call him Merlin, for I am sure he is the same wizard who put in an appearance in the legend of King Arthur. King Arthur may have been a mythical figure, but my Merlin was real flesh and blood. It is extremely difficult to find Merlin, for he travels the continents.

I put out the word to some of my undercover contacts that I needed him, and then I waited. Merlin would find me.

In the meantime I decided that I needed to take control of my work environment. Elmarie and I were swamped. At that stage we were handling fifteen active serial killers between us, of whom seven were in my head.

Elmarie had a case in Thohoyandou in the Northern Province involving a man who had killed eight people. He targeted couples making out in cars. Within a week of setting up a task team, headed by Superintendent Tollie Vreugdenburg, Captain Kwarra Muthavinsindi, Inspector Jan van der Merwe and Sergeant Herman Espach, as well as some detectives whom I had not trained, they had arrested the man, David Mbengwa. Another world record was broken. Elmarie and Tollie interrogated David and got a confession within a couple of hours. But the very next day, a new serial killer filled the place that this one had vacated.

I made an appointment with General Suiker and pleaded for more personnel. He made an appointment with the other commissioners and I was promised that they 'would look seriously into the situation'. I had been promoted again to deputy director, which is the equivalent of senior superintendent or full colonel in the old ranking system. I waited for Merlin.

Merlin found me within two weeks and he took my hand and led me out of the abyss. He showed me a shortcut too.

I took leave for the month of August and spent it quietly at home. I regained my strength and meditated on the positive advice Merlin had given me. He gave me guidelines on how to focus my senses, how to differentiate between my own thoughts and those of the serial killers and to regain the boundaries within myself again. As the wind brought the first breath of spring, I fell in love again. I had survived another winter. I think Merlin and his magic had something to do with this, as I had been so disillusioned with love that I would not have been able to fall in love all by myself.

O happy living things! no tongue
Their beauty might declare:
A spring of love gushed from my heart,
And I blessed them unaware:
Sure my kind saint took pity on me,
And I blessed them unaware.

The self-same moment I could pray;
And from my neck so free
The Albatross fell off, and sank
Like lead into the sea.

– **Samuel Taylor Coleridge, 'The Rime of the Ancient Mariner', 1798**

I returned to work at the end of August, revitalised and ready to face the serial killers one by one. Reyneke reported to me that the army had moved into Piet Retief at the beginning of August again, which probably explained why the Saloon Killer had not struck during that month. The lull lasted only until the last weekend in August when he wounded a woman and her daughter and killed a young man riding a bicycle on the same road where Jacob Ngobesi and Paulo Manana had been attacked. Koos went to Piet Retief to assist Inspector Jan Hattingh, who had taken command of the team while Danie was on a course. I could not join them, as I had to finalise my arrangements for my trip to Liverpool.

At 6 a.m. on 10 September my cellphone rang. It was Koos. He told me calmly that they had arrested the Saloon Killer that morning at a quarter to four at a shebeen in Phoswa Village. They'd had information from an informer who thought he knew the killer. The man had admitted to the murders and they had found the weapon in his house. He admitted that had they arrested him at his house, he would have shot them, as I had predicted. Koos said they were already on their way to Pretoria to bring him to me.

I was elated, and I felt so free. I knew that this time they had arrested the right man. I don't remember how I whiled away the hours until they arrived at my office at 10 a.m.

I interviewed the suspect, thirty-two-year-old Velaphi Ndlangamandla, for the rest of the day. My predictions in the profile were mostly correct. He was not a soldier, but he yearned to be one. His nickname was 'Soldier'.

No wonder the phrase 'he is a soldier' had occupied my mind during the investigation. It was his name, not his occupation. The closest he could get to being a soldier was a job as a security guard. He lived in Phoswa Village with his girlfriend, as I predicted. He loved to walk in the forests among the trees, where he felt safe. He buried the weapon next to his house, to keep it close to him and out of sight of others. He often walked with bullets in his pockets and would then think about his previous victims. I had predicted this.

He had been to prison on a housebreaking charge and had been charged with assault and rape, as I predicted. He was sodomised in prison and contracted a venereal disease. After this he suffered from impotence and the .22 rifle became a substitute for his penis. He said when he was with a woman his body became dead and he could not get an erection, but the moment he held the weapon in his hands, his whole body became warm and alive. He treasured the rifle and buffed it often. The rifle confirmed his masculinity to him and was an extension of his personality, as I had said it would be. He blamed the rifle for the murders and said he was glad the police had taken it away from him.

As soon as someone angered him, he would don his army coat and balaclava, dig up the rifle and hunt for a suitable victim. He blamed the male victims, for they represented the men who had sodomised him and stolen his manhood; and he blamed the females, for they represented the women who belittled him when he could not get an erection. It is interesting that although there was no sex involved in the actual murders, it played a symbolic role in his motivation.

Soldier told me that he had a recurring nightmare in which he walked on a high mountain with a deep dam below him. He was very frightened of falling into this deep gorge. To me, his dream personified the abyss. I remembered the dream I'd had of walking knee-deep in maggots and diving down a deep gorge into the abyss, but I did not tell him this.

It did not amaze me that we had shared the same nightmares, for this man had haunted me for so long. I could not believe that it was finally over and that he was sitting in my office, talking to me. Koos and his men had not slept for quite a while and the stubble of their beards was showing, but the arrest had given them such a mental high that they kept going through the long interview.

The interview ended at 4 p.m. and Koos and his team took Soldier back to Piet Retief for him to make a full confession to a magistrate. I went home and packed my bags for my trip to Liverpool the following day. At last I could leave my post for a few days knowing that this one was in the bag and that he would not haunt me again. I slept soundly without any nightmares that night. The detectives had come through for me again. I knew they would catch me a killer.

ELEVEN

The Capital Hill Serial Killer

Her lips were red, her looks were free,
Her locks were yellow as gold:
Her skin was white as leprosy,
The Nightmare LIFE-IN-DEATH was she,
Who thicks man's blood with cold.

– Samuel Taylor Coleridge, 'The Rime of the Ancient Mariner', 1798

I lectured at the Serial Killer Conference in Liverpool, meeting profilers, detectives and experts on serial killers from all over the world. It was fascinating listening to their presentations on investigations and seeing some of the sophisticated programs they had at their disposal. When I arrived back in Johannesburg, Elmarie fetched me at the airport. I switched on my cellphone to find that a multitude of journalists had been trying to reach me. I asked Elmarie if there was something I should be aware of, but she said it would be best if I went home first to unpack. I replied that it would be best if she told me what had happened, and she informed me that a number of decapitated bodies had been found in Delmas in Mpumalanga.

I spent the last days of September 1998 in Delmas and Secunda working on the case. The headless bodies were dispersed all over an open veld and the heads were found in a river a few kilometres away. Most of the heads and bodies matched, but in the end one head had no body and one body had no head. Superintendent Koos Fourie and I consulted local sangomas in the area and came to the conclusion that the bodies were the result of muti murders and not the work of a serial killer. I was glad to step away from the case and packed my bags again.

On 7 October 1998 I flew to Paris to deliver a lecture as a keynote speaker at the Centre International des Sciences Criminelles et Pénales (CISCP). There were hundreds of representatives from all over Europe in the audience, and I felt privileged to talk to them. The CISCP spoilt me and introduced me to foie gras. As in Mitchells Plain, I lost my heart to a city, Paris. Luckily, I had studied French at university, so I could communicate a few words to the charming French. From then on, I was invited to Paris annually to train European profilers, detectives, lawyers and even judges in the investigation of serial killers, and of course to enjoy Paris.

When I was a ten-year-old girl riding her first horse, I had always dreamt of playing with the wild white horses on the Camargue in the south of France. I had read that the horses belonged to Gypsies and ran wild on the beach. I also remembered my mother telling me that I could become anything I wanted, if I believed in myself. I made a mental pact with the horses that one day I would find them and play with them. Then life got in the way.

One year, while I was lecturing in Paris, the French journal *Paris Match* contacted me for an article. They wanted to take my photograph with the wind blowing in my hair. That particular day, the wind was only blowing in the south of France. So they boarded me on a domestic flight and flew me down to the south, where I met the photographer, and we drove to a beach in his SUV.

On the way, I read the signboard: Camargue. I'd had no idea this was where we were heading, but an excitement welled up inside me – just maybe, I hoped. And then, as I stood on the dunes with the wind blowing in my hair, they came. Over the dunes a whole herd of wild, white Camargue horses galloped up to me and nuzzled me in my neck. 'You promised us you would come one day, and we waited for you,' they seemed to communicate to me. 'And here you are.'

The photographer snapped away – he could not believe it and neither could I. Who would have thought my hard work and deep diving into the abyss of serial killers would one day lead to my childhood dream coming true. This has become my inspirational message for my motivational talks: If someone believes in you and you believe in yourself, the river of life might take some strange bends, but it will take you where you dream of going. Never give up!

In November 1998, I testified in the trial of Nicolas Ncama. One day, one of the detectives and I were having a coffee in a café on the beach in Port Alfred. It was a dismal afternoon, cold and rainy. My cellphone rang, and when I answered I was surprised by a woman, speaking in a strange accent, who told me she worked for a television programme in Hungary called *Frei Dossier*. She invited me as a guest on the programme in February 1999, all costs covered! As I sat staring at the misty sea through the curtain of rain, once again I wondered at the dichotomies in my life. I never imagined I would sit in a forlorn little café in the Eastern Cape and receive a call like that from the other side of the world. My work on serial killers has taken me to Scotland, England, France, Hungary, the United States, Greece, Swaziland and Namibia.

I spent Christmas with my father and his wife in Knysna, but mostly I locked myself in my room for I was not good company. How could I participate in festivities when people were being tortured to death? My post-traumatic stress was still riding high.

On 4 January 1999, Pretoria Murder and Robbery summoned me to a murder scene on Capital Hill, overlooking the city centre. Elmarie accompanied me, and as I parked the car in the street, I realised we would have to climb the hill. I was wearing high-heeled shoes, but fortunately my gym clothes were in the boot of my car, so I donned my tracksuit pants and my sneakers. We climbed the hill to meet my old friend Captain Fabby Fabricius at the top.

He informed me that Captain Henning van As had been called to the hill two days earlier when a Mr Rautenbach had discovered a body under a tree while walking his German shepherd. Captain Van As and his team processed the scene and found that the body was lying on top of an older decomposing body. Both victims were men, and the bottom body had no skull. Captain Van As directed the detectives to search for the skull, which they found not far from the tree. Van As had a nagging feeling and told them to extend the search. An hour later, about six hundred metres from the first scene, they found the third body of a male. All three bodies were removed from the scene.

The scene we were inspecting on 4 January was that of a woman, lying under the tree – the exact same spot where the two men had been discovered two days prior. Although this body was fresh, the maggots from the previous two bodies were feasting on her flesh. A pair of panties with faeces was found lying on her back.

Fabby decided to call for a police dog to come and search the area for more bodies. He was informed that a police helicopter would bring the dog. I thought that in my next life I would like to be a police dog who gets a helicopter ride, while I'd had to climb that hill. Elmarie and I sat down on the ground next to the body, taking notes as we waited for the dog to arrive, while the detectives hung around a little way off, smoking. Suddenly the police helicopter was hovering just a few metres above the crime scene. Gusts of strong wind showered bucketfuls of maggots all over us. In the chaos I grabbed the panties to prevent them from blowing away, as they might contain evidence. The detectives frantically waved the helicopter away. Then I saw a mass of maggots squirming in Elmarie's hair and I realised I must have looked the same. Maggots had blown into my blouse and Fabby dug handfuls of them from my cleavage. I was stunned but held on to the panties, which left my hands covered in shit. There was no water on the hill to wash my hands. Other detectives were trying to shake the maggots from Elmarie's and my hair. The dog was lowered along with his handler, and the helicopter left.

Then we heard another helicopter in the air. The national commissioner, George Fivaz, had been informed about the crime scene and commanded a chopper to take him to see it. I could clearly see him in the passenger seat next to the pilot. At that stage I really resented him up there, clean and far removed from the nitty-gritty, while we were down here covered in maggots and smelling of shit and decomposing corpses. Nobody pays me for this, I thought. The abyss had quite literally vomited all over me, and this was my sign that I should really retire and find a clean life.

I sent Elmarie home to recover and worked on the hill for the rest of the day. We found a little abandoned room with signs of someone living there. I suggested to Fabby that someone should keep watch on the mountain that night, as the killer would certainly return.

That night, as I drew my bath and undressed, maggots were still falling from my tracksuit pants onto the bathroom floor. I sat on the toilet seat, smoking a cigarette, watching them crawling over the tiles. I was quite numb when I cleaned the bathroom floor. Finally, when there was no sight of any maggots, I broke down. It felt as if I was crying my intestines onto the floor. I knew I could not carry on any longer. I was broken.

The morning of 6 January 1999, Fabby called to inform me that they'd requested the Special Task Force to stay on the mountain the night before, and, as I predicted, the killer had returned. Samuel Sidyno was arrested on the mountain. I congratulated Fabby. He and his team established that Sidyno, a former security guard, had raped a woman in January 1995 and was sent to prison. He was released in July 1998 and lived illegally in that little room on Capital Hill. Sidyno's wife lived in Valhalla, but he had abandoned his family. He sold vegetables and worked as a car guard at the zoo.

On 14 December 1998 the body of Elizabeth Senwamadi, Sidyno's first victim, was discovered. The bodies of two of the men found on 2 December were identified as Sipho Mavuka and Tsholofela Maoka, but the third, a teenager, remained unidentified. The female we'd discovered on 4 January was Paulina Ledwaba.

Sidyno was very hostile at first, but eventually pointed out the crime scenes to Superintendent Poerie van Rooyen. He could not remember the names of the victims and gave them fictitious names. He told Superintendent Poerie van Rooyen that he had killed a 'Petros' on the hill in November 1998, and that two weeks later he had killed a 'Timothy'. In the last week of November he killed a man he called 'Oupa'. All the victims were strangled. In the last week of December 1998 he killed a 'Hilda'. When he noticed that the bodies of Timothy and Oupa had been removed, he left Hilda on the same spot under the tree. He also took Superintendent Van Rooyen to another place where he claimed he had killed a boy. Van Rooyen found the remains of a human head and realised that this scene had not yet been processed. This boy was killed in the first week of January 1999. Lastly, Sidyno pointed out a scene where he killed a 'Rosina' (identified as Elizabeth Senwamadi) in October 1998.

On 11 January 1999 I was on a first-class flight to Hungary. The contrast could not be more stark: a week earlier I had maggots in my hair at a hot, dirty crime scene on a mountain in South Africa, and now I was booked into a five-star hotel with a chauffeur and a tour guide treating me to the sights of snow-covered Budapest. I was entertained there for four days – the television interview only taking two hours – and I requested to see the archaeological sites.

Two days after my return to South Africa, the public discovered another of Sidyno's victims on the mountain. He told Fabby that he had killed a certain 'Mannetjie' but when Superintendent Vinol Viljoen took him for the pointing out, he directed Vinol to a different mountain.

Sidyno was found guilty on seven counts of murder and one of robbery in September 2000. He received seven life sentences.

Back in January 1999, I presented another training course in Paarl. Fabby arrived a few days late, but presented his case to the class. In February and March 1999 I accompanied a French television company who were making a documentary on the Phoenix, Saloon and Stewart Wilken cases.

In April 1999 I flew to Los Angeles to attend a course on stalkers presented by Gavin de Becker. I was the first South African ever to attend this course. After a thirty-six-hour flight, I checked into an airport hotel – my first night in the United States. This was just a few days after the Columbine school massacre and I sat on my hotel bed eating pizza, watching the horror replay on the television. The next day I was whisked off to a secret location somewhere in the mountains. For the second time that year, I found myself in a snowscape. We stayed in cosy bungalows and sat around the fireplace while Gavin de Becker taught us how to profile stalkers and people who threaten presidents and celebrities, and we also profiled the school massacres. For the first time, I met real-life LAPD officers. It turns out that cops are cops all over the world. As I had a few hours to kill back in Los Angeles, I took one of the tourist bus drives around Hollywood. At last I could walk the Hollywood Walk of Fame, and I saw Magnum P.I.'s home from the outside. I bought a few T-shirts in Venice Beach and then I flew home.

In June and July 1999 I selected more detectives for my courses and testified in the trial of Jan Abraham Christoffel Nel in Upington. On 3 November 1984, Chris Nel – as he was known – had attended a disco in Postmasburg. He raped a young girl, as well as a woman named Rika Fouché, whom he stabbed twenty times with a knife and then cut her throat. In June 1986, the Honourable Judge Basson decided not to sentence him to death, but passed a life sentence of twenty years. Nel went to prison for twelve and a half years and was released on parole in January 1997. He moved to Upington where he worked as a car mechanic. Ten months after his release, on the night of 11 November 1997, he picked up eighteen-year-old Hermien Maasdorp and raped her in the veld. Then he crushed her skull with a log. In December 1997 he picked up twenty-two-year-old Belinda Visagie, a sex worker, and sexually assaulted her with a bottle. She managed to escape. On 18 March 1998 he picked up thirty-year-old Janetta Meintjies, also a sex worker, and murdered her on the same spot where he had assaulted Belinda. He hit Janetta so hard in the face that she gagged on her teeth. Nel was arrested on 23 May 1998 by Sergeant Jacques Visser. I testified that there was no chance that Nel would ever be rehabilitated and the Honourable Judge Kriek sentenced him to life imprisonment. Nel is an example of why serial killers should never be granted parole. As FBI profiler John Douglas said, why give a serial killer a second chance at life, when you are giving an innocent person a first chance of dying? I completely concur, and so do profilers all over the world. It is time Correctional Services pay heed to us.

In August 1999 I gave another training course to the detectives, and in October I presented another course in my favourite city, Paris. By now my French had improved. While I was there, we arranged for a contingent of French delegates to visit South Africa in February 2000. They would be on a fact-finding mission, exchanging expertise with the Departments of Correctional Services, Safety and Security (Police), and Justice, as well as visiting psychiatric clinics and other private institutions.

In November 1999, I was contacted by a private security firm, Associated Intelligence Network, and invited to a braai they were hosting at the International Police Association (IPA) house in Pretoria. I was sitting under the lapa when I noticed a man looking a little lost, wandering around. I recognised him as the new national police commissioner, Jackie Selebi. Realising that no one else had recognised him, I introduced him to the other detectives. At this function the directors of Associated Intelligence Network made me a very lucrative job offer. General Suiker Britz, who had recently retired, as well as some of the other detectives I knew, had already joined them.

In January 2000 General Leonard Knipe from the Western Cape had been appointed to General Suiker's position, making him my new boss. He agreed that I could work until the end of February, take leave in March and April, and resign by the end of April. In effect 29 February would be my last work day in the South African Police Service.

I entertained and accompanied the French contingent in February when they visited Durban and Cape Town. In Durban, I contracted Allan Alford and Bushy Rambhadursingh, who had both resigned from the SAPS, to be our security guards, and in Cape Town it was my friend AJ Oliver, who had also resigned, who accompanied the French contingent. At one stage we were joking around and told the French that there was no crime on Wednesdays. We said that the country had grown tired of crime and so the police and the criminals had agreed on a truce every Wednesday. One day, we took the bus out to the Mitchells Plain dunes to show them the Station Strangler's crime scenes, but the bus got stuck in the sand. Some of the French began digging at the sand, but to no avail. AJ then called some of his friends and some cops to come and assist us. A short while later, the policemen arrived in a police van and AJ's friends arrived on the back of a truck. AJ's friends were playing loud music and wore bandannas on their heads. They immediately jumped out and began digging the sand around the bus, while the policemen stood against the van, watching them with their arms folded. The French asked who the bandanna bunch were, and AJ answered they were local drug dealers, winking at me. The French asked why the policemen were not arresting them, and we both answered: 'But it's Wednesday!' The policemen and AJ's friends, who were definitely not drug dealers, just laughed and played along.

Eventually the 29th arrived, which coincided with the last night of the French visit. We had arranged a festive farewell dinner for them at the Police Training Centre in Silverton, Pretoria. With a glass of real French champagne in my hand, surrounded by French detectives, I celebrated my last day in the South African Police Service. I was on leave for two months, and on the morning of 30 April, shortly before 7 a.m., I slipped into Knipe's office to hand in my resignation – I didn't want to run into any of my colleagues. He accepted the resignation, shook my hand and said: 'Good work.'

It was slightly more than six years since joining the Police Force, and almost a year since the maggot shower, that I finally left. It took three months of intensive psychological therapy with Dr Susan Kriegler to get the worst of my post-traumatic stress symptoms in hand. It took another three years before I could say that I was mostly symptom-free.

Then I wrote this book, and another childhood dream came true: I became an author.

Conclusion

My six years in the South African Police Service were a time of great change. The socio-political landscape altered when the African National Congress became the ruling party after the April 1994 elections, with Nelson Mandela as president. Crime increased, as would be expected in any country undergoing a period of transition. Power bases shifted, and the Rainbow Nation of South Africa tried to figure itself out, with some people coping and adjusting, and some not at all. Apartheid came to an official end, but racism did not.

The South African Police Force became the South African Police Service, and community policing and a policy of transparency were implemented. Through the policy of demilitarisation, the ranks were changed to a more civilian structure, although military ranks would be reinstated in 2010. The initial distrust and antagonism I experienced from the detectives transformed to an *esprit de corps*, based on respect, honour, loyalty and a sincere recognition for my work, for which I am grateful.

Where the interest in serial killers started out as a project in the Psychological Services of the South African Police Force, with the support of General Suiker Britz, I founded an independent unit called the Investigative Psychology Unit, which formed part of the Serious and Violent Crimes component of the Detective Services. This represented the general change in attitude. I was promoted from a rank equivalent to captain to the commander of a unit and a deputy director, which was equivalent to full colonel.

The SAPS regarded serial homicide seriously. I developed two courses for training detectives in Investigative Psychology and we trained hundreds of detectives. They were mainly members of the various Murder and Robbery Units in the country, who were activated as soon as it became known that a serial killer was active. Later, members of the Forensic and Criminal Record Unit and covert intelligence units were included. By investing funds in their training, the SAPS was committed to arresting serial killers as soon as possible.

I was promised more staff members, who would mainly focus on researching serial killers. In cooperation with Dr Mark Wellman of the

MTN Centre for Crime Prevention Studies at Rhodes University, we were planning to establish a data bank on serial killers by the end of 2000. This data bank would have been a sought-after commodity by the rest of the world, since South Africa had the second-highest number of serial killers.

Arresting serial killers, while important, is a reactive approach. I had hoped when more members were appointed to my unit, we could address the problem on a proactive basis by lecturing to community leaders and members of the health, education and correctional services on how to identify possible traits of serial killers in young children. I endeavoured to educate the public on this phenomenon through the press, public lectures and this book. By the time I resigned, the Investigative Psychology unit consisted only of three persons.

While in the SAPS I was trained in covert interrogation and interviewing techniques by various international institutions and I trained covert units. My expertise expanded from profiling violent criminals to white-collar criminals, stalkers, intelligence operatives and competitive intelligence in the corporate arena. After my resignation I continued lecturing to government institutions in several countries, including police, justice and correctional services, and to private institutions, universities and the general public.

Personally, I have matured and have grown much stronger through my work. I have made mistakes, but I have also learnt the value of true friendship, the brotherhood – which includes women of course – and team spirit. I have learnt to manage my post-traumatic stress to a large extent and to help others afflicted with this disorder. At one point, I thought my job had ruined my chances of maintaining a love relationship, but now I am more mature.

In 2002 General Suiker Britz and I established our own private investigation firm for a few months, but eventually I had had enough. I joined my friends, actress Sandra Prinsloo and TV producer Jan Groenewald, to produce several crime documentary series. Then I joined my therapist Dr Susan Kriegler in her practice as a psychologist – after all, I have a doctorate in psychology – and eventually I opened my own private practice and consultancy for several years. I wrote more books: *Strangers in the Street, Fatal Females, Profiling Serial Killers and other Crimes in South Africa*, an Afrikaans novel called *Sorg*, and *Heroes: A Psychological Insight into Men's Perceptions on Relationships*.

Later, I completed my honours degree in archaeology, closed my private practice, sold my house, relocated to another country, and began travelling the world to visit and write about archaeological sites. I still consult for governments, legal fraternities and film companies, I present corporate work-shops, and I am a motivational speaker. I will always be an author. I have changed my abode, country and career several times and I am carrying on with my life! Then in 2023 a TV series based on *Catch Me a Killer* was produced, featuring the wonderful actress Charlotte Hope in the role of Dr Micki Pistorius. It is a great series, but it took some adjustment to get used to the idea that the TV series is not the accurate historical truth, and I trust that the public will realise that.

Since I first wrote this book, General Suiker Britz, Superintendent Piet Byleveld, Captain Fabby Fabricius, Captain Wouter Mentz, Inspector Coen Maritz, Bushy Singh, Inspector AJ Oliver and many other colleagues have passed away. So has Robert Ressler. I am privileged to have walked with heroes. Kudos to all of them.

To the reader:

> *O Wedding-Guest! This soul hath been*
> *Alone on a wide wide sea;*
> *So lonely t'was that God himself*
> *Scarce seemed there to be.*
>
> *Farewell, farewell! But this I tell*
> *To thee, thou Wedding-Guest!*
> *He prayeth well, who loveth well*
> *Both man and bird and beast.*
>
> *He prayeth best, who loveth best*
> *All things both great and small;*
> *For the Dear God who loveth us,*
> *He made and loveth all.*

To the victims and their families:

> *T'was not those souls that fled in pain,*
> *Which to their corpses came again,*
> *But a troop of spirits blest:*

For when it dawned – they dropped their arms,
And clustered round the mast:
Sweet sound rose slowly through their mouths,
And from their bodies passed.

Around, around flew each sweet sound,
Then darted to the Sun;
Slowly the sounds came back again
Now mixed, now one by one.

Sometimes a-dropping from the sky
I heard the sky-lark sing:
Sometimes all little birds that are,
How they seemed to fill the sea and air
With their sweet jargoning!

And now t'was like all instruments,
Now like a lonely flute:
And now it is an angel's song,
That makes the heavens be mute.

To the serial killers:

They groaned, they stirred, they all uprose,
Nor spake, nor moved their eyes;
It had been strange, even in a dream,
To have seen those dead men rise.

'Is it he?' quoth one, 'Is this the man?
By him who died on cross,
With his cruel bow he laid full low
The harmless Albatross.'

The other was a softer voice,
As soft as honey-dew:
Quoth he: 'The man hath penance done.
And penance more will do.'

And to the detectives:

> *He went like one that hath been stunned,*
> *And is of sense forlorn:*
> *A sadder and a wiser man,*
> *He rose the morrow morn.*

– Samuel Taylor Coleridge, 'The Rime of the Ancient Mariner', 1798

A Psychodynamic Explanation
of Serial Killers

The origin of serial homicide has been an enigma that has eluded theorists since the 1970s. Several different theories have evolved in an attempt to make sense of the tormenting riddle of why a human being would want to kill several strangers and sometimes also hideously mutilate his victims.

Besides investigating the origin of serial homicide, theorists have also grappled with a sensible definition of serial killers. During the 1980s, authors such as Leyton (1986), Cameron and Fraser (1987), Holmes and De Burger (1988), Leibman (1989) and Hollin (1989) merely differentiated between *serial killers*, *spree killers* and *mass murderers* by focusing on the time lapse between murders and the sexual element of the crimes. Except for Holmes and De Burger, who described characteristics of serial homicide, the rest did not elaborate on what would constitute serial homicide. In the 1990s, Levin and Fox (1991) and Lane and Gregg (1992) also seemed to be caught up in the differentiation between serial, spree and mass murderers, rather than expanding on serial homicide as such.

Robert Ressler and his colleagues at the FBI defined a serial killer as *a person who kills more than three victims, during more than three events, at three or more locations with a cooling-off period in between*. There is also premeditated planning and fantasy present. The problem that I have with this definition is that a serial killer can in fact be identified after his *second* murder and he may limit his crime scenes to a centralised location. Although Ressler and his colleagues introduced the important element of fantasy in their definition, they omitted the very important element of motive or, rather, lack of apparent motive.

How would one differentiate between a robber who murders more than three victims during more than three events, at three or more locations, with a cooling-off period in between, and a serial killer who does the same? The robber also meticulously plans the crime and fantasises about the power that money will bring him. The difference is that the robber is prompted by financial gain, which is a discernible motive, while the serial killer is motivated by a deep psychological gain, which is difficult to ascertain.

I define a serial killer as *a person (or persons) who murders several victims, usually strangers, at different times and not necessarily at the same location, with a cooling-off period in between. The motive is intrinsic, an irresistible compulsion, fuelled by fantasy, which may lead to torture, and/or sexual abuse, mutilation and necrophilia.*

This definition covers the possibility that serial killers may operate in groups, although this is rare. They may murder people they know or are related to, although this too is rare, and they may centralise their crime scenes, which is not so uncommon.

The motive is settled deep within the subconscious psyche, and the serial killer is unaware of this. By 'irresistible compulsion' I do not mean that serial killers have absolutely no power over their urge to kill. Many of them experience the urge as an external force taking control of their own will and forcing them to commit murder, a force they perceive they cannot resist. But the urge is their own subconscious, which they *can* control, as proven by the sometimes long cooling-off periods during which they commit no murders, and by the fact that some of them refrain from murdering all their victims. Whose subconscious is it, after all? As I explained before, should a policeman stand next to them, they probably would not kill. Rarely is a serial killer so disorganised or mentally ill that they kill due to hallucinations or delusions – and then they should be institutionalised for life. It is still not an excuse to kill.

Now that the problem of definition has been looked at, I would like to return to the more important issue of *the origin of serial homicide*, since the answer to this problem provides the means of trying to understand serial killers. Again, understanding them does not mean sympathising with them. As a psychologist I need to understand human behaviour, in order to explain it, to a judge and the public.

The first of the theories on the origin of serial homicide to emerge were the socio-cultural theories, which proposed that serial homicide was the result of a violent culture combined with dysfunctional early relationships during the serial killer's youth. Cruel and violent parents and exposure to external violence were cited as common reasons.

Ressler and his colleagues at the FBI proposed the motivational model, which comprised five stages, namely the ineffective social environment, formative years, patterned responses, action towards others and feedback. In this model emphasis was again laid upon the child's early developmental years in which he was exposed to direct or indirect trauma, causing distorted thought patterns which he acted out towards others and himself, eventually grading his performance in an attempt to improve on it. Deficiencies in families such as violence, alcohol and drug abuse, as well as mental illnesses and sexual, physical and emotional abuse of the child, were highlighted in this theory.

The systemic theories on the origin of serial homicide examined the role that the complete system, comprising the nuclear family, the educational system, social structures like religion and welfare, law enforcement, the judicial system and correctional facilities, played in the development of a serial killer. In most cases these theories illustrated how these substructures failed to recognise, address and rehabilitate deviant behaviour in children. The theories also indicated how the media plays a role in sensationalising and encouraging serial killers.

The theory of demonic possession has also been explored in the context of the origin of serial homicide. But, no matter how horrendous their deeds, serial killers are not possessed by the devil. Symptoms of supposed demonic possession are a radical change of personality, loss of self-control, blasphemy, dissociative states, voice changes, and auditory or visionary hallucinations of demons. Some serial killers may be blasphemous, some may lose self-control, but not all of them manifest with all of the symptoms. 'The devil made me do it' is no excuse.

Serial killers belong to different religious denominations. Norman Afzal Simons converted from Christianity to Islam and then back to Christianity; Mhlengwa Zikode was Catholic; Nicolas Ncama and Bongani Mfeka both studied to be Methodist ministers. Some serial killers may be Satanists, but not all.

Another important difference between Satanists and serial killers is that if Satanists commit murder, they do so to honour the devil, but serial killers commit murder for their own subconscious psychological gain. Satanists operate in cults, enjoying an audience and showmanship, while serial killers mainly work alone and in solitude. They rarely recruit others into their activities.

Neurological theories have attempted to find a link between neurological damage and serial homicide. Unfortunately not all serial killers have neurological damage, and fortunately not all people with brain damage are serial killers. Nor could a genetic link be identified among serial killers.

Even psychologists are unable to define serial killers according to the *Diagnostic and Statistical Manual of Mental Disorders*, where all mental illnesses and personality disorders are classified. Serial killers tend to have personality disorder tendencies like antisocial, borderline, schizoid, schizotypal and paranoid personality disorder, but there is no common category that they all share. The disorganised serial killers tend to be schizophrenic or delusional, but again, not all of them are. Many serial killers try to plead dissociative personality disorder (previously called multiple personality disorder) in court. But they all fail dismally in this desperate attempt to avoid responsibility for their crimes. Not all serial killers can be diagnosed with antisocial personality disorder (psychopathy) and not all so-called psychopaths are serial killers.

In my opinion, MacCulloch, Snowden, Wood and Mills had a breakthrough in 1983 when they identified fantasy as an important element of sadism. Prentky, Wolbert-Burgess, Rokous, Lee, Hartman, Ressler and Douglas elaborated on the fantasy element in 1989 when they found that an intrusive fantasy life manifested in serial killers. They found that serial killers act out their fantasies on the crime scenes. This is ultimately true.

What they failed to establish is what *causes* these particular idiosyncratic fantasies and why they have no inhibiting factor, such as a *conscience*, to prevent them from acting out these fantasies in reality. Lastly, they do not explain sufficiently why the serial killer commits *a series* of murders.

After I had studied all the available theories on the origin of serial homicide as I have explained them so far, one valid question remained: If two boys in the same family are both exposed to family abuse, be it emotional, physical or sexual, and both are equally exposed to violent and criminal external factors such as crime, faction fighting, terrorism, illness and poverty, why does one develop into a serial killer and the other not?

I asked myself this question after reading each of the theories. If violence and dysfunctional developmental years cause serial homicide, as the sociocultural theories would profess, why do we not have many more serial killers?

Not every abused or mistreated child turns into a serial killer. Some severely abused children lead very successful and productive lives.

Nor could any of the other theories solve my dilemma. Not all serial killers are Satanists, not all have neurological dysfunctions, or any other physical ailment or genetic deviation for that matter, and not all of them suffer from the same mental illnesses or personality disorders.

To my mind, the answer lies within the individual's internal reaction to all these adverse circumstances and not in the external adverse circumstances themselves.

I had to find a tool, a medium, by which I could delve into the soul of the serial killer to try to decipher his particular reaction, and this tool had to be of such a nature that it could generally be applied to all serial killers. I discovered the tool in some of Freud's psychoanalytical theories on the psychosexual developmental phases and the topology of the psyche, and I found that I could generalise these theories to the more than three hundred case studies I have studied on serial killers and all the cases I have personally worked on. I think I have found the answer.

It is all very elementary and I will explain it in the simplest of terms, illustrating the theories by using examples from the personal histories of some of the serial killers I have personally met and worked with and whom you have met by reading this book.

In a nutshell, my theory is that a serial killer fixates in one of the psychosexual developmental phases. This fixation is the seed from which his particular fantasy germinates within the subconscious. The serial killer does not socialise like other children and does not develop a conscience. Due to the lack of conscience, the fantasy is allowed to emerge from the subconscious to the conscious. As soon as the serial killer's self-esteem is challenged or threatened, he has to act out his fantasy in order to restore the mental homeostasis and there is no conscience to prohibit the acting out of this fantasy. There is a correlation between the serial killer's early fixations and the fantasy he acts out on his crime scene.

My theory can answer the three questions I posed regarding Prentky and his colleagues' research. It takes us a step closer to the enigma.

Freud's theory on the psychosexual developmental phases provides an answer to my first question as to where the serial killer's fantasy originates.

This theory states that every human being passes through *five psychosexual developmental phases*. They are the *oral phase, anal phase, Oedipus or phallic phase, latency phase* and the *genital phase*. A person can fixate in any of these phases and failure to resolve the fixation would be cause for pathology. A layman's term for a fixation would be a mental short-circuit. It is an individualistic reaction to being exposed to too much or too little of something.

The first phase is the *oral* or breastfeeding phase, existing from birth to about two years. All the infant's basic needs – such as survival, hunger, love and security – are satisfied orally by the mother's milk. The oral phase is divided into two stages, namely oral erotic, which is the sucking stage, and oral sadistic, which is the period when the infant bites the mother's nipple. An infant can fixate in this phase by either not getting enough milk or by getting too much. If the infant feels that he is not getting sufficient milk, he perceives that his needs are not satisfied. The infant will develop into an adult who is forever searching to have his needs gratified and who is over-sensitised to rejection. He is, after all, totally dependent on the milk for all his needs. If he perceives that he is getting too much milk, he will develop into an adult who expects the whole world to attend to his needs immediately. Preverbal sexual and aggressive fantasies already exist in the infant's subconscious, since sex (procreation and pleasure) and aggression (defence and conquering resources) are the two most basic instincts we are born with.

The *anal phase* is the so-called 'potty-training phase', existing from approximately two to four years. This is also called the control phase, since the toddler is learning to control his own bodily functions, he is exercising control over his environment by becoming more mobile and less dependent on his parents, and he is learning to control his parents. The toddler is engaged in a battle of power with his primary caretaker, usually the mother, who tries to teach him to use the potty. He can sit on the potty for hours and either 'give' or 'retain' faeces which he perceives to be a product of his own body and of which he is very proud. The mother patiently waits, usually on her haunches in front of the mighty toddler (sitting on the throne), for him to give or retain. Fixations can occur if children are forced to use the potty before they are physically ready to, or a toddler can fixate on the immense feeling of power. The passive infant is developing into an active toddler. The sexual and aggressive fantasies in the subconscious become more defined since the toddler is learning how to speak and how to interpret symbolism.

The *Oedipus or phallic phase*, existing from approximately four to six years, is a most interesting phase when the little boy subconsciously falls in love with his mother and hates his father. A father can be replaced by any father figure and need not necessarily be the biological father. He vies for his mother's attention and has subconscious sexual fantasies about her and subconscious aggressive fantasies towards his father. This is also the period during which children show a natural curiosity in the difference between the genders' genitals. The little boy discovers that the little girl has no penis and cannot imagine that she was actually born like that. He subconsciously perceives her to be castrated and consequently fears castration himself. A fixation occurs when a boy may beat his father in the battle for his mother's affection, or where he perceives himself mentally castrated either by the father or the mother. The father might castrate him for coveting his wife and the mother might castrate him by rejecting his adoration. At the end of this period, the little boy decides it is safer to identify with his father in order one day to marry a woman like his mother. As a result of this identification with the father and the fact that the boy is ready to go to school and socialise, a *conscience*, or *superego* as Freud called it, develops.

The *latency phase* exists from the ages of approximately six to twelve years, beginning at the time when the boy is sent off to school. All sexual thoughts and subconscious fantasies from the previous phases are repressed as the boy concentrates on socialising, developing empathy for others, sharing, incorporating moral and ethical values and thereby developing his internal conscience or superego. Fixation in this phase would mean the boy fails to socialise and empathise, and the primitive sexual and aggressive fantasies are not repressed. He also fails to develop a conscience. A fixation could also occur when the conscience develops too strongly, in which case the boy will develop into an adult who is tortured by feelings of guilt.

During the *genital phase*, existing mainly during the teenage years, the boy becomes sexually orientated again, but this time he enters into a sexual relationship with an appropriate partner and he has a last chance at resolving issues resulting from fixations that developed during the previous phases.

Children are very sexually orientated during the first three phases and masturbation is a natural occurrence and a manner in which they explore their bodies. Most of us do not remember the explicit sexual and aggressive fantasies we had then, since most of them have been repressed to the subconscious and our incorporation of moral and ethical values has banished these fantasies as taboo. Masturbation and accompanying sexual and aggressive fantasies are repressed during the latency phase, but re-emerge as censored and as more subliminal versions during the genital phase. In cases of neurosis, these fantasies may re-emerge as neurotic symptoms.

I will demonstrate with case histories how particular serial killers fixated in these phases, and how these fixations manifested on their crime scenes, after I have discussed more of Freud's theories. (The development of female serial killers is discussed in my book *Fatal Females*.)

Freud's theory on the topological structure of the psyche, namely the *id*, *ego* and *superego*, provides an answer to my second question, namely the lack of an inhibiting censor, such as a conscience, to prevent the serial killer from acting out his fantasy.

This theory postulates that every human being is born with an id. The id is situated within the subconscious and contains the instincts and all the energy needed to have the instincts satisfied. The first basic instincts are sex and aggression. Sex comprises all the instincts based on the reproduction of the species and aggression comprises the instincts based on survival (securing resources), attack and defence of the self. Both have to do with self-preservation. The id is like the witches' cauldron in Shakespeare's *Macbeth*. It bubbles, toils and is full of trouble. It knows no time, no morality, and cannot discern between good and bad. There is no logic in the id. The id operates on the pleasure principle and it wants all its needs satisfied immediately. The id is like a very demanding baby, and like a baby it cannot verbalise its needs and frustrations. Since the id is situated in the subconscious, it communicates with the ego by means of dreams, symbols and symptoms.

From the id develops the ego, the second structure. The ego is the executive manager of the psyche. It adheres to the reality principle and understands logic. It can communicate in language. The ego exists within the conscious. Its main task is to act as negotiator between the id, the superego and external reality. Since this is such a difficult task, the ego has an army of mental defence mechanisms to assist it. One of the main defence mechanisms is its ability to repress anything it finds threatening to its self-preservation to the subconscious. Unfortunately, the subconscious demands that the ego deals with whatever it has repressed and this can cause pathology.

At about the age of six, during the commencement of the latency period, the superego, or conscience, develops as a result of an identification with the father figure and the incorporation of society's norms and values. The superego sets up an ideal self, by which it measures the ego. Should the ego fail to meet the standards of this ideal self, or fail to comply with the superego's moral and ethical values, the superego punishes the ego with guilt feelings. The superego is situated partly within the subconscious and partly in the conscious. Sometimes we know why we feel guilty and sometimes we cannot pinpoint the exact source of our guilt feelings, because the reason has been repressed to the subconscious by the ego. Where the id says 'yes' to everything, the superego says 'no' to everything, and it can be just as unrealistic in its demands on the ego as the id.

The id's sexual and aggressive fantasies, which all children experience during the first three developmental phases, cause anxiety to the ego due to the development of the child's superego during the latency phase. In an adult the superego has grown much stronger and will force the ego to repress any upsetting need or urge originating from the id. These fantasies are then repressed to the subconscious.

The serial killer has a particularly strong and dominating id and consequently very ardent sexual and aggressive urges. Owing to a lack of bonding with his mother or primary caretaker, or due to a symbiotic situation in which he fails to differentiate his own personality from his mother's, he has a weak ego. Furthermore, the serial killer has no positive father figure with whom to identify during the latency period and he does not manage the socialisation process, and therefore does not develop a superego, or develops only faint traces of a superego. The fixation he experienced during any of the developmental phases germinates into a fantasy which becomes more defined and more conscious as the child becomes older. As a result of his weak ego and virtually non-existent superego, these pervasive and invasive fantasies cause no anxiety to the ego and are therefore neither repressed nor are they sublimated into more acceptable versions. The serial killer is in absolute command and is omnipotent in his own fantasies. As soon as the adult serial killer's fragile ego and self-esteem are threatened by any form of rejection or pain, the original childhood agony is triggered and he feels the irresistible urge to act out this powerful fantasy, which is the only way he perceives to restore the psychological imbalance.

All serial killers fixate in the latency phase, although they will also fixate in one or more of the other psychosexual phases. They always feel like outsiders. The case history of any serial killer will indicate that the father figure was perhaps physically, and definitely emotionally, absent when the boy was in his latency phase. As a boy, therefore, the serial killer had no positive father figure with whom to identify.

The case histories will indicate that serial killers report themselves as very lonely children who felt alienated and isolated from their peers. During their latency phases they did not learn to socialise, they did not learn to empathise with others, and they did not incorporate moral and ethical values. Because they failed in their socialisation process, serial killers treat their victims as mere objects that exist for the gratification of their own needs. They show no empathy for the victim.

Serial killers can either be *egodystonic* or *egosyntonic*. Egodystonic serial killers have a very slight sense of conscience and cannot associate themselves with the killing of other humans to relieve their own suffering. They may indicate slight guilt feelings, especially after their arrest, but the guilt is not strong enough to motivate them to refrain from killing. Egosyntonic serial killers have no conscience whatsoever and do not feel the slightest sense of guilt or remorse.

The last question I asked after studying the work of Prentky and his colleagues was why serial killers feel compelled to repeat the acting-out of their fantasies and commit repetitive murders. Freud's theory on the compulsion to repeat provides an answer to this tendency.

The theory states that the ego experiences any trauma passively, but in order to master the trauma, it repeats it actively in a weakened position.

Anyone who has observed children will notice that they tend to repeat any new experience. If they learn a new word they repeat it often, or if they learn to tie their shoelaces they will tie and untie them a hundred times until they get it right.

The passive–active role reversal can easily be illustrated by the example of a husband returning home in a foul mood because his boss has berated him. He criticises his wife as he walks in the door. The wife yells at their little boy for not doing his homework and the boy kicks the dog for being in his way. The dog chases the cat (and the cat, of course, is smart enough to understand the whole situation and merely shrugs the dog off). The point, of course, is that all the role-players converted their passive victim positions into active aggressor positions in order to master their anxiety. (Except the cat – the cat is a master unto herself.)

The serial killer does the same. He repeats what was done to him either directly or symbolically in order to master it and he will keep on repeating it until he gets it right. Unfortunately, he will never get it right for he is using the wrong method to master it. Prentky and his colleagues, especially Ann Burgess, correctly assessed this process when they pointed out that reality is never as perfect as fantasy.

The passive–active role-reversal process and compulsion to repeat the trauma also influences the serial killer's idiosyncratic selection of victims. As I have said, he can either directly repeat what was done to him, like Simons, and will then most likely choose victims who represent himself, or he may symbolically avenge his suffering, and will then be more likely to select victims who represent the original tormentor.

It is my job as an investigative psychologist to try to decipher the serial killer's particular fantasy from his crime scene. The fantasy will point to the fixation that will give us a key to understanding the killer we are investigating. The better we understand him, the more likely we are to catch him and to formulate a tailor-made interrogation strategy for this particular individual. I would like to select the case studies of Norman Afzal Simons, Mhlengwa Zikode and Stewart Wilken, with a few references here and there to others, to illustrate how my theory works in practice.

Norman Afzal Simons fixated in the anal phase. An element of a fixation in the anal phase is perfectionism. This manifested in Simons's crime scenes. No clues were left behind – the crime scene of Elroy van Rooyen was particularly neat. The fact that the victim was a little boy who was tied up and therefore forced into a passive, helpless position also indicated that power was very important to the killer. Simons was a strong man and did not need to tie the boy up to control him. The bondage indicates a need to control. Therefore I described him in my profile as a person who would be a perfectionist and very neatly dressed. Simons is a perfectionist and attentive to his own appearance.

Simons admitted to being sodomised as a young boy, during which he was the passive victim. The only way he could master this abuse was by repeating it, and by identifying with his tormentor by becoming the active aggressor. He reversed the passive–active roles. The moment his self-esteem was threatened, it reminded him of the time when he was not in control of his life or body, which was the time he was sodomised. He needed to regain control and the only way he felt he could regain homeostasis of his ego state was by doing to others what was done to him.

Control and power go hand in hand, and there is no greater power than power over life and death. The moment one has another's life literally in one's hands, one is ultimately powerful, almost godlike, omnipotent. When one is in this position, one is no longer the victim, since someone else has become the victim. Simons selected a victim just like himself, namely a coloured schoolboy between the ages of eight and fourteen. Symbolically he committed suicide when he killed that boy, for he was killing his childhood self.

Simons was an egodystonic serial killer. Perhaps because of his intelligence, his superego had developed an ideal self, whereby he saw himself as a community leader who helped other people. He was indeed a community leader and a very good teacher. It could be that he rationalised, which happens to be a very intelligent mental defence mechanism, that altruistic behaviour towards others might counterbalance the murder. Simons could not identify this ideal self-image with the dark side of his personality – the side that murdered. He attributed the identity of his original aggressor, namely his brother, to the murderous side of himself and said in his statement to the detectives that it was the spirit of his deceased brother who ordered him to murder the children.

Simons was not hallucinating or suffering from a dissociative personality disorder when he made this statement: it was merely an intelligent man's way of trying to make sense of what had happened. In his statements he apologised to the community and to the citizens of South Africa for murdering the children and said that he was relieved to have been arrested. This indicates guilt feelings and a small sense of conscience. The conscience was not enough, however, to prevent him from killing, nor was it enough to motivate him to give himself up to the detectives in Mitchells Plain.

Simons professed his innocence in jail, although his initial appeal failed and his sentence was converted to life by the Appeal Court. The fact that he could not reconcile his ideal self with a murderer makes sense, since he continued his altruistic work even in prison. It is ironic that before his arrest he assisted in the rehabilitation of released prisoners and helped them to settle back into society. Simons again applied for parole in his late fifties, still convincing himself that he was innocent – displaying typical egodystonic dynamics. It is no wonder Mitchells Plain is not ready to forgive him, as he shows no true remorse. Then, in July 2023, he was released under strict parole conditions. I oppose this decision and Mitchells Plain is still reeling from shock.

Mhlengwa Zikode of Donnybrook fixated in the Oedipus phase. His father was paralysed and Mhlengwa won the favour of both his mother and his older and only sister, who was his primary caretaker. He had a symbiotic relationship with both these women and could never really succeed in differentiating his own personality from theirs. He did not perceive his father or his brothers to be any competition regarding the attention he received from the two primary females in his life.

Therefore, as an adult Mhlengwa did not consider any male as competition to challenge him. In the course of his crimes he did not have any scruples about approaching a woman he wanted, even if she was in the company of another male. When he entered the huts at night, he immediately and efficiently eliminated the males by killing them first, so that he could have access to the females.

His fixation in the Oedipus phase also manifested in his selection of victims. They represented his sister. The female victims were mostly women in the prime of their lives, except for the little girl who happened to be present when Mhlengwa raped her mother. Only the last three victims were in their forties and fifties, indicating that subconsciously his anger had shifted from his sister to his mother. Fixation in the Oedipus phase meant that subconsciously he was still caught up in the unresolved love affair with the mother figure.

He experienced a severe rejection when his sister left the family when he was ten years old. She had abandoned him and he was very angry with her. Mhlengwa chose victims who represented his sister and raped them to act out the sexual fantasies of the Oedipus phase and he killed them to act out the aggressive fantasies that resulted from his anger at being rejected.

When I asked Mhlengwa who was responsible for the murders, he replied that it was his sister's fault because she should have been the one to introduce him to females on a social level.

Mhlengwa also had another fixation. Because he was only sent to school at fourteen and had no contact with any peers, or females for that matter, until that age, he had a retarded Oedipus phase which lasted until his fourteenth year. His father was not a factor during his life and his brothers had also left home, so he had no father figure with whom to identify. He was deprived of the circumstances and opportunities of socialising during the latency phase because he did not go to school.

When he was eventually sent to school, Mhlengwa had to mentally confront the latency phase, while his body was entering the very sexual genital phase. He was developmentally retarded in comparison with his peers and did not have any social skills regarding the forming of friendships or relationships.

At the age of nineteen, when his mother brought home the pin-up pictures, she inadvertently activated his seething fantasies. Mhlengwa felt the urge to have sex but lacked the social skills to form a relationship. He was also a very angry young man.

Both sexuality and anger exploded in his murders. It was the only way he felt he could express himself and his needs. His victims were found with their legs spread-eagled and their genitals exposed. They were left exactly as they died. This indicated his total lack of socialisation, and it is typical that he treated his victims as mere objects to gratify his needs. Mhlengwa did not develop any superego whatsoever and did not show any regret or guilt when he was arrested. He said it was his mother's duty to apologise to the families of the victims.

Another South African serial killer who fixated in the Oedipus phase was the Cape Town Prostitute Killer. He had, however, lost the battle for his mother's affection and felt mentally castrated by her rejection and her preference for other men. He compensated for this castration by shoving a bottle up the vagina of one of his victims, thereby symbolically giving her a penis. Seeing the 'penis' inside the woman relieved his fear of losing his own penis. It was a clear example of acting out his fantasy to compensate for castration anxiety. Insertion of sexual phallic objects into vaginas is very common among serial killers, to compensate for their inferiority complexes regarding their masculinity.

Stewart Wilken, alias Boetie Boer, is an example of a serial killer who fixated during the oral phase. He was abandoned as a baby, and as a result was deprived of being breastfed by his mother. His basic needs as an infant regarding hunger and security were grossly neglected. The oral fixation manifested already as a toddler when he bit anyone who angered him, including his adoptive mother. This is an example of oral sadism. Eventually his oral fixation manifested on his crime scenes when he admitted to biting several of his victims on their genitals, breasts and toes and finally when he ate the nipples of Georgina Zweni. He cut open her breasts by removing the nipples in a symbolic attempt to get to the milk, which he subconsciously had missed all his life. He ate the nipples, which is a primitive but symbolically powerful manner of expressing his need for mother's milk.

But Wilken also fixated in the anal phase. The elements of sadism support a fixation in this control-orientated phase. Roy Hazelwood, retired FBI agent specialising in serial rapists, taught me that sexual sadists prefer anal sex, since it causes pain to the victim as well as humiliating them. Wilken preferred anal sex with all his victims. The pain they showed when he penetrated them anally heated his sexual arousal and caused him to commence strangling them. This caused what he called the 'jellybean effect', which brought on his ejaculation.

Wilken manifested with a very interesting choice in his selection of victims. He had two types of victims. The prostitutes resembled the women who had rejected him, and he acted out his agony and anger in a symbolic manner on these victims. The boys represented himself and, like Simons, he acted out his childhood passive suffering directly on these victims.

The abandonment by his biological mother, his lost sister, the punishment he received from his adoptive mother and the fact that his two wives apparently refused him sex, correlated with Wilken's first selection of victims, namely the prostitutes. He unleashed his sexual frustrations on these women, but they also provided a means of venting his Oedipal anger at the mother figures for rejecting him, so he strangled the life out of them. By sodomising the boys, Wilken fell into the typical pattern of passive–active role reversal by identifying with the aggressor and selecting a victim like himself. When he sodomised and strangled twelve-year-old Henry Bakers, he even told Henry that he was going to do to him what was done to himself when he was Henry's age.

Wilken professed to feel guilty about his daughter Wuane's death, indicating a very, very slight conscience, but he was vehement in his hatred of the prostitutes and showed absolutely no remorse. He loved his adoptive father, who did not abuse him, but he had died when Wilken was nine years old, in his latency phase. The opportunity of identifying with a positive male role model was therefore denied, and there were no positive male role models in the reformatories he was sent to. The other adult males whom Wilken had met – namely the man who originally took him in, as well as the deacon – proved very negative tormentors. Wilken was ostracised by his peers, who teased him about his adoptive status. He also had to fight for survival in the reformatory, where he was sodomised. He had little chance to socialise and learn empathy for others. Wilken's wives both reported that there were times when he was very generous and kind-hearted, especially to children.

The fact that Wilken was prepared to return to the decomposing bodies of some of his victims in order to commit necrophilia indicates the extent to which he regarded them as objects for the gratification of his own needs and pleasures.

As I have said in the chapter on Wilken's case, since he has been confined to a single prison cell, he has reverted back to the passive role, and in his hallucinations he is being persecuted by his victims, who have taken on the roles of active aggressors. Since Wilken was never able to master the trauma in his life, he is still caught up in the compulsion to repeat it, albeit this time as the victim once more. It would be extremely dangerous for the community if he is ever paroled or released.

It should be clearly understood that I am not inferring that all people who were not breastfed are likely to become serial killers. What I am saying is that to become a serial killer, a person must have fixated in one or more of the psychosexual developmental phases, which caused a fantasy to evolve in the subconscious. Secondly, this person must also have a weak ego, virtually no superego and a domineering id, which means that the fantasy will not be inhibited but will be acted out. Thirdly, the person's ego needs to feel threatened by some event that causes a psychological imbalance. The psychological gain he receives from the murder is the restoration of the mental homeostasis, and of course most of them also experience sexual gratification.

Serial killers themselves do not understand this process and often seek an acceptable explanation for their murders, such as justifiable vengeance – in their minds. Moses Sithole, for instance, said he murdered the women because they reminded him of the woman who in his opinion had falsely accused him of rape and was the cause of his being sent to prison. He does not understand that this woman merely triggered the original rejection and Oedipal fixation he experienced as a child.

Lastly, I would like to comment on the possibility of the rehabilitation of serial killers. It takes a person about twenty years to develop into a serial killer. The process begins during the first five years of his life, whereafter he nurtures the most horrendous sexual and aggressive fantasies in which other human beings are subjugated to mere objects. He rehearses these fantasies as a teenager and eventually acts them out, as one after the other innocent person becomes his victim, without the slightest regard for their pain or the agony of the families and loved ones they have left behind.

He realises that he has a problem, he knows right from wrong, but the psychological gain and, of course, the sexual gratification are so great that he refuses to give it up and seek another, more humane, manner of addressing his pain.

So he carries on until he is eventually arrested and sent to prison. Most incarcerated serial killers have admitted that as soon as they are released they will murder again, and many have done so. In addition to the time it takes someone to develop into a serial killer, he may be active for many years before he is arrested. Theoretically, then, it would take a very determined therapist twenty years or more of intense psychoanalytical therapy to completely rehabilitate a serial killer and to restore his disturbed object relations. This is practically impossible and I hope it is an experiment that will never be executed.

The best way of preventing a person from becoming a serial killer is for the trained professionals in the social services, and even for concerned members of the public, to learn to identify the little dreamers who flee into their fantasy worlds to escape abuse and to refer these children for therapy. Bad performance at school, excessive daydreaming, the absence of friends, the triad of bed-wetting, fire-setting and cruelty to animals, as well as signs of abuse and neglect and continuous masturbation during the latency phase, should alert adults to the possibility that a child may be a potential serial killer. Children often give clues that they are disturbed in their play and in their art. Therapists should explore the sexual and aggressive fantasies of children and should not be so naive as to think that children as young as five do not have the capacity to fantasise about raping and mutilating their mothers. They do, believe me.

Teenagers who recognise these fantasies in themselves should urgently consult a trained therapist and candidly and courageously talk to them. A person can be helped before he acts out the fantasy; and a person cannot be arrested for having murderous fantasies. Once the murder has been committed, it is too late.

I agree with John Douglas, a retired FBI agent and contemporary of Robert Ressler and Roy Hazelwood, who stated that he would rather not give a serial killer a second chance in life, for he might be giving someone else a first chance of losing their life.

I asked all the serial killers I interviewed what their worst childhood memory was. One would expect someone like Stewart Wilken to report that his custodian father had burnt him with cigarettes on his genitals. But, to a man, without conferring with the others, they all answered their worst childhood experience was that their parents told them they were useless and worthless! Contrary to popular belief, it is a myth that all serial killers were abused as children, but it is a fact that they were all neglected as children.

I would like to leave you with this thought: Some grown-ups should know better! What are we doing to our children? Neglecting them, indulging their tantrums, not encouraging them to speak (too many parents indulge toddlers who whine and scream instead of teaching them to verbalise and express their needs), and failing to discipline them and guide them to become productive considerate human beings, due to fear of a raised eyebrow of societal disapproval. By not teaching them to discuss and consider the long-term consequences of their actions and indulging their immediate gratification, parents are breeding generations of self-indulgent, inconsiderate, dangerous individuals with weak egos and no inhibitions or consciences. As a society, we should all take responsibility and be accountable. Children need to be loved and they need adults to guide them, to teach them social skills, tolerance, and the extended gratification of needs. They have voices – let them speak – not scream in frustration.

I hope my book and my life can inspire people to stand up and stand together – to fight injustice, whether it is child abuse, child neglect, domestic violence, sexism, supressing women, demeaning good men, interpersonal violence, corruption, robbery, riots, drugs, denial of education, animal abuse, bullying at schools and workplaces, and environmental destruction (including archaeological sites). Where have all the heroes gone? It is time for people to stand up and be counted.

References

Cameron, D., and Fraser, E., 1987. *The Lust to Kill*. Cambridge: Polity Press.

Douglas, J., and Olshaker, M., 1997. *Journey into Darkness*. London: Heinemann.

Freud, S., *The Complete Works of Sigmund Freud*. London: The Hogarth Press.

Hollin, C.R., 1989. *Psychology and Crime*. London: Routledge.

Holmes, R.M., and De Burger, J., 1988. *Serial Murder*. Newbury Park: Sage Publications.

Lane, B., and Gregg, W., 1992. *The Encyclopedia of Serial Killers*. London: Headline Book Publishing.

Leibman, F.H., 1989. 'Serial Murderers: Four Case Histories', *Federal Probation*, 53 (4): 41–45.

Levin, J., and Fox, A.J., 1991. *America's Growing Menace – Mass Murder*. New York: Berkley Books.

Leyton, E., 1986. *Compulsive Killers: The Story of Modern Multiple Murder*. New York: Washington Mews Books.

MacCulloch, M.J., Snowden, P.R., Wood, P.J.W., and Mills, H.E., 1983. 'Sadistic fantasy, sadistic behaviour and offending', *British Journal of Psychiatry*, 143: 20–29.

Pistorius, M., 1996. *A Psychoanalytical Approach to Serial Killers*. DPhil thesis. Pretoria: University of Pretoria.

Prentky, R.A., Wolbert-Burgess, A., Rokous, F., Lee, A., Hartman, C., Ressler, R.K., and Douglas, J., 1989. 'The Presumptive Role of Fantasy in Serial Sexual Homicide', *American Journal of Psychiatry*, 147 (7): 887–891.